" MORE

Club Histor ... s:

Bedford Avenue.

Lovell's Athletic.

Romford.

Rugby Town.

Slough Centre.

West Stanley.

- -

Written and Published by: Dave Twydell.
12, The Furrows, Harefield, Middx. UB9 6AT.

Printed By: JUMA.
Tel.: 0742 720915.

ISBN 0 9513321 3 9.

CONTENTS:

"DEFUNCT F.C." - Erratum.

In view of the many diverse, and often knowledgeable readers of the original 'Defunct F.C.' Book, it is gratifying to record, that the only errors (in relation to the factual aspects) that I have been notified of - and therefore hopefully can be regarded as a complete list - are as follows:

Rear Cover and Page 3: Chippenham Town should read
Chippenham United.
Page 2: Old Carthusians are not defunct (as intimated) - currently members of the Arthurian League.

Page 39:   Bedford overall Champions by virtue of 2-1 win play off with Hereford (North-West Champs).
Page 40:   Managers commence dates: Hayward (Feb.1964), Burgess (Jan.1966), Wright (Mar.1969-Play/Man.).
Page 42:   Fahy not Fahey; Heckman not Hickman.
Page 53:   Bedford 1 - Arlesey 6.
Page 55:   Dog Farm not Dog Lane.
Page 57:   Harrowden Lane, Cardington - not Cardington Road.
Page 59:   Add; Overall South.Lge.Champs. 1958/59.
South.Lge. (Midland Div.) runners-up. 1980/81.

Page 94:   First game 1947, not 1948.
Page 132: Previous F.A.Cup victories over Snowdon Colliery and Sittingbourne.
Page 138: Floodlights opening game was 1960 (not 1961). Venues of Matches versus Tunbridge reversed (Away game first).
Page 143 & 144: Brentford and Newport in Fourth Division.
Page 147: First home game was versus Hastings.

Page 182: Sir Harold Thompson died aged 75 years.
(Various pages) Pegasus opponents:
Bishop Auckland not Aukland. Bishops Stortford not Bishop.
Boldmere St.Michael not Micheal.
Corinthian-Casuals. (with 'hyphen')
'F.A.Boys Week Xl' and similar - team names are as those recorded in Pegasus Minutes Book.

Two update points: Harborough Town (Leicestershire Senior League) currently play on the old Symington's Ground, but the original changing room block has now been demolished. 'Bedford Town' have now been reformed under the title of 'Bedford Town (1990)' and hope to enter competitive football in the 1990/91 season.

Much of what follows in this introduction was written in 'Defunct F.C.', but is repeated here in view of it's equal relevance.

To set about writing the History of YOUR Football Club is a daunting prospect. To attempt to write the Histories of six Clubs, whom you knew little about - other than a general interest - magnifies the difficulty of the task. I do not claim that this Book contains the full, definitive, histories of these Clubs, but I believe that it does fill a gap in the World of Football which would otherwise have been ignored. Each of these Clubs, despite their variable support and seniority, had fans and administrators - plus many more who followed the Clubs progress via the local Press - etc. In the rare event of Football League Clubs going out of existance, these have either already been covered by others, were contained in my books 'Rejected F.C.' volumes 1 and 2, or, in the future will no doubt be written. In the non-League World, Club histories of defunct Clubs are seldon, if ever, covered.

The Clubs I have chosen, and many more like them, have never had their past fully recorded; now defunct they would in all probability have passed into virtual oblivion, like Turton, London Caledonians and Nunhead, to name but three teams of distant yesteryear. I have attempted to bring back to life the days of six Clubs, hopefully written factually and objectively, but at the same time with a hint of emotion by expressing the feelings, aspirations and disappointments; as one would, who was closely associated with that Club. To have completely documented every match, every highlight and every lowlight would have been next to impossible to achieve, and I believe would have made boring reading. I have attempted to carry the reader through from beginning to end, emphasising special matches, particular points of interest and humourous points along the journey. I have, with notable exceptions, avoided naming names - if this had been an extensive list, many would have inevitably been omitted!

To any readers who knew these Clubs intimately, I apologise for any - in your eyes - omissions and (hopefully) few errors.

It will not have gone unnoticed that five of the chosen Clubs are from the Southern half of England! The reasons are twofold; firstly my better accessibility, and secondly, and more importantly, is the rather strange fact that there appears to be more 'ex' non-League Clubs down South than in the North.

I would like to record my thanks to all those who brought 'Defunct F.C.' (now out of print), and who consequently have made this book both financially possible, and through whose encouragement have made the writing of 'More.... Defunct F.C.' that much more rewarding. One should always strive towards perfection, and whilst this will never be reached, I hope that the improved type face and the hopeful lack of spelling and grammatical errors, is at least a step nearer towards this ultimate goal!

Finally, an old cliche, but particularly true once again: I should like to thank the following principal sources of reference and individuals for their help and interest in making this Book possible. Much of the research was undertaken at the same time as that for 'Defunct F.C.', therefore my apologies for any ommisions that have been forgotten during the interim of several years!
(Random order) Selwyn Kemp, John Grimme, Mark Grabowski, Mr.B.Van Meeteren, Brian Abraham, Alec Reeves, Mr. W.J. Burrows, Mr. J. Thompson.
The Staff and facilities provided at The British Library (Newspaper and Map Libraries), plus the Public Libraries (Reference/Local Studies section) of Bedford, Newport (Gwent), Rugby, Romford, Slough and Stanley (Co.Durham)
The following were the principal books that were used for reference:
'Seventy Five Years of Southern League Football'. (Lionel Francis)
'Southern League Football - the post-war years.' (Paul Harrison)
'Non League.' (Bob Barton)
'Non-League Club Directories.' (Tony Williams)
'Romford Facts and Figures'. (Leigh Edwards and John Haley)
'History of West Stanley'. (Fred Wade)
Also many newspapers (particularly those that relate to the towns covered).
Thanks finally to the many unnamed people for the occasional item of information.

Last but far from least, my wife...Fay.

****

Every effort has been made - where applicable - to acknowledge the source of and/or seek permission for the reproduction of specific items, and to ensure that copyright has not been infringed.

Bedford Avenue

1962: The last Major Honour, United Counties League Div.2 Champions.

(Standing, L.to R.): T.Shadrake, A.Reeves, L.Jones, G.Dazley, N.Russell, E.Abraham, B.Ames, R.Griffiths, M.Rutter, C.Ames, M.Adams, S.Shadrake.

(Seated, L.to R.): D.Ashby, R.King, B.Abraham, T.Cocoran, P.Burrows.

Bedford Avenue.

(Bedford Queens Park Rangers 1905 — 1945)
(Bedford Avenue 1945 — 1982)

****

1905/06.	Friendly Matches.
1906/07 — 1910/11.	Bedford League Div.2.
1911/12.	Bedford League Div.2 (South).
1912/13.	Bedford League Div.1.
1913/14.	No Competition.
1914/15 — 1918/19.	No Competition.*
1919/20.	Bedford & Dist. Lge. Div.3.
1920/21 — 1925/26.	Bedford & Dist. Lge. Div.2(North).
1926/27.	Bedford & Dist. Lge. Div.1 (East).
1927/28 — 1938/39.	Bedford & Dist. Lge. Div. 1.
1939/40.	South Midlands Lge. Div.2.**
1939/40 — 1944/45.	Bedford Combination.
1945/46.	United Counties Lge.***
1946/47 — 1947/48.	Corinthian Lge.
1948/49 — 1949/50.	Central Amateur Lge.
1950/51 — 1955/56.	United Counties Lge. Div.2.
1956/57 — 1960/61.	United Counties Lge.***
1961/62.	United Counties Lge. Div.2.
1962/63 — 1964/65.	United Counties Lge. Div.1.
1965/66 — 1970/71.	United Counties Lge. Div.2.
1971/72.	United Counties Lge. Div.3.
1972/73 — 1979/80.	United Counties Lge. Div.2.+
1980/81.	Bedford Senior Lge. Div.1.++
1981/82.	Bedford Senior Lge. Div.2.++

+++

*   Team Named 'Bedford XI' competed in the Bedford
Combination which included players from several
Bedford teams, including those from Bedford Q.P.R.
(Bedford Avenue).
**   Few games were played by teams in this League
before War intervened.
*** During this period, only a single division in the
League operated.
+   Divisions of League re-numbered from 1972/73,
such that 'Div.2' was in effect the Third Division.
++   Divisions of League such that 'Div.1' was in
effect the Second Division, etc.

Bedford Avenue.

Main Facts and Achievements.

Grounds:
Queens Park Recreation Ground.
Russell Park. Cardington Road.
Newnham Avenue. (Enclosed Ground)
Newnham Avenue. (Open Ground)
(From 1950, the occasional 'big' match was played at
enclosed Grounds in Bedford)

Colours:
Blue and White. (Initially 'hooped' shirts, latterly
Royal Blue Shirts with White Collars)

Nickname:
'The Bolos' or 'The Rangers' — As Bedford Q.P.R.
'The Avenue' — as Bedford Avenue.

First Game:
Season 1905/06 — Friendly. (Details Unknown)
Last Game:
Dunton Reserves 2. Bedford Avenue 7.
(Bedford Senior League — Div.2. 7th May 1982).

Record Attendance:
3,500 versus 'An Army X1'. (Kilby Cup. 4th May 1945.
N.B. 2,800 — Bedford Minors (Juniors) last match 1947.

Major Honours:
Bedford Lge. Div.2: Runners-up. 1906/07 to 08/09 incl.
Bedford & District League Champions:
Div. 3   —   1919/20.
Div. 2 (North) — 1925/26.
Div. 1 (East) — 1926/27.
Bedford Comb. Champions: 1939/40 to 1942/43 Incl.
United Counties Lge. Champs: 1961/62.
                            1945/46 (Div.2).
Reached 4th Qualifying round of F.A.Cup — 1945/46.
Juniors — Undefeated for three seasons in the 1940's.
Cup Winners: (In brackets — full dates not known)
Bedfordshire Senior Cup : 1940/41. 1942/43.
Bedfordshire Hospital Cup: (1932 1935).
Bletchley Hospital Cup : (1931).
Hinchingbroke Cup   : (1930).
Kilby Cup   :(1946).
Luton Hospital Cup:(1946).
Bedford League Cup Div.1 :   Winners. 1933.
Bedfordshire Minor Cup (Juniors) :   1948.

-6-

Bedford Avenue.

The rise to Senior status was as long an uphill struggle for Bedford Avenue, as was their drop to obscurity and final demise.

Soon after the turn of the Century, a number of youngsters would play their own, disorganised, style of football in the Queens Park Recreation Ground - an area which still exists to this day just to the South-West of the centre of Bedford. Most of these lads were apprentices at the nearby works of W.H. Allen, Sons and Co.Ltd. Eventually these footballers decided that they should organise themselves into a proper team, and invited a Mr. Bob Hamblett to be their Honorary Secretary - a wise decision in the event since this gentleman was to devote a lot of time and enthusiasm to the post. A Mr. Harry Harvey was asked to be their Chairman - he accepted the and remained in that capacity for many years. Mr. Harvey also became the Chairman of the Bedford & District League for a long period of time, and in addition was a qualified Football Referee. His officiating included three F.A.Amateur Cup ties.

1905 - 1919.

The first season, 1905/06 saw the Club play just friendly games, most of them away from 'home' - at this time 'home' games consisted of any readily available pitch ! No formal record of these games was made, nor any written record of the Club's first game or team line-up. However amongst the team on that (probable) September day were:-
Freddy Smith, 'Ginger' Chapman, Harry Mardle (the latter two were both to become Luton Town professionals).
'Napper' Chapman (later of Bedford Town), Reg. Shadrake (A family name to eventually become synonimous with the Club), Dick Jones, Harold Smith and George Green.
The original name of the Club was variously Bedford Q.P.R., Queens Park Rangers (Bedford), and the probable formal name of 'Bedford Queens Park Rangers'. This title was evolved more from the area of their origins rather than from the somewhat more illustrious London Club! Another popular reference was simply 'Q.P.R.' which could no doubt lead to confusion for other Football Historians!

Bedford Avenue.

In 1905 (it was still three years before the eventually famous 'Bedford Town' came on the scene) there were many 'Bedfords' around already including; Bedford Queens Park Excelsiors, Bedford Socials (who could attract crowds of several hundred to their home games in Russell Park), Bedford Athletic, Bedford Rose and Bedford Falcons.

The game, in those far off days, was played with more of a spirit of enjoyment rather than rigid rules and the demands to win. Two examples illustrate this philosophy. In the inaugural Season, a friendly match was arranged at Biggleswade, but the horse-brake (the equivalent of the present-day 'team coach') broke down at Sandy, some three miles from the Ground. There was no option for the team and supporters to walk the rest of the journey. But despite this additional exercise the game was won, and the long walk had to be repeated back to the transport, which by this time had been repaired. The second incident related to the home game versus Cranfield, which occured during the Club's first season in League football. 'Home' on this occasion was Russell Park. However, at the last minute the pitch was discovered to be unavailable, and an alternative venue was rapidly arranged at the 'Church Lads' ground. Unfortunately not all of the team were aware of this re-arrangement, and come the kick-off, only seven Rangers players were present; not to be deterred, two volunteer footballers were found from the spectators and the nine men managed a creditable one all draw!

Although the Queens Park Recreation Ground, also known as 'The Slipe', was the Club's original home venue, this was changed after a few months to Russell Park. This unenclosed Park still exists, and provides several pitches and facilities for different sports. In these very early days, the Club were soon able to attract a great deal of support - despite their Junior rating - and often several hundred spectators were present at home matches. This encouragement led to inevitable progress, and the Bedford & District League was first entered in 1906.

The competition included most of the previously mentioned Bedford teams and also Kempston Rovers, who achieved Senior status in 1927 and joined the Bedfordshire (later South Midlands) League.

Bedford Avenue.

The Bedford Avenue 'Bolos' (a strange and not readily identifiable nickname) enjoyed immediate success in League competition and finished as runners-up in each of their first three seasons. This achievement, which did not include any official awards for their efforts, prompted the local M.P., Mr.W.Attenborough, to present the Club with a set of consolation medals.

The 1909/10 season commenced in fine style, and by the 15th of October the Avenue led the table without having conceded a single goal. The winning run did not continue however and the Championship eluded the team yet again.

For two seasons a period of re-organisation was undertaken in the League when a regionalised Second Division was created. This move did not bring much success to the Avenue as only mid-table final positions were attained in the South section.

In the Autumn of 1912, following the resignation of several clubs, Bedford Q.P.R. competed in the First Division. Not the honour that it may have appeared since only five clubs competed with each other, namely: Bedford Q.P.R., Biggleswade, Harrold United, Luton Amateurs, and Wooton Blue Cross. The season was a near disaster, for by the end of the year the Club were in the second from bottom position, and in their final placing ended as wooden spoonists. To make matters worse, two points were deducted for playing an ineligible player (obviously the rules had been tightened up by this time!). The team's one win was therefore cancelled out, producing nil points in eight games, with 43 goals having been conceded.

The following season also saw the start of the First World War and the League was completely reorganised, Bedford Q.P.R. played a few friendlies before their activities were curtailed for the duration.

A team under the heading of 'Bedford X1', which included several of the Rangers players, competed for the next five seasons in the renamed 'Bedford Combination'.

1919/20 - 1928/29.

After the Great War, the Club was in effect reformed, but retained many former Officials, Players and Supporters. A meeting was held at the home of the Chairman in December 1918 when the decision was made that the Club would start again. Friendly games were played for the few months, before matches were recommenced in a

League for the 1919/20 season. A start was made at the bottom of the ladder once again, with entry into the Bedford & District League Division 3, with a second string in the 4th Division. Success was immediate with both teams becoming Champions in their respective divisions, and in September 1920 the first game in the Second Division was played. For five seasons the position remained fairly static until further progress was made with a promotion to the 1st Division (East) in the 1926/27 Campaign. Despite it's 'Junior' status, the Bedford & District League was highly regarded, with many of it's members over the years rising to well established Senior Club level. Support from the public was forthcoming and it was not unusual during the 1920's for Second Division games to attract crowds in excess of 500.

League competition was now played under strict rules, unlike the earlier pre-war encounters. In March 1924, in the home game versus Bedford Clarence (which was lost by the Bollos by 1-2), Phillips of the Q.P.R. was sent off. Play was resumed, and despite pleas by the home Captain, Phillips was determined to rejoin his team on the pitch. Eventually the referee blew time after 89 minutes, and subsequently the miscreant received a 28 day suspension!
Initially Queen's Park Recreation Ground was once again used for home matches and it was not until the mid-1920's that a move was made, back to Russell Park. High scoring was a common feature of matches, and one of the most impressive victories for the Club was a clear 14 goal thrashing at Biddenham in January 1920. Entries into local Cup Competitions were made which were generally only of a minor nature. An exception being the moderately prestigious Bletchley Hospital Cup which was first played for in the 1921/22 season and eventually won by the Q.P.R. nine years later.
The promotion season of 1925/26 was completed with a 4-1 win at Shortsands over the Reserve team of St.Neot's; two seasons later the Saints first team 'made' it to the South Midlands League. Just one year was spent in the 1st Division (East), for immediate promotion to the 1st Division proper was made by virtue of the final runners-up position out of the twelve teams. Other Clubs in this higher company included the second teams of Buckingham, Arlesley and Sandy Albions. A reserve team was dispensed with at the end of the 1924/25 season.

Bedford Avenue.

The previous ten years of football could be looked back on as being a successful period, but it was to be a further ten before Senior Football was achieved by the Q.P.R. The first half of the 1930's started with some notable successes, followed by a second period of mediocrity.

1929/30 - 1938/39.

In successive seasons starting with 1929/30, the following cups were won for the first time in each case: Hinchingbroke, Bletchley Hospital, (this, the first time the Cup had left Buckinghamshire) Bedford Hospital and finally the Bedford & District League Cup. The success in the Bletchley Hospital competition was achieved by a 4-2 victory over 'Luton Amateurs and Ramblers' of the South Midlands League, in the Final. This season also produced the best League position to date, that of third, and several 'home' games were played at Bedford Town's Eyrie Ground. One of the Club's League opponents was the Bedford North End team, who not only had their own ground - at Astell's Meadow in Cardington Road - but by this time were also entering into the F.A.Cup, an example of the status of this 'Town' League.

Most of the 1930's passed by without any honours in the League competition, although membership of the First Division was maintained throughout. But in 1938, a turning point in the Club's long held ambition to achieve Senior status was realised by the aquisition of their own Ground. Ambitious Junior Club's are so often thwarted by this problem of the use of an enclosed playing pitch, and Bedford Q.P.R. were no exception, and in later years this point was to lead directly to their own demise. The site of the Club's Ground was, as for Bedford North End, in Cardington Road but in this case was owned by Whitbread's Brewery. In recognition of this Company's help, Major Simon Whitbread became the President of the Football Club.

During the 1938/39 season a great deal of work was put into this new venue by the many stalwarts of the Club, whilst on the field a satisfactory 6th final placing in the League resulted. The sound footing that had by now established the Club led to their upward acceptance into the South Midlands League Division 2.

RANGERS OF THIRTY YEARS AGO

The Queen's Park Rangers (Bedford) A.F.C. team and officials of the 1906-7 season, many of whom are still keenly interested in local football. Back row (left to right): Messrs. Bob Hamblett, J. Freame, E. Phillips, H. Higman, A. Wildman, R. Chapman, A. Luddington, and A. Riches. Middle row (left to right): P. Chapman, W. King, J. Malpass, A. Thompson, and J. Reed. Front row (left to right): D. Jones, H. Mardle, and F. Smith.

(Bedfordshire Times and Standard)

Although the quality is poor, the significance warrants inclusion of this rare 1906 team group of the 'Rangers', as they were then known.

Bedford Avenue

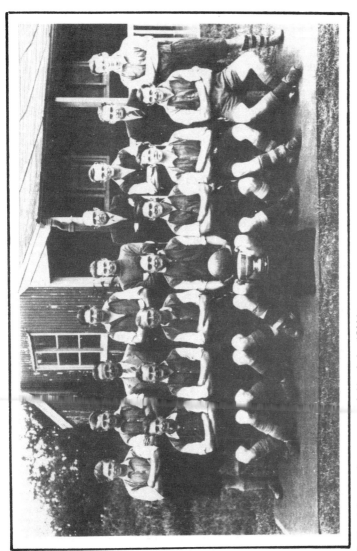

Bedford Avenue team group of the late 1940's.
(Note the pavilion, at the enclosed Newnham Avenue Ground)

(Back, L. to R.): T.Harris, D.Oakley, G.Golder, R Johnson, P.Ames, B.Salisbury (Chairman), R.King, C.Ames, P.Gilbert.

(Front, L.to R.): J.Frost, T.King, B.Staughton, B.Watts, E.Abraham, P.Dynes, D.Marriot.

Bedford Avenue.

Despite all the enthusiasm and work that had been put
into the Club over the years, this rise in status was to
no avail - at least for a few years - for the Second
World War intervened before the 1939/40 season had barely
started. A delay in arranging alternative competitive
football led to the playing of several Friendly Charity
matches at Cardington Road, and for the first time in the
Club's history they were able to charge an admission fee.
A competition was finally evolved in the Bedford area,
which continued for the duration of the War. The Bedford
Combination was in fact reborn, being the name that had
been chosen originally for the Wartime League during the
earlier Great War.

1939/40 - 1944/45.

The Bedford Combination provided competition of a
high standard since the established Senior Leagues in the
area ceased to function during the wartime period,
resulting in a number of well known Clubs (who continued
for these years) joining forces. Additionally, Servicemen
in the area - often established professionals - were
happy to offer their skills at this level.
Bedford Q.P.R., as members of the Combination, came
into their own during these war years, and coupled with
at last having their own enclosed ground enjoyed their
most successful period, which led to higher status
football when peacetime returned. The second World War
proved in some cases the making of, or conversely the
finish of many Clubs. Further South, London Caledonians
and Nunhead for instance never re-appeared after shutting
up shop in 1939, whilst Lovell's Athletic (perhaps the
most successful of all 'Work's teams') leapt to prom-
-inence during hostilities and carried on in a higher
status after.
Bedford Q.P.R. dominated the Bedford Combination
during seasons 1939/40 to 1942/43 being Champions on all
four occasions. The first of these Campaigns saw the Club
in the final of the Bedfordshire Senior Cup, only to be
denied a win by Waterlow's (Dunstable). The following
season however the Club went one better and became the
first Bedford based winners since the Bedford Montrose
triumph way back in 1899. The next season the honour
passed to Bedford St. Cuthbert's only to return to the
Q.P.R. and so record a hat-trick of successes for the

town after so many unsuccessful years. It is a strange
fact that the most Senior team in the area for so many
years, Bedford Town, never achieved this honour.
   Although finishing in high final positions in the
Combination table, the next two seasons saw the title
pass from the Club. However 1945 produced the capture of
the Bedford Hospital Cup following a remarkable win in
the final. The decider was played over two legs, and
Potton won the first by two goals. the return at
Cardington Road was attended by 1,265 spectators, at
which the Q.P.R. recorded a 9-2 victory !
   Despite the efforts put in by Club Members it became
apparent that the home Ground was not going to be
suitable in the long term, due to it's low lying location
close to the River Ouse, and the continuous problem of
drainage and flooding. Also at this time the home venue
was in a very open area and subject to vandalism; over
the years a small fortune could be envisaged for the cost
of replacing broken goal-posts !
   In the final event, the move to a Council owned site
in Newnham Avenue was offered and accepted by Bedford
Q.P.R. This new Ground was located where the present
Athletics Stadium is positioned, just a few hundred yards
from the Club's earlier 'home' in Russell Park. Whilst
still very near the River, it was at a higher elevation,
and therefore the water problems previously encountered
down the road were not repeated. In 1945, work by
enthusiastic members commenced in earnest to create
another enclosed Ground in order to provide Senior status
football, and within a short time a fenced enclosure with
a roped off pitch and a Pavilion were provided.
   The end of the war coincided with the arrival of Alec
Reeves from London, a man who was to have a large effect
on the Club's future progress. Reeves was a pre-war
Wimbledon and England Amateur International player, and
his experience and enthusiasm were soon channeled into
his newly adopted Club.
   In April 1945, it was proposed by the Bedfordshire
F.A. that the Club should be granted Associate Membership
of the Football Association, and this was readily
accepted - a rare distinction for an Amateur Club. This
newly found status warranted a change in name from the
somewhat unwieldy and confusing 'Bedford Queens Park
Rangers', and the Club requested that the name should be
changed to 'Bedford Association F.C.', but this proposal

was turned down by the Bedfordshire F.A. The Club finally
settled on 'Bedford Avenue' at the suggestion of Alec
Reeves.

The name admirably suited the Club who were now based
in Newnham - Avenue - although it may also have been
evolved from London based Walthamstow Avenue.

By the Spring of 1945, a number of 'serious' Friendly
matches were arranged at the new Ground, and the public
responded by turning up in force at the new Headquarters.
On the 9th of May, an Army X1 were in opposition, and
included several players from Football League Clubs,
including pre-war Welsh International - Perry - who had
been playing for Brentford during the hostilities. The
official attendance was 3,500, with gate receipts of £51,
and represented new records for the Avenue. A report
stated that: "The largest Football Crowd to assemble in
Bedford for many years...", were present (The largest in
fact since 1934, when Bedford Town made their debut in
the F.A.Cup first round proper). The Avenue delighted
their followers with a single goal victory in a highly
competitive game, that was full of missed chances, with
the visitors being the worst culprits! The game was for
the 'Kilby Cup', with profits going to the Red Cross and
the St.John's Prisoner of War Fund.

An amusing incident can be retold which occured in a
friendly match arranged by Alec Reeves, that was played
in London. Tooting & Mitcham of the Athenian League, then
holders of the Surrey Senior Cup who were enjoying a run
of 16 undefeated games, were the hosts. The Avenue had
only recently undergone their name change, but the
fixture that was advertised outside the Ground referred
to the visitors as 'Queens Park Rangers', presumably due
to outdated information. A number of spectators were
known to have entered the ground in the belief that they
were to see the locals play in opposition to the Reserve
team of the more illustrious London based League team! A
fact that may well have boosted the attendance. This
misconception was believable from the result, since with
just four minutes left the Avenue were winning, but the
final outcome was a very creditable three all draw.

Bedford Avenue.

1945/46 - 1947/48.

The Club's wartime abilities were recognised by their
admittance to the United Counties League, with a Reserve
team in the South Midlands League - the latter of which
had hosted the Avenue's first eleven just a few years
earlier. A Junior team was also formed for 15 to 17 year
olds.

It was The Avenue's ambition to join a more 'notable'
London based Amateur League, but, with Britain still on a
wartime type footing and with the attendant travelling
difficulties, the more local United Counties competition
was a suitable compromise. Even with only eight teams in
contention, the standard was high and included the first
teams of Corby, Wisbech and Kettering.

The first game brought Kettering to Newnham Avenue and
a 'large crowd' was present, as there was for the
following fixture against the Northampton 'A' team. A
good record was maintained throughout the next few months
and the season was an unqualified successful introduction
into Senior Football. Bedford Avenue became the Champions
with ten wins and two draws in their 14 fixtures. One of
the two defeats was an amazing ten goal reverse at
Peterborough, although the return - and final match - was
a 5-1 win to the Bedford team.

The two major Cup Competitions were entered for the
first time, with something of a sensation in the F.A.Cup.
The 1st qualifying round produced fitting opposition with
neighbours Bedford Town visiting Newnham Avenue. The two
Clubs had always been on the best of terms despite the -
theoretical - large gulf between their abilities. The
Town had by now moved up to the highest non-League
echelon, that of the Southern League, and were obviously
clear-cut favourites to win. 2,500 spectators packed into
the small enclosure and were amazed to see the minnows
hold the 'giants' to a goalless draw. The replay at the
Eyrie a few days later, was expected to be a mere
formality - not so much 'if' the Town would win, but by
how many! The three thousand crowd were stunned when The
Avenue romped away with a four goal clear cut victory!
This win was to prove to be the Club's most notable
victory in their history. The result was no 'one-off'
since Hitchin Town were the next victims (away from
home), followed by another 2,000 plus crowd to see the
3rd qualifying round home victory over Letchworth.

Bedford Avenue.

There was now just one hurdle to overcome before the entry of the Football League Clubs. But no fairy-tale ending was to be, for the Avenue were firmly put in their place with a 1-6 defeat at the hands of Grantham.

Surprisingly in what should have been the easier Competition, that of the Amateur Cup, little success was forthcoming. A lucky - by all accounts - 3-2 victory over Leighton United in the first qualifying round was followed by a home reverse with the same score to Luton Amateurs before another 2,000 crowd. Some measure of satisfaction was obtained over the Luton team when they were defeated by 4-2 at Newnham Avenue in the final of the Luton Hospital Cup which produced a £53 gate.

Several prestigious friendlies were played, notably a ten goal thrashing over Windsor and Eton of the newly formed Corinthian League before 1,000 spectators. Other matches included an entertaining five all draw with the '101 Military Convalescent Depot - Kempston' (not with the inmates !), and a game versus RAF Henlow. Despite a 2-5 defeat in the latter, the match was memorable in view of the opposition which included the renowned Laurie Scott of Arsenal fame (who was unfortunately injured in the match) and W.G. Richardson of West Bromwich Albion.

This post-war successful season led the Club into the Corinthian League for the next campaign. The initial nine Club entry in 1945, was increased to thirteen, with additional Senior Clubs regaining their post-war footing, and included such names as Slough United (later 'Town'), Maidenhead United and Walton & Hersham. With the increasing return to 'norm' came the attendant return to the fold of quality teams and their attendant amateur players, and The Avenue came down to Earth in no uncertain terms! By May 1947, the Club were shown to have been out of their depth, when, with only nine points to their credit they were clear-cut wooden spoonists.

Despite this major setback, the Cup Competitions were not without success. In the major competition, victories were recorded over near neighbours Kempston Rovers and an excellent away victory by seven goals to one over Biggleswade Town before over 1,000 spectators. The run ended with a home defeat to Hitchin Town. The 4th qualifying round was reached in the Amateur Cup (this was to be the team's best ever run), with victories that included an exciting 5-4 result against Queens Works (of Bedford) and a 4-2 home success over Chatteris Town in the Divisional Final. A halt came at the hands of Lowestoft Town, who went on to reach the quarter-finals of the Competition.

The Junior team were to make an impact locally, and achieved the first of their many successes when they became the Champions of the Bedford Minor League. Their final match producing an incredible attendance of 2,800 and receipts of £99.

The 1947/48 season was even more disastrous, for the Seniors and a dreadful League campaign was matched with no success in the Cups. The Corinthian League had one addition, in Chesham United, but The Avenue could only record four victories (three at home), and with just eight points were left ten points clear at the bottom of the table. In contrast the Youth team maintained their progress.

After many years in Junior Football, Bedford Avenue had had a brief encounter with Senior Amateur football at a high level but they were now on the path of an equally slow slide into oblivion.

1948/49 - 1960/61.

A suitable Competition had now to be sought which was compatible with the Club's potential and coupled with more local teams, since travelling in the Corinthian League had been an excessive expense for a team from Bedford. The less prominent Central Amateur League accepted their application, and they joined just eight other Clubs including Boldmere St. Michael's, Lockheed Leamington and Coventry Amateurs - hardly local derbys but generally with less lengthy journeys to away fixtures. This League existed for a total of only nine seasons, (each side of the Second World War) with that of 1948/49 being the penultimate.

The Avenue had been invited to join the newly formed Metropolitan League, but declined since the travelling would again have been excessive. The other nine far flung Clubs consisted of, Callendar Cable Athletic, Chingford Town, Chipperfield, Dagenham, Dickinson (Aspley), Hammersmith, Headington United (Reserves), Hove, St. Neots & District and Twickenham. A greater mixture of Clubs would be difficult to find in one League, with new and old established teams, Reserves, Professionals and Amateurs and all from such diverse areas !

Bedford Avenue

The present Stand at Newnham Avenue – on the site of the Avenue's former Ground.
(Photo: Dave Twydell)

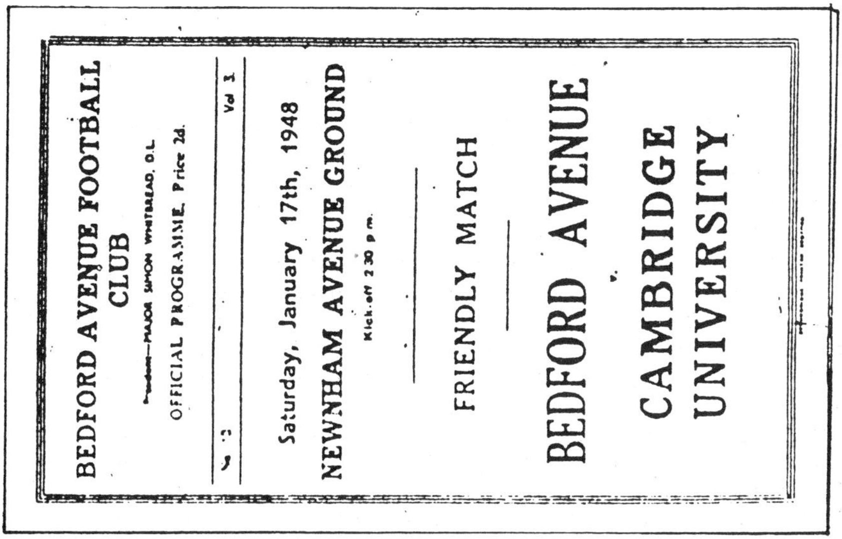

Bedford Avenue

BEDFORD AVENUE FOOTBALL CLUB

President—MAJOR SIMON WHITBREAD, O.L.

OFFICIAL PROGRAMME. Price 2d.

Vol 1

Saturday, January 17th, 1948

NEWNHAM AVENUE GROUND

Kick-off 2.30 p.m.

FRIENDLY MATCH

BEDFORD AVENUE
v.
CAMBRIDGE UNIVERSITY

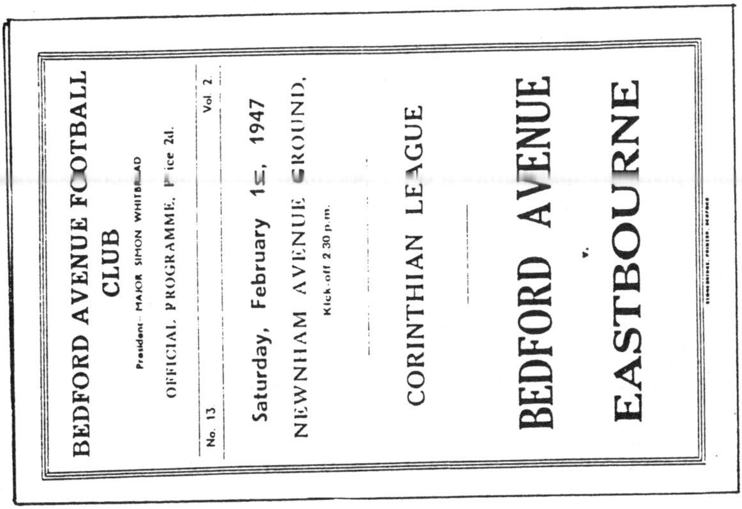

BEDFORD AVENUE FOOTBALL CLUB

President—MAJOR SIMON WHITBREAD

OFFICIAL PROGRAMME. Price 2d.

Vol 2

No. 13

Saturday, February 1st, 1947

NEWNHAM AVENUE GROUND.

Kick-off 2.30 p.m.

CORINTHIAN LEAGUE

BEDFORD AVENUE
v.
EASTBOURNE

Regular four page programmes were issued for a few post-war seasons.

-21-

The Central Amateur League, despite it's expected more suitable status for the Club, proved a far from easy competition, and the Club only managed to achieve a mid-table final placing.

Trouble was already brewing with regard to the Newnham Avenue Ground, where the Club was attempting to secure exclusive use of the venue (during the football season). This failure did not help in their attempts to regain a higher status.

The 1949/50 campaign was the Avenue's second (and last), in the Central Amateur League - and also the last season of this competition. But no honours were won, and there were equally no successes in the two major Cup Competitions. The first game in the F.A.Cup - when Bedford Town's Eyrie Ground was used as the Avenue's 'home' Ground - was lost. In the Amateur Cup, the Club bowed out with defeat at Wolverton - in theory an 'inferior' South Midlands League team - by six clear goals!

A change of League was therefore forced upon the Club, and the only reasonable choice was the United Counties once again, where they were readily accepted, but in the newly formed Second Division. For ten seasons, successes were rare with final positions usually well down in the bottom half of the table. However for five years the Club's status was raised when, from 1956/57, the League operated only one Division. For a while they were able to rub shoulders with the likes of St. Neots Town, Kettering Town Reserves and the Northampton 'A' team. The reinstatement of a Second Division for the 1961/62 campaign to which the Avenue became members again, produced the only real success for years when the Championship was won; this just one year after finishing fourth from bottom in the single division League of 17 teams.

The 1950/51 season was to be their last entry in the F.A.Cup. In the extra preliminary round, neighbours Bedford St. Cuthberts - who were at this time competing in the South Midlands League - were opposed for the second season running, and on this occasion defeated by 6-1, with the match played at Kempston Rovers Ground. Wootton Blue Cross then overcame The Avenue by four goals. The Amateur Cup Competition was competed for until the end of the decade but successes were rare. The 1st qualifying round was reached in 1951 when they were beaten by Luton Amateurs, and at the same stage one year later they succumbed to Shefford Town by six clear goals; this later match was preceded by earlier wins over Kents Athletic (played at the R.B.S. Ground, Kempston) and a second match in Kempston over the Rovers. But defeats became the norm, 4-6 to A.C.Delco of the South Midlands League in the 1954/55 season - following a goalless draw - and a 2-7 thrashing dealt out by Stotfold four years later, being typical of the Club's reduced ability.

Even local Cup Competitions resulted in few honours, although the Scott Gatty Trophy was won in 1950, only to be lost the next season with a defeat by St. Neots St. Mary's - wooden-spoonists in the South Midlands League Division 1.

A Bedfordshire Senior Cup game during the 1951/52 season was ordered to be replayed for a rather unusual reason, and one that highlighted one of the problems besetting Bedford Avenue. The match in question was played at Newnham Avenue against Harrold United, a village team that had enjoyed recent successes in the lower divisions of the South Midlands League. A 3-1 victory to the Avenue ensued, but Harrold complained, stating that the rules of the Competition required that Gate money would be taken; Bedford Avenue were unable to comply with this requirement since the terms of their Lease from the Local Corporation now allowed only a collection to be taken (hence the reason for major Cup-ties being staged on alternative Grounds). A replay was ordered, in which the Avenue were leading 3-2 with one minute to play; Harrold equalised, and then went on to win by the odd goal in nine at the end of extra time.

Despite having an enclosed Ground, the restrictions on it's use - and eventual loss - was one of the main factors that led the Club down the Senior Football 'ladder'. An approach was made to the Council during the summer of 1946, for covered accommodation at the Ground, but despite the Club's success at this time, the request fell upon deaf ears. Attempts were then made in May 1949 to secure the sole use of the Newnham Avenue enclosure, since despite being an Amateur Club, without the financial gain of 'gate money' it was impossible to make ends meet at Senior level football. Once again the Club were given no encouragement. A typical loss on a season (1952/53) of £25 was a not inconsiderable sum at that time.

The only prolonged success came from an unexpected quarter, for despite competition from elsewhere - not least at Bedford Town F.C. - the Club were able to maintain a Junior side of quality. The Junior team were undefeated for three years, and back in 1948 not only won the Bedfordshire Minor Cup, but also defeated a full Northamptonshire Youth X1 by three clear goals at Kettering Town's Ground. The two outstanding players in the team were Percy Ames, who, whilst still a Junior, played for the full County side and later played for Tottenham and Colchester United; and Bill Abraham (Great Britain National Association of Boys Clubs Captain at Wembley in 1948) who had trials with West Bromwich, but later died at an early age, after playing a football match.

1961/62 - 1979/80.

In 1961, hopes of a revival in the Club's fortunes were soon dashed from an unexpected area. It was decided by their Landlords that the Newnham Avenue Ground - that had suited them in a reasonable fashion - was to be developed. It was decided that a brand new Athletics Stadium would be built, and it was understood by Bedford Avenue that they would be able to continue to play at this venue within the area bounded by the running track.

With the future superior changing facilities, concrete terracing on one side and partly covered seated Grandstand, the future looked bright. The inconvenience suffered whilst the Stadium was being built required the team to use the adjacent unfenced football pitch, but this, at the time, seemed to be a small price to pay. However on completion of the new Ground, the Club were devastated to learn that objections had been raised regarding it's use as a Football Ground. In addition the insurmountable problem was discovered that the central area was too small to stage Senior Football. This hopeless setback resulted in the start of a long drawn out end for the Club.

Despite winning the 1960/61 season League title, promotion was denied the Club, due to their inferior and unenclosed facilities. With the new Stadium denied to them, a grade 'C' classification, the lowest acceptable to the League ruled out any possibility of a rise in status either then or in the future.

The 1961/62 title was followed by a third placing, followed by regular lowly positions near the foot of the table. A good start was made at the start of the 1968/69 season, but a 2-10 defeat in late September was the start of a disastrous year which resulted in rock bottom position by the end of the campaign. A Third Division had now been introduced and although relegation was not automatic at this time, two years later - in 1971 - a second from bottom final position and the conceding of 127 goals in 34 matches sealed their fate and a drop down to the League's lowest group. Due to re-classification of the different Divisions in 1972, and hence the Avenue becoming members of the 'Second Division, the fact remained that this was still in reality, the 'Third' Division.

New faces in United Counties League football included Belsize, later Milton Keynes Borough - who became Champions in 1973 - Deanshanger Athletic, and V.S. Rugby. For the next few seasons it was still a struggle even at this lower status, and only in the 1974/75 season was a respectable mid-table placing of eighth achieved. Five new Clubs tried their hand in the United Counties League between 1970 and 1978, namely Blisworth (until 1978), Buckingham Town - from the South Midlands League, Leighton Town who remained for only two years, plus Newport Pagnell Town and Vauxhall Motors.

The 1978/79 campaign was awful with the Club finishing in third from bottom position and even worse one year later, at one place lower; the latter year saw the Club concede 99 goals in 28 games!

Ironically a lifeline was thrown to The Avenue towards the end of this disastrous season, when the possibility of an area for the sole use of the Club arose. However, this was not pursued since the team's dwindling fortunes on the pitch was matched by equally reduced support, and the money for such a project was just not forthcoming or conceivable for the future.

For a number of years the Club had hung onto their United Counties League membership, despite the lack of minimum facilities - another 'open' pitch in Jubilee Park was also used for a time. For the 1980/81 season, a further re-organisation of the League resulted in their being no place for Bedford Avenue, for the Second Division was dissolved, and was replaced with a section for Reserve teams of higher division Clubs.

Bedford Avenue.

1980/81 - 1983/84.

With now only a small nucleus of support for the Club, they soldiered on, but now as a Junior Club. The Bedford Senior League was entered, but only at the First Division level, and not the higher Premier section. Even this level of football proved to be too much for the Avenue, and relegation to the Second Division was the final result, at the end of this first season in Junior football. The final active time for the Club was played at a very minor level, competing against obscure Clubs - at least to those outside of Bedford - and versus the Reserves of obscure Clubs! Despite a nine goal defeat in one game, the 1981/82 season ended with the following record: Played- 26. Won- 12. Drawn- 5. Lost-9. Goals: 64 - 55. Final position 6th of 14 teams.

The last match for the team resulted in a 7-2 win, away to Dunton Reserves, watched by a handful of Officials and a few casual observers;

"Avenue returned to their winning ways with an emphatic win over Dunton. The Avenue opened the scoring after just two minutes when Rob Johnston put the ball in the back of the net from a rebound. Dunton equalised eight minutes later due to slack marking by the Bedford defence. It was hard going for both teams with a pitch like concrete. Dunton took the lead midway through the first half from a free kick, but on the stroke of half-time Bedford Avenue were awarded a penalty which was converted by Eddy Clarke.

The second half was all the Avenue, and with the wind behind them goals came in quick succession; from Rob Johnston, Mark Stupple (two), Beattie and Sargent. In fact Bedford could have had more, especially Iain Clarke who shot wide on several occasions."

In many ways the fall and eventual demise of Bedford Avenue could be compared with their more famous neighbours Bedford Town: Their last game was played with no foreknowledge that it was to be their final one, it happened in the same season, and the root of both Clubs problems was the lack of a suitable home Ground.

Bedford Avenue.

For two more seasons the name of Bedford Avenue still existed - in a non-playing capacity. In the summer of 1984, the Club amalgamated with old rivals Bedford North End, and the Club became 'Bedford North End Avenue'. The new Club played in the Bedford Senior League with the home Ground being an open pitch, adjacent to the Newnham Avenue Athletics Stadium!

Personalities.

In the foregoing History of Bedford Avenue a number of names have been mentioned, to whom the Club owed a debt of gratitude, however the record would not be complete without further reference to the Shadrake family. For many years the three Shadrake brothers were THE Club. All three were founder-members back in 1905. Ted (including the role of Secretary) was a member for more than 60 years. Brothers Syd and Len were also actively interested in the Club for a long period. Two notable players have already been referred to, others that made their mark included; George Watson (Bedford Town and Tottenham Hotspur trialist), Roy Johnson (Bedford Town and Arsenal trialist), Len Newnham (Northampton Town), Roger Simmonds (Welsh Amateur International), Ken Lee (West Bromwich Albion) plus Harry Lee and Arthur Cornell - both Luton Town.

Programmes.

From the Club's entry into Senior Football (immediately after the Second World War) until 1962, the Club regularly issued programmes. Despite this long period few copies appear to have survived.

Attendances.

During pre-war - Junior status - days, 300 to 400 hundred spectators were not uncommon around the unroped touchlines. Whilst playing at the Newnham Avenue Ground in the late 1940's and early 1950's, similar numbers were normally present with many more for important matches. But, from the late 1950's, support, in common with most Clubs, began to dwindle but particularly after the enclosed Ground was lost, and by the early 1970's the normal attendance could be counted in tens.

Bedford Avenue

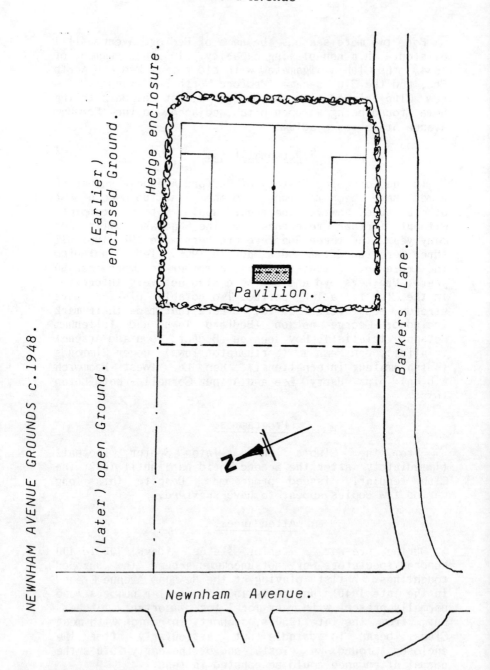

Newnham Avenue.

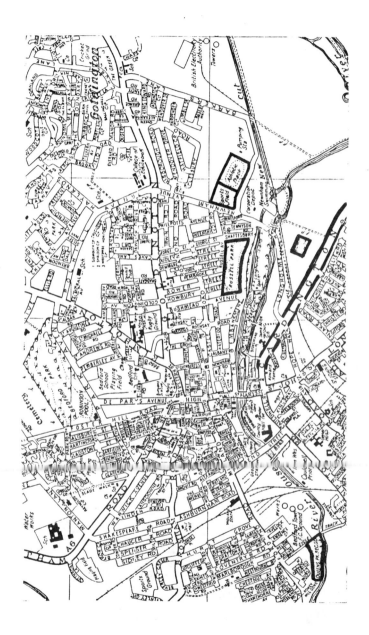

Ground Locations.

Lovell's Athletic.

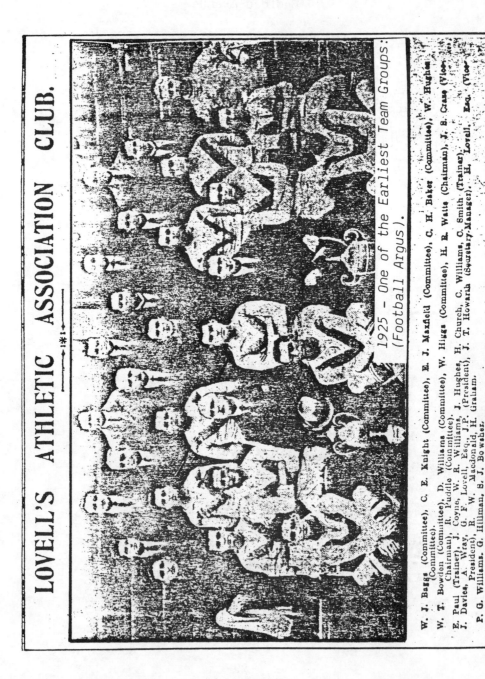

LOVELL'S ATHLETIC ASSOCIATION CLUB.

1925 – One of the Earliest Team Groups:
(Football Argus).

W. J. Bagg (Committee), C. E. Knight (Committee), E. J. Maxfield (Committee), C. H. Baker (Committee), W. Hughes (Committee).
W. T. Bowden (Committee), D. Williams (Committee), W. Higgs (Committee), H. E. Watts (Chairman), J. B. Crane (Vice-Chairman), R. Puddle (Committee).
E. Paul (Trainer), J. Coyne, W. R. Williams, J. Hughes, H. Church, C. Williams, C. Smith (Trainer).
J. Davies, A. Wray, G. F. Lovell, Esq., J.P. (President), J. T. Howarth (Secretary-Manager), H. Lovell. Esq. (Vice-President), R. W. Macdonald, H. Graham.
P. G. Williams, G. Hillman, S. J. Bowsher.

-30-

Lovell's Athletic.

(1918 - 1969)

:::

1918/19 - 1919/20.	Friendly Matches.
1920/21 - 1921/22.	Newport & Dist. League Div.1.
1922/23 -	South Wales Amateur League.
1923/24 - 1924/25.	Western League.
1925/26 -	Western League Div.2.
1926/27 - 1927/28.	Western League Div.1.
1928/29 - 1929/30.	Southern League (West Div.)
1930/31 - 1931/32.	Western League Div.1. *
1939/40 -	Southern League (West. Section) **
1940/41 - 1941/42.	(Wartime) Welsh League and Western Regional League.
1942/43 - 1944/45.	Football League - West.
1945/46 - 1946/47.	Welsh League Div.1.
1947/48 - 1957/58.	Southern League.
1958/59 -	Southern League (North-West).
1959/60 - 1963/64.	Welsh League Div.1.
1964/65 - 1968/69.	Welsh League Premier Div.

During the seasons 1924/25 to 1938/39 the Club's first team also competed in the Welsh League Div.1.
* First team also in London Combination.
** Wartime Competition.

:::

Summary of Main Facts and Achievements.

Ground: Rexville, Newport, Monmouthshire.

Colours: Varied considerably over the years, but generally:
Red Shirts (with Blue and/or White).
Black or Blue Shorts.

Nickname: The Toffeemen.

Record Attendance:
10,000 versus Cardiff City. 31st March 1945. (Football League North Cup. 1st Round, 2nd Leg)

Lovell's Athletic.

Major Honours:

Western Regional (Wartime Football League) Champs.:
1940/41. 1941/42.
Football League West Champs. : 1942/43. 1943/44.
Southern League (West. Section) Champs.: 1939/40.
Western League Champs.   : 1923/24.
Western League Div.1 Champs. : 1938/39.
Welsh League (South. Section) Div.1 Champs.: 1931/32.
1937/38. 1938/39. 1945/46. 1946/47. 1965/66.
(Reserves) 1947/48.
Premier Div. Champs.: 1965/66.

Welsh Senior Cup Winners. : 1947/48.
                 Finalists.: 1958/59.
Welsh Amateur Cup Winners.: 1925/26. 1926/27. 1927/28.
1953/54.
Monmouth. Sen. Cup Winners:
1929/30. 1930/31. 1936/37. 1937/38. 1938/39. 1946/47.
1948/49. 1949/50. 1951/52. 1954/55.
South Wales & Monmouth Sen. Cup Winners.:
1930/31. 1934/35. 1936/37. 1948/49. 1954/55.

(English) F.A.Cup.:
3rd Round: 1945/46.
1st Round: 1955/56.

Welsh Internationals:
(Full): Eddie Jenkins (v. England 1924/25)
(Amateur): From 1924/25 to 1965/66 a total of 28
different Players.
Great Britain (Olympics):
Idwal Robling, 1952. (Only Welsh Player)

Harry Clarke transferred to Tottenham Hotspur (and
later England) in 1948/49 season, for £6,000 plus
Benefit from a Friendly match — played at Spurs (the
choice of venue produced only a poor attendance)!

Wartime 'Guest' Players included:
(Scottish Internationals) Bill Shankly and Archie
Macaulay, plus Bert Turner of Wales.

The Club had, during their fifty-one years, just five
different Managers.

Lovell's Athletic.

The emergence of Lovell's Athletic F.C. in 1918 came at a time when Soccer was at a high in South Wales. The Southern League abounded with Clubs from the South of the principality with four in the First Division (shortly to become the new Football League Third Division), whilst the Second Division was an almost total Welsh affair!

Lovell's started as a pure amateur 'Work's' team and was created by Harold Lovell. Messrs. G.F.Lovell & Co. Ltd. were Manufacturing Confectioners, makers of "Toffee Rex" - the 'King of Toffees' as they were to be known - and were located at Rexville, an area near to the town centre of Newport, Monmouthshire. Mr. G.F.Lovell, Head of the family business, soon became the Football Club's President; his son Harold, was to later show his passion for the sport, eventually becoming a Life Member and President of the Welsh Football League, plus - for a long period - a Councillor on the Welsh Football Association. All in addition to a lifetime interest in the Lovell's Club. Tragically, Harold's football playing days were ended almost as soon as he founded the Club, for in the first ever match played by Lovell's Athletic F.C., he was injured, and never played again.

By late 1918, Britain was slowly recovering from the Great War, and on Christmas day, Newport County played their first post-war match - a Friendly. However, it was not until the 1920/21 season that local football in the area once again became properly re-organised, when the Newport & District League started afresh. The intervening period saw Lovell's finding their feet, and playing just friendly matches. The firm provided a Ground for the Club - opposite the Factory - and at the first meeting of the new League, on the 19th of June, Lovell's were represented. The Club were elected to the First Division, along with such Clubs as Y.M.C.A., Rivet Warmers Institute, Newport United and Caerleon, in all a 16 strong competition.

The first representative honour for the team came with the Club Captain, Jim Davies, being made Captain of the League side versus Newport County Reserves in a pre-season friendly game. September the 4th saw the team play it's first competitive match, which resulted in a 3-2 win at Llantarnam. One week later, another victory, at home, was recorded over Newport United, by 5-2. The first seven League matches were all won, but this dream

Lovell's Athletic.

start for the new Club, became a nightmare for a time as
games were then frequently lost. Nonetheless by the
season's end, the Club finished as runners-up to Risca
Park Stars. The Toffeemen also made their mark in the
prestigious 'Woodcock Cup', by reaching the final, which
was lost to Abercorn Welfare. But evidence of the Cup's
popularity could be seen in the gate money taken at the
semi-finals and final match when a total of £250 was
realised. The Monmouthshire Senior Cup was also competed
for, and in the first match, at home to Abercorn Welfare,
before a 'good crowd', six goals were shared. But the
Toffeemen lost the replay 2-9!

The following season also started well with four
victories and only one defeat, although by Christmas
through having played less games than their opponents,
only a mid-table League placing was held. As the games in
hand were played, and won, the Club rose up the table, to
become finally the Champions, having suffered only two
League defeats. Whilst the enthusiasm was building up for
the Toffeemen and monetary support was forthcoming from
the Parent Company, the same could not be said for many
other Clubs. Financial difficulties were suffered by most
Clubs, most of whom played on park pitches and therefore
could not rely on paying spectators. Aided by unem-
-ployment, that was rapidly becoming a feature of the
area, by the season's end several Clubs disbanded or were
expelled from the League for not completing their
fixtures. The Woodcock Cup was won at only the Club's
second attempt, but the gate receipts for the final were
well down on the previous years's figure.

The Club's potential was realised with their
acceptance into the South Wales Amateur League, that was
dominated by Cardiff based Clubs, and with the Reserve
team taking over from the first eleven in the Newport &
District League (First Division). A third team was also
formed, and a total in excess of 50 players signed on for
the Club. Extensive alterations and improvements were
made to the Ground at Rexville which, especially in view
of their still moderate status, by now was well equipped
for both players and spectators, whilst another pitch was
acquired near the Glassworks. The Club were determined to
rival their neighbours Newport County - who were now in
the Football League - and no less than five different Cup
Competitions were entered for.

On September the 2nd, a visit was made to Caerphilly Albions for the first match in the new League. A good start was made in both Cup and League matches, although a sign of the times was apparent when the Cardiff United team came to Rexville with only ten players; the spirit of the game was demonstrated with a Lovell's player filling the vacant position! Although no honours were won, the Toffeemen gave a good account of themselves over the season, with the highlight being an appearance in the final of the National Amateur Cup. The support for the team was also encouraging, and a (an unrecorded number) record attendance was present for the League game versus Cardiff Corinthians on the 18th of November, when eight goals were shared.

The Club was rapidly going from strength to strength, and by the 1923/24 season were being referred to as 'The Famous' Lovell's Athletic! This campaign produced another elevation in status, with the Club competing alongside such Clubs as Yeovil & Petters, Minehead and Poole, in the Western League. There were only eleven Clubs in League opposition, but even so by February after 13 games - with only one defeat and a single draw - the team were three points clear at the top. This position was held at the season's end, and the Club also caused some surprises in Cup competitions. In the South Wales and Monmouthshire Senior Cup, Merthyr Town of the Football League's Third Division South were held to a draw, and then beaten 4-3 in a thrilling replay - "Never have such scenes of excitement been witnessed at Lovell's Ground" - despite being two goals in arrears at one time. The Final of the Welsh Amateur Cup was again reached, but lost to Mold, with earlier victories that included a semi-final victory over Chirk at Oswestry. The Monmouthshire Challenge Cup was the only Trophy that was won, but deservedly so, with a victory over Newport County in the Final, and before another new record attendance. The Club were also losing finalists in the Monmouth. Senior Cup, the local Hospital Cup, and the South Wales & Monmouth Senior Cup. The latter final being lost by 0-3, but to Cardiff City of the Football League. High scoring victories included 10-0 over Careau, six unopposed goals versus Mid-Rhondda, whilst four Lovell's players became Welsh Amateur International Trialists. Only six years had passed since their formation, and the Club were well and truly on the football map!

Lovell's Athletic.

The serious intent for progress was shown with further Ground improvements and the acquisition on the playing front (from Cardiff) of Eddie Jenkins the Amateur Int-ernational. From the 1924/25 season, and playing in parallel with the Western League, the Club were also represented in the Welsh League. The National League eleven was run as a virtual joint first team, and included a number of young players with the aim of them progressing into the Western League. A highly successful season was enjoyed in the Welsh League, which started with a 3-2 win at the Pengam Athletic Grounds of Cardiff Corinthians and by November, 8 victories, 5 draws and only one defeat had been recorded. By the season's end the Club showed that they were a force to be reckoned with.

The Western League showing was, however, a different matter! Far from retaining the Championship, the Club's playing ability in this League was lamentable, and the first game - 3-1 at home to Radstock - proved to be the only victory of the season. This inexplicable change of form was all the more frustrating since the many defeats were usually close affairs, apart from a 1-7 hammering at Welton Rovers.

The semi-finals of the Welsh Amateur Cup were reached, ending with a single goal defeat to Northern Nomads at Pontypridd (after a scoreless draw at Oswestry). The Club's first appearance in the Welsh Senior Cup ended in the third round defeat at Barry by three unopposed goals.

The success of one 'first' team coupled with the failure of the other, produced poor home attendances (with few exceptions a situation that was to remain with the Club until their demise), although the Club's prowess - at least in the Welsh League - ensured good crowds on their travels.

The bad Western League showing resulted in the Club having to play in the newly constituted Second Division for the 1925/26 season. Although no honours were won, a high, final place in the League was achieved, and some further 'shuffling' of the Clubs resulted in the Club being re-admitted to the First Division for the next campaign. The first game was played at Poole (before a 3,000 crowd), and the last game was also with the same opponents - the eventual Champions.

The main honour of the season went to the Toffeemen's winning of the Welsh Amateur Cup for the first time. The

holders - Northern Nomads - were beaten at the semi-final
stage, and before a 4,000 crowd at Hereford, Holywell
were defeated in the final.

The 1926/27 season saw the Club's first entry into the
(English) F.A.Cup, when two games were won. The extra-
-preliminary round required a visit to fellow Western
League opponents Minehead, when, after taking a two goal
half-time lead, the Toffeemen were eventually fortunate
to run out as 3-2 winners. Keynsham were beaten in the
next match, but the first qualifying round was lost at
Barry by 0-2.

The Club now had teams in four Leagues; the Western
Division 1 and Welsh, a Reserve eleven in Division 2 of
the Western League and the Juniors in the Newport &
District League Division 1. By the turn of the year, the
Club were lying second in the National League, 4th in the
Western Division 1 (mid-table in Division 2), whilst the
Juniors topped their League. The Club's continuing
achievements brought forth the comment: " Week after
week, Lovell's continue their onward advance..."

Surprisingly by the season's end, there were few
honours. Although satisfactory final placings in the
Leagues were achieved - including an unbeaten Western
Division 1 run that extended from the 14th of October to
March the 16th - the only real achievement was the
retention of the Welsh Amateur Cup. A run that extended
to the 7th round of the Welsh Senior Cup included a 9-1
thrashing of Pembroke Dock, when Howarth was on target on
seven occasions. The Club's ability was also noted by the
Welsh selectors, for Hillman was capped in an Amateur
International, and Lovell's provided two players for the
Welsh League representative team.

One year later, things had taken a backward step. The
teams did not maintain their high placings in their
respective Leagues, apart from the table topping debut of
the third eleven in the Monmouthshire Senior League.
However, the Amateur Cup was won for a record breaking
third consecutive time, a feat that has never been
equalled. Although little headway was made in the
F.A.Cup, the Toffeemen's fame was spreading and in the
preliminary round on September the 17th, the match at
Clevedon was eagerly anticipated by the locals, as one of
the highlights of the season. The match was won, 7-1, by
the visitors. The last two home Western League (Div.1)

matches were lost, 3-6 to Bath and 1-6 versus Weymouth.
However, these heavy reverses did not deter the Club, and
a successful application was made for entry into the
Southern League - the peak in non-League Football.

August the 25th 1928, not only marked the first ever
Football League numbering of players shirts ('1' to
'22'), but also Lovell Athletic's first Southern League
(Western Section) match - a single goal and unlucky
defeat at Bath City. But the Club made amends in their
first home match when the Bristol Rovers Reserve team
were beaten 2-1. Early results were poor in the Welsh
League - still a joint first team competition - for a
crushing 1-5 home defeat to Cardiff City was first
suffered followed by a second reverse, to Newport
County's Reserve eleven. The latter game, although a
local derby, was 'remarkably well attended' when a crowd
of 2,000 were present. This measure of support was far
and above the norm, for with competiton from a Football
League team in the town, and continued high unemployment
in parts of Wales, it was only the continued financial
support of the parent Company - and the special interest
of Harold Lovell - that was able to keep the Club at such
a Senior level. The attendance for the Monmouthshire
Challenge Cup Final at Brynmawr, delayed until September,
was broken down as follows; men - 283, unemployed - 710,
Ladies -19 and Boys - 39; this total crowd of just over
1,000 was, at this time, considered a 'fair crowd', and
gives an illustration of the unemployment that was
prevalent in the area.

The Toffeemen went out of the F.A.Cup at the first
attempt - 1-2 after six goals were shared at Barry Town;
the same team who beat Lovell's 8-0 in a Southern League
match! By the season's end it was a case of mixed fort-
-unes. The, albeit much higher standard, Southern League
results finished with the team in 8th place of 14 teams;
the Welsh League matches were generally disappointing but
the Reserves in the local County (Monmouth.) League
became Champions - despite losing their first three
games. The only other trophy won, was the Monmouthshire
Amateur Cup - the Club's higher status barred them from
the National non-professional competition.

The 1929/30 season saw Howarth, the Club's consistent
prolific goalscorer, hang up his boots, while Miles and
Western were transferred to Charlton Athletic; Good
arrived from Raith plus Gardiner from Clapton Orient.

Lovell's Athletic.

This Campaign resulted in a similar position as a year
earlier, with a hat-trick of successes achieved in
Monmouthshire - the County League, plus the Senior and
Challenge Cups. Despite the good football displayed, the
Southern League results were generally poor - a repeat
final placing of 8th - matched by likewise disappointing
home attendances!

A change was made for the 1930/31 season, when the
Toffeemen resigned from the Southern League and instead
opted for the, geographically surprising, London Combination. The reason given being the higher standard of
Competition - a case perhaps of being over ambitious
since the team had struggled somewhat in their former
League! The First Team continued with a dual role, in the
London Combination and the Welsh League, but in both
competitions results were poor. The wooden spoon was
their reward in the English competition, and a mid-table
placing in the National League. Playing against such
teams as the Reserves of Football League Clubs, Thames
and Northampton plus Guildford City and Aldershot Town it
was a hard struggle in the 'foreign' competition.

There was, however, some success in Cup Competitions.
The Monmouthshire Senior Cup was won - when Excelsior
were beaten 4-1 at Newport County's Ground - as was the
South Wales and Monmouth Senior Cup - the first time that
this had been achieved by a team in the town. In both the
Welsh Amateur (the Reserves) and the Senior Cups, the
semi-final stages were reached. Therefore, the year had
been neither a disaster nor highly successful.

The move to the London competition was a short one,
and for the 1931/32 season the Club moved back to the
Western and remained in the Welsh League. Although
attendances were generally poor, the spectators were
often entertained by the local Band. In the F.A.Cup, the
familiar faces of Barry were beaten, for a change,
followed by a four goal win at Hanham. The next game
brought Yeovil to South Wales, when the locals lost by
the only goal of the game; victory would have meant a
prestigious and financially beneficial journey to Fulham.

However, in the Leagues the season was a great
success. With three games remaining the team were
confirmed Welsh Champions after a long undefeated run,
and in the eight-club Western competition a healthy third
place resulted. Top marksman was Gardiner with 38 goals
in the Welsh League, and 17 (of 33) in the Western.

There were no Cups won, but-all-in it was a memorable season for the town, as Newport County after not being re-elected to the Third Division South in 1931, bounced straight back after just one year's absence - despite finishing in only sixth place in the Southern League!

The next season saw the Reserves playing in the Newport and District League after a non-productive period of Friendly only games. No real successes were achieved during the campaign, and as ever the low attendances gave great cause for concern:

"Away from home Lovell's have often found themselves playing before a four or five thousand 'gate', yet the following week would find but a mere handful of their own townspeople watching them...."

With the Toffeemen making steady progress on the field but not on the gate, it must have been particularly galling for the Management to see that their neighbours Newport County attracted 10,000 spectators to their first game back in the Football League. The 1933/34 season did not start well for the Works team since despite holding Ebbw Vale to a scoreless draw on their own pitch in the preliminary round of the F.A.Cup (before a crowd of only 300 - there was a Carnival on in the town) and they lost the home replay. An inconsistent start in League matches gradually improved, with a final third place in the Welsh competition. There were only seven teams in the Western League (Division 1), although in a final third from bottom place, the team were only five points behind the Champions Bath City; Tail-enders Taunton Town lost all of their twelve games!

The most notable events of the year, were the transfer of Jack Weare to Wolverhampton Wanderers and Gardiner to a Swiss team (before moving onto Ipswich), plus Channel Island tours for the Club at Christmas and at Easter. Five well attended matches were played 'abroad', versus Rangers, Guernsey Islanders, Guernsey, Northerners (a combined team) and Jersey Island, out of which only one game resulted in a defeat.

Several new signings were made during the close season, but the goalkeeping position was a problem, with Weare having departed and the reserve, Young, deciding to retire. The Club had to sign on Boots, an amateur from Newport County, who was not upto the required standard.

Lovell's Athletic.

However, a good start was made, but mainly in respect of Cup matches only, for in the Leagues only one game in each was won from October to January. It was ironic that a dismal campaign in these Leagues finished with the 'wooden spoon' in the Western (including a 1-9 defeat at Swansea) and a mediocre placing in the Welsh, for all eyes were on the various Cup Competitions where the team fared far better. In the F.A.Cup, Cadbury Heath Y.M.C.A. were first thrashed by 6-0 (R.Williams netting three), followed by a 'revenge' victory - with interest - over Ebbw Vale by five unopposed goals. The Vale had received a bye in the preliminary round as they were due to play former Football League Club, Merthyr Town, but the latter disbanded before the encounter. In the 2nd qualifying round the Toffeemen lost to Barry Town by the only - disputed - goal of the game.

A run through to the seventh round of the Welsh Cup was achieved, at which stage the team encountered Tranmere Rovers. The team raised themselves to the occasion and forced a shock 1-1 draw with the Third Division North leaders. The replay in Newport was expected to produce a record attendance of around 3,000, for the early Monday evening match. However, poor weather produced a poor gate, but the stayaways missed what was described as Lovell's greatest game. A thrilling encounter was all level at full-time, but the non-Leaguers finally succumbed to a last minute free-kick equaliser, and lost by 5-6.

The 1935/36 season saw a vast improvement in the Western League, with a runners-up placing, but only a short run in the English Cup. An almost regular fixture with Barry, resulted in the normal defeat, although after beating the same team in the Welsh Cup - and with only 10 men for 80 minutes - a victory was expected. But one year later, they overcame their fellow Welshmen, but only to lose in the 2nd qualifying round at Cheltenham. The somewhat yo-yo existance in the Western League continued, for by April 1937, they were back in bottom position! This season produced little all round, (apart from the capture of the South Wales & Monmouth.Cup) and with severe injury problems, 24 different players were used in the eight League matches.

LOVELL'S ATHLETIC A.F.C.

●

THE TRINIDAD
FOOTBALL ASSOCIATION
TOURING XI.

v.

LOVELL'S ATHLETIC

●

REXVILLE, NEWPORT, Mon.

SATURDAY, 5th SEPTEMBER, 1953

Kick-off 3.15 p.m.

●

SOUVENIR PROGRAMME

PRICE - THREEPENCE

A Friendly match that attracted a (rare) good gate.

LOVELL'S ATHLETIC A.F.C.

Rexville  Newport

WELSH CUP
5th ROUND

SWANSEA TOWN

Versus

LOVELL'S ATH.

....

SATURDAY, 1st FEBRUARY
1964

Kick-off 11.15 a.m.

OFFICIAL PROGRAMME - 3d.

One of the last Programmes issued by the Club.

Lovell's Athletic.

Before the 1937/38 season, the Club's founder, Harold Lovell, received the reward he richly deserved, with his election as the South Wales member for the Welsh F.A. Council. Harold Lovell's playing career with the team lasted just one game due to an injury, but off the field he had thrown all of his energy - and no little money - into 'his' team. The Club, by this time, whilst only rarely capturing the eyes of the National Press, were nonetheless regarded as one of the foremost Works teams in Britain.

The season was to prove that the Club had become one of the best in Welsh non-League football. Once again the team finished bottom of the Western League, but with only eight games (five teams) there was little opportunity to recover from a few defeats! Additionally the opposition were very strong, consisting of the Reserves of Bristol Rovers and City, Torquay, plus Yeovil & Petters first team. The Club's real worth was shown in the Welsh League when for the second time they became Champions, heading off the strong challenge of the Cardiff and Swansea Reserve elevens. They amassed a record 50 points (only 4 draws and 5 defeats in 32 games), and scored 109 goals, with Anthony claiming 34 of them. All this was achieved by Manager Eddie Jenkins who was faced once again with a long injury list. Further honours came by way of both Fisher and Clarke representing the Principality in the Amateur International with England.

There was even a reasonable run in the F.A.Cup, with wins over the newly formed Ebbw Vale - before a pathetic crowd of less than 100 (and with several of their opponents having only just finished their shift in the Mines) - another victory over Barry, and a single goal being enough at Gloucester. The end came in a replay with Llanelly in the 3rd qualifying round. The Monmouthshire Senior Cup Final was won at home over Newport County (before a rare, large crowd). The formation of a Supporters Club - not confined to just the Firm's employees - helped no doubt towards a long overdue rise in attendances, although these were still poor for a team of this status.

The last season before the War was to become the best in the Club's history. With the Reserves elevated to the Welsh League Division 2 East, the two teams swept nearly all before them, and captured the 1st Division Champion--ship, and were Runners-up in the Second.

Perhaps more creditable was their triumph in the Western League also, when in ten games (Bath City Reserves had joined this small exclusive group) they lost just one game. There was little doubt of their intentions in the Welsh League Division 1, when they beat Nantymoel 9-0 in the first match and went on to score five goals or more in nine other matches. Their own previous record was surpassed with 56 points obtained (eleven points clear of the nearest challenger), and the goal difference was an incredible 110 - 29. In view of these achievements it was surprising that little was achieved in the various Cup games. Defeat came in the 2nd qualifying round of the F.A.Cup - at Barry (!), and the sole capture was of the South Wales and Monmouth Cup, for the third season running.

It was a time of great celebration for the football fans in the town, for added to Lovell's successes, was the achievement of Newport County who achieved promotion to the Second Division. The Toffeemen's achievements did not go un-noticed, for they were elevated to the highest level in non-League football, with their election into the Southern League. The only blot on the horizon, apart from the greater stormclouds heralding an impending war, was the ever present question of poor gates, which had risen slightly, but were still low.

The expected 1939/40 season finished almost before it started, when a long interval for 'normal' football was signalled with the start of World War Two.

Wartime Competitions were hastily arranged, and while the County took part in the eight team South West League, the Toffeemen continued in the Southern (Western Section). Although this Wartime competition, which started in early November, only contained eight teams, all of the Club's opponents were of an already proven high status, yet to the amazement of the local football scene, they became comfortable Champions, three points above runners-up Worcester City. If this rapid rise in stature was a pleasant surprise, even better was to come in the next few years.

Although the Club were about to embark on their most successful period ever, and to reach heights that not in their wildest dreams could they have forseen, there were two important factors that substantially enhanced their chances. Newport County, who had only played three matches in the Second Division before the war intervened, ceased playing after the short 1939/40 Emergency Season. By virtue of the Toffeemen now being the only Senior Club in the town, the Factory team were able to command better support and were even able to recruit several County Players on a long time temporary basis. In addition, and in common with most Football League Clubs during the War, they were also able to call upon quality Players from other teams, that were based in the area.

A number of Friendly games were played before and after their successful sortie into the Southern League, but on the 1st of February 1940, it was announced that the Club would be invited to join a new Western Regional League. Cardiff City, Swansea Town and Bristol City were somewhat isolated, and they formed the Football League contingent, along with the Toffeemen, plus Bath City, Aberaman and Cardiff Corinthians.

In just a few months, the status of the Work's team had risen to the extent that they were now on a par with Football League teams, and honours to suit this elevation were to come. The first match in this new Regional League started with an excellent 3-1 victory at Bath City on March the 28th, followed by a 6-1 home thrashing of an understrength Aberaman team. Within a few weeks, the Club were amazingly riding high at the top of the League. It wasn't until the 3rd of May that the first defeat came, when the Toffeemen lost by the odd goal in three, at home, to Bath. Yet the attendance of 1,000 plus, may sound poor, but was good for the team that always struggled for spectator support. By this time, despite the defeat, the Club were favourites for the Championship, which they won, over their amazed Football League opponents.

Entrance costs to games at Rexville at this time was 6d. (2.5p), and double this amount for a seat in the Stand, while boys and Members of the Armed Forces were admitted free. It was perhaps something of an encouragement to spectators, that Lovell's were able to proudly announce of their... " Own Air Raid Shelters Available..." !

It was no understatement when the local Press stated that "Rexville is the home of First Class Football in Newport, with many games with notable teams. A remarkably successful season.

Lovell's Athletic.

The 1940/41 season was something of an anti-climax with the Club only playing in the Wartime Welsh League, but Football was still in some turmoil, and it wasn't until the 1942/43 season, that the Club once again really made their presence noticed on a more National level. The likes of Cardiff City and Bristol City in the West, were still isolated from others, and with the difficulty of travel in wartime Britain, it was not practical for them to continue in the Football League 'South' section, where far flung opponents such as Leicester and Norwich were encountered. Therefore for the 1942/43 season, a new 'West' section was formed, with Lovell's joining up together with Bath, Cardiff City, Bristol City, Swansea Town and Aberaman - once again they had become a 'Football League' team.

The Toffeemen started in fine fashion with a 2-1 win at Bath, and as other victories followed, they sustained an almost unbroken succession of wins that had extended back to the beginning of the previous season! The return with Bath was expected to attract a record attendance, but with under 2,000 present - even so, far in excess of the previous norm - it must have been most discouraging for the Management. Harold Lovell's passion for the game entailed great financial sacrifices in order that the game was kept alive in Newport during the dark War years. The Bath game produced a two goal victory for the homesters, but with the visiting team arriving with only nine players, a 'spare' Lovell's man took his place in the visitors goal, and by all accounts had a good game!

On the 3rd of October, Lovell's sustained their first defeat for over a year when they lost 1-3 at Cardiff, but after seven games, they were riding high at the top of the table. After victories at Bristol City (attendance of 2,000) and Swansea - a poor crowd of only 1,200 - they were four points clear. Two goals were then shared in Newport, with Cardiff City, before at last an encouraging gate of 3,000. But in a second game at Ninian Park (Clubs played each other upto four times), a single victory was marred by a fight on the pitch, which was only subdued when the home Club Chairman called on the Players to shake hands at the end of the game.

A second home match with Bath City on November the 21st attracted a record attendance of 4,000, with Lucas scoring the winning goal for the Toffeemen. The team continued in their winning vein, and by the 'season' end (at the turn of the year), they once again staggered everybody by becoming Champions, two points clear of runners-up, Bath City. Much of the Club's success was of course due to their enlisting some notable players, including; Witcombe (West Bromwich and Wales), two other Welsh Internationals, and three Newport County men. Remarkably only 18 different players were used in this short season.

After Christmas, the qualifying competition got under way for the League North Cup. A final, but somewhat artificial, table was produced from the 54 entrants, in which teams played just a few games with local opponents, and in which goal difference played an important role. With seven victories and only one defeat, the team finished in an unbelievable fourth position, one point less than Manchester City, Rochdale and Liverpool, and above the likes of Huddersfield, Manchester United and Newcastle United. Of course with so many teams in this 'table', in which few played each other, it could hardly be considered a true reflection of a Club's ability, but nonetheless to be 'rubbing shoulders' with so many Football League teams, it must have been a very proud Harold Lovell, who saw his humble 'Works Team' in such an elevated position. When the Club were presented with the Football League Cup at the end of January 1943, they were spoken of as "One of Britain's leading Clubs."

The first round (first leg) proper of the League North Cup, brought familiar opponents Bath City to Rexville on March the 6th, and the match produced a new record attendance of 5,000. But with at last such good support, the homesters lost 1-2 after many missed chances, including a penalty; with the second leg ending in a 1-1 draw, the Toffeemen made their exit. There was now the Football League West Cup to compete for, at which the Club again excelled. They reached the final, only to suffer a surprise 2-4 home first leg defeat to Swansea (admission was raised to one shilling and threepence). The second leg was won by 4-3, before an excellent attendance of 8,500, and hence the Works team lost on goal difference. This may have been a disappointment, but overall the season had been little short of sensational.

The 1943/44 season contained the same teams in the League West as before, and it was not long before the reigning Champions - the Toffeemen - showed that they

intended to keep their title, with the addition of
Thompson (Sheffield United) and Wood from Halifax in
their line-up. Their close rivals, both geographically
and in the League table were Cardiff, and a rare defeat
was suffered when the Work's team lost by two unopposed
goals at Ninian Park. But with Palfreman injured early
on, the ten man Toffeemen were hardly disgraced. Earlier,
on the first day of the season, Cardiff had been beaten
at Rexville (by 3-1) before an excellent attendance of
4,000, and by now the admission costs were 1/6d (7.5p)
with an extra shilling to sit in the Stand.

After a single goal victory at Aberaman on the 11th of
September, the team topped the table, only to suffer a
2-3 defeat in the return game the next week (attendance
3,000). Another 3,000 crowd was present for the visit of
Bristol City, when the Work's team were on song to the
tune of 6-0. But this scoreline paled in comparison with
that for the visit of the young Swansea Town side. There
was an attendance of only 2,000, and they saw the home
team go into a moderate two goal interval lead. But the
inexperienced Swans collapsed in the second half to a
final nine-nil scoreline. The Toffeemen lost their table
topping place to Bath after a 1-3 defeat in that City -
watched by 5,000 - but regained their form, and their
place at the top, with a brilliant 5-0 victory in the
return match before an enthusiastic gathering of 4,000.
This wasn't the end of the big scorelines, for Swansea
were again thrashed, on their own pitch (7-1), and a
second home game with this team led to a 5-2 win, but
before only 2,000 fans.

The 'season' ended at Christmas, and for the second
time in as many years, the Newport Work's team again
staggered the football World when they once more finished
top of the League West, just one point clear of second
place Cardiff City. Cardiff City featured prominently in
the Club's fixtures for they were also played in two
encounters when the two teams were fighting for the
qualifying places in the League North Cup 'League'. By
now the Newport football public were at last appreciating
that they had a team in the town that were worthy of
support, and when Cardiff came to Rexville in the last
Cup qualifying match, there was a new record attendance
of over 6,000 present. The game was won by the homesters,
but both Clubs qualified to go on to the final stages.

Lovell's Athletic.

The frequent meetings with their, peacetime, Football League opponents and neighbours continued still further, when ironically they were also drawn to play each other in the first round proper of the Cup!

Cup-tie 'fever' gripped the town, and the attendance record was broken once again, when over 7,000 fans packed into Rexville to see the locals beat the team from the Capital by 2-0. But there was also further cause for celebration that day, when the League West Championship Cup was presented to Lovell's Athletic. Although the second leg of the League North Cup was lost by the only goal, at Cardiff, the Toffeemen continued onto the second round by virtue of their better goal difference.

Their opponents at this stage were another familiar team, Bath City, but the match finished with mixed blessings. The interest was such that yet another new record crowd was present, this time 7,200, but the result and the incidents near the end of the game did nothing to enhance Lovell's Athletic's good character. With ten minutes remaining, and the score at 1-1, a disputed penalty was awarded to the visitors. The goal was duly scored, but Ferguson of Lovell's continued to argue with the Referee to such an extent that he was eventually ordered off the pitch. The homesters lost with a final score of 1-3, and the home fans - with a sense of injustice - invaded the pitch and booed the Referee, who had to be escorted from the field, by the police. The Toffeemen were unable to pull back this deficit, in the second leg, and so did not progress further in the competition. Once again the team captured the League West Cup, and good crowds were by now being regularly attracted to Rexville, as evidenced by the 3,000 for the match in mid-April - versus Cardiff City. The season had overall been an unqualified success, and to cap it, Lucas (of Lovell's and Swindon Town) played in the full International match with England.

The 1944/45 season did not get off to the expected start, when the first match was lost at home (attendance 3,000) to Bath, but the team redeemed themselves with a good 4-2 away victory over the much improved Swansea team. The past year's performances continued to attract the fans, with 4,500 present for Bristol City's appearance and the home draw with Cardiff which drew 5,500 to Rexville. A further win over Bristol City was obtained on December the 2nd, when, despite having to

recover from a two goal deficit, the homesters finished
3-2 to the good, before a 4,000 crowd. The last League
match was played out over Christmas - when Cardiff were
beaten 1-0, as were Aberaman (in the League Cup by 6-1),
plus Hereford in a friendly match on Boxing Day.

*"Lovell's and Bath City have met over thirty
times to date during the War, and no other sides
outside of the Football League have done so much
to keep the the game alive during this period.
Their performances should earn Bath City League
membership one day, and for Lovell's perhaps an
honourable F.A.Cup exemption from the preliminary
rounds."*
So stated a local reporter. Despite later attempts,
Bath City never achieved this goal, and the statement
perhaps put things into their true perspective; for
despite their remarkable achievements, Lovell's Athletic
were only a 'Work's' team, and destined to fight in
non-League football with the return of peace.

But the bubble was about to burst! With a gradual
return to normality as the War drew to an end, the Guest
Players started returning to their own Clubs, and the
Toffeemen had to struggle towards the end of the season.
The final League West placings put Lovell's in third
place, with Cardiff as Champions and the Bristol team in
the Runners-up slot; poor old Swansea were still
struggling though as they finished bottom! But all was
far from doom and gloom, for after a quite outstanding
series of matches in the qualifying League North Cup,
seven victories and only three defeats were recorded.
These achievements placed the little Work's team in the
amazing position of third in the 52 strong League 'table'
(which contained only three peacetime non-League Clubs),
just one point behind the Champions, mighty Liverpool,
and by virtue of goal difference, just one place behind
Runners-up Stoke City! The enthusiasm and excitement at
this time was well summed up by the local press:
*" A packed Ground, rosetted spectators, the
crowds breaking through the touchline fences, a
Player collapsing insensitive in the last minute,
the Police calling for a loudspeaker van to guide
home the crowd - all this was not a dream of
pre-war cup-ties, but what happened at Rexville*

*where Lovell's Athletic beat Cardiff City 1-0 in
the War Cup qualifying competition. Lovell's are
at the head of the table with Liverpool. How is
it done then? Guest Players? Partly, but mainly
because Lovell's handle a football team with a
spirit and experience unique for a non-League
Club."*

Cardiff were played yet again, in the first round
proper. In the first leg, before 12,000 spectators, a
closely fought match resulted in a one goal win to the
City. Sensing the chance of further progress, and aided
by the gradual return of the menfolk - eager for
entertainment after the long War - all previous
attendances were shattered at Rexville, for the return
tie, on March the 31st. An estimated crowd of 10,000
crammed into the little Ground, but the one goal deficit
could not be made up, and the scoreless draw meant that
the Toffeemen were out of the Cup.

The last game for the Club as a 'Football League' team
was played on the 19th of May, when Swansea were beaten
3-0, and the return game one week later was the final
match at this elevated level.

The 1945/46 season heralded a virtual return to
normality, and the team (and Reserves) were back in the
1st and 2nd Divisions of the Welsh League! But with
War-time players Eddie Jones, Billie Guest and Welsh
International Billie Lucas, all accepting jobs at the
Lovell's Factory, the Club were not short of 'quality'.
But with a number of pre-war Lovell's Players having not
yet returned from combat, the team was supplemented with
several promising Amateurs.

The first game was played on August the 25th with a
visit from Cearau Athletic. But it must have been very
galling for the Work's team, for after all of their
previous achievements, and the praise that had been
justifiably heaped upon them, the return of Newport
County onto the scene, resulted in scarcely a mention of
the team that had done so much to keep alive football
during the dark War years! Yet the Toffeemen soon proved
that they were far above the standard of the National
League, and after the first five games - that were all
won - they had recorded a goal difference of 40-4. Not to
be outdone the Reserves were heading their Division, also

with five straight wins - and a goal tally of 26-7.

On November the 16th, Lovell's entertained Bournemouth in the F.A.Cup first round, and with further Ground improvements that had gradually been made, a crowd of over 10,000 was expected and could easily have been accommodated. But the poor weather produced only 3,000 at the start, which improved to 4,000 by half-time. Making the best of every opportunity the non-Leaguers pulled off a shock 4-1 win. But even this 'cushion' began to look doubtful in the return leg, when the team went behind after just two minutes, and at one time were 0-3 to the bad. Yet with incredible spirit the Toffeemen fought back to produce a final scoreline of 2-3 and so progressed onto the next round.

Once again poor weather reduced the attendance for the visit of Bath City in the next round, when the homesters ran out 2-1 winners after trailing at half-time. In the second leg, the Toffeemen soon took control and coasted home with a 5-2 scoreline. For the first time ever, the Club had reached the third round of the F.A.Cup, and luck decreed that they would first entertain the renowned Wolverhampton Wanderers. Nearly 10,000 fans turned up to see a thrilling encounter with the illustrious team that contained three full England Internationals. Despite nearly scoring early on, for much of the first half the local team were somewhat overawed by the occasion, but only until one minute from the interval, when a goal from Morgan set the crowd alight. Yet more excitement was to come, for a successful shot from Hardwicke - and now a two goal lead - "sent the fans hysterical." But the Wolves were far from finished, for they gradually started to dominate the game, and scored four late goals. The chance of glory had passed, for in the second leg, the Toffeemen were overwhelmed by Billy Wright and Company, and succumbed to a 0-4 defeat.

But another memorable season ended with some staggering records. The first team were undisputed League Champions, finishing 8 points ahead of Runners-up Merthyr, with 31 wins, 3 draws and only 2 defeats. The Reserves, not to be outdone by the Senior team, also only suffered two defeats in their 28 League games, and topped the table, one point ahead of challengers Tynte Rovers. In all matches the first team scored no fewer than 193 goals, with Holland leading the goalscorers with 45!

But the team were all but deserted by the Press, and to a large degree the football public in the town. Despite their complete domination of the Welsh League, the fickle fans preferred to watch the more Senior team in Newport, and the best League attendance of the season was only 4,000 (although this figure was way and above the pre, and later, post-war crowds), for the match in mid-February with title challengers Merthyr Tydfil. Whereas in a miserable, (and solitary) Second Division season for neighbours County, they none the less managed to attract a crowd of 15,339, for the visit to Somerton Park - of Wolves!

Yet true Sportsman to the end, in October 1946, Lovell's donated £500 to their struggling neighbours 'New Players Fund'. It could have almost been an epitaph to the Club when the local Press acknowledged this gesture with the following:

"Lovell's kept the football flag flying on a high mast, when the County had to put up the shutters during the War. Aided by a number of English League Players as guest Stars, Lovell's became one of the leading lights in the War-time Competitions."

But the Toffeemen refused to let the continued lack of publicity and recognition deter them, and once again, they stormed through the 1946/47 season. Victories upto Christmas such as the 6-1 win at Cardiff Corries., and 7-1 at Garw plus the demolition of Ebbw Vale by 8-1 on Boxing Day were commonplace, and defeats were rare. The Winter of 1947 was a very harsh one causing the postponement of many games, and by mid-May - with still seven matches to play - the team required only two points to ensure the Championship again. Needless to say this goal was easily achieved, with a final nine points more than their nearest challengers, and a record after 36 games of 133 goals scored. Perhaps the greatest snub to the Club, despite their recent distinguished footballing record, was their requirement to enter from the 2nd qualifying round stage of the F.A.Cup. To make matters worse this game was lost at Merthyr (who were now in the Southern League) by 2-4.

It was quite obvious that their abilities were far above the standard of the Welsh League, and their application to join the Southern League was, as expected, readily accepted. Their election created a new record,

Lovell's Athletic.

since they were the first pure 'Work's' team to be allowed into the fold.

Several new Players were signed for the new season, not least George Poland, a former Liverpool, Wrexham, Cardiff and Welsh Amateur International goalkeeper. By now it was obvious that the Club could not rely solely on non-Professionals, and so for a number of years the team consisted of a mixture of genuine amatuers - from the workforce - and paid Players.

The campaign got off to an away match at Exeter (Reserves) on the 23rd of August followed by another visit, this time to Gloucester. In the latter match the team were two goals in arrears, but then scored four times in 15 minutes to record a 4-2 success. An early exit was made from the F.A.Cup (to Merthyr once again), but in the League, their record was impeccable, for by early November they were at the head of the table. By Christmas a slight loss of form made them drop into the second slot, behind Hereford United, who brought 500 fans for the match at Rexville. The second half of the season was something of a disappointment for they slipped to finish sixth; albeit a far from unsuccessful start in this top non-League competition.

However, their pride was restored when for the first time they won the Welsh Senior Cup, which completed a record of having - on at least one occasion - won every Welsh Competition that they had ever entered! The team's route to the final included the elimination of Cardiff City and South Liverpool (in the semi-final). The Final, which was played at Wrexham, attracted a gate of 10,000, and included four coaches of Toffemen supporters. Despite a knockout injury to goalkeeper Holland early on in the second half, the Player gamely played on, and was rewarded with his team's victory over the Midland League leaders Shrewsbury Town.

The end of the season saw the Club make their boldest move to date when they applied for election to the Football League. They only received one vote - as did the likes of Peterborough, Workington and Wigan - but in any event the commercial nature alone, of the Club, would no doubt have precluded them from being accepted.

The Club's exploits in the F.A.Cup at last saw them beat Merthyr Tydfil in September 1948, and they progressed onto the fourth qualifying round.

Lovell's Athletic.

Telegrams
LOVELL, NEWPORT

FOUNDED 1918
Colours : RED, WHITE & BLUE HOOPS

Telephone 59666

LOVELL'S ATHLETIC FOOTBALL CLUB

President :
J. F. LOVELL, O.B.E., J.P.

Vice-Presidents :
G. G. LLEWELLIN.
SIR MAYNARD JENOUR, T.D., J.P., V.L.
M. G. THOMAS, F.C.A.
R. W. MACDONALD.

Chairman :
G. MORGAN.

Hon. Treasurer :
K. SCREEN.

Hon. Secretary-Manager :
S. KEMP.

Office and Ground

REXVILLE
NEWPORT

MONMOUTHSHIRE

Members of the
Football Association of Wales
Welsh Football & Mon. Senior Leagues

WINNERS
Welsh Football League 1931-32, 1937-38, 1938-39
1945-46, 1946-47, 1947-48
1965-66
S.W. & Mon. Senior Cup
1930-31, 1934-35 1936-37, 1948-49, 1954-55
Mon. County Senior Cup
1929-30, 1930-31, 1936-37, 1937-38, 1938-39
1946-47, 1948-49, 1949-50, 1951-52, 1954-55
Welsh Amateur Cup
1925-26, 1926-27, 1927-28, 1953-54
Mon. Senior League 1927-28, 1928-29, 1929-30
1960-61, 1965-66, 1966-47
Mon. County Amateur Cup 1925-26, 1928-29
Mon. Challenge Cup 1923-24, 1929-30
Western Football League 1923-24, 1938-39
Southern League 1939-40
Football League West 1942-43, 1943-44
Welsh Cup 1947-48

7th May, 1969. 19

Dear Sir,

We are very sorry to inform you that we have decided to disband Lovell's Athletic Football Club as from the end of this season. Over the past few years serious thought has been given to the future of the Football Club and we have now, very reluctantly taken into account various factors; these are the possible future development plans of the ground, which is a valuable site, lack of support at the gate and the increasing financial burden to the Supporters Club.

Our club in recent years has almost entirely been financed by the Supporters Club and due to their great efforts has not experienced any financial difficulties and could, if necessary, have carried on next season.

The Supporters Club have indicated their willingness to continue for the benefit of members of Lovell's Social Club, who now have 500 members enjoying its facilities.

Mr. Selwyn Kemp, Honorary Secretary and Honorary Player/Manager, has done a splendid job this season and it is largely due to his efforts that the club has enjoyed a very successful season, culminating in their challenge for the 'runners-up' position of the Welsh League.

We would like to thank the Football Association of Wales, the Welsh Football League, the Monmouthshire League, the Football Association, our Vice Presidents and Committee Members, players past and present, Supporters Club, the Press and Member Clubs for the great interest they have always taken in Lovell's Athletic Football Club, which will always be remembered by myself, family and colleagues.

Yours faithfully,

J.F. LOVELL
President.

The letter that marked the end of the Club.

Lovell's Athletic.

Proudly on view at the Company's New Factory: The Honours Board.
(Photo: Dave Twydell)

Lovell's Athletic.

A large attendance - by now an unheard of occurence at Rexville - was expected, especially since the visitors, Yeovil Town, brought with them several train loads and coaches of fans. But the large gate never materialised, and the homesters lost the match. The Club were to later realise that they had already passed their peak, and with a final League position of 16th (of 22) they were heading on a slow route to final oblivion.

A slight improvement came at the end of the 1949/50 season with a final 12th Southern League placing, and also a reasonable run in the F.A.Cup. In the latter competition, victories were achieved over the now forgotten teams of Weston St.Johns (7-2, away), 4-2 at home to Mount Hill (Bristol) and the somewhat more familiar Merthyr Tydfil. But the end came at home to fellow Leaguers Gloucester City by three unopposed goals. The next season an early exit was made at Stonehouse after a 2-2 home draw. This latter campaign produced another plunge down the League to a final, and worst to date, 20th of 23 teams.

The F.A.Cup trail was again left at an early stage in the 1951/52 season following a 0-2 defeat at Llanelly in the 1st qualifying round - despite an earlier 4-3 win there, and later a 6-1 home success in the League games! With regular low gates of around 1,000 (the lowest in the League and poor for such a Senior Club) there was a dramatic boost for the Club's Treasurer when 7,000 attended the Festival of Britain game with the Gold Coast. This match, which was something of a novelty, ended in a 5-3 victory, and a special Souvenir programme was produced for the event. Although there was little to enthuse over, at least the final Southern League placing was a slight improvement on the previous two seasons.

The first match of the 1952/53 season required the Toffeemen to visit Kettering, where they lost by 1-3. The attendance was 4,804, an undreamed of number for a League match at Rexville, where the attendances were dropping yet further. Even the local Press took up the case for the Club, stating that they were deserving of far more support in view of what they had done to encourage football in the area, particularly during the War, just a few years earlier. But the team could do little to encourage more fans. After six games they lay fifth from bottom in the table, and the F.A.Cup offered no solace. Llanelly, accompanied by many supporters, visited

Rexville, and went home happy with a single goal victory;
a particularly bad result for Lovell's since the visitors
had been reduced to only ten men for much of the game.

The dismal run continued upto the end of the campaign,
with a final table placing of 17th, a position that was
repeated one year later. But at least during the 1953/54
season there were some bright spots. The Welsh Amateur
Cup was won - by the Reserves - for the first time since
1928 (when the Club completed a hat-trick of successes),
and the second string also put up a creditable performance in the Welsh League. At one time they led the table,
but were not destined for any final honours in a
Competition that the Club's First X1 had dominated from
1938 to 1947 with four consecutive (peacetime) Champion-
ships, followed by the success of the Reserves in 1948.

The Club were also honoured with the staging of the
Wales versus England Amateur International on the 24th of
April 1954. A healthy crowd of 5,000 came to the match,
with the Welsh team including three Lovell's players in
their line-up. Back in 1947, the Factory team had hosted
the same fixture

During the summer of 1954, it was necessary for 100
tons of drainage soil to be placed on the Rexville pitch
in order to cure it of repeated flooding. But the better
surface did not prevent the team from starting the new
season with a series of poor results at home. Ironically
an early two goal win at Tonbridge - the Kent team's
first home defeat for 16 months - gave a false impression
that the coming months were going to be more successful.
It was only an end of season improvement that lifted the
Club from well below halfway in the table, to twelfth. To
catch up on a backlog of fixtures, the Club's two teams
had to play no fewer than 16 games during April. Back in
September, during a Welsh League game at Barry, an
individual scoring record for the Club was created when
Selwyn Kemp (who later became the Manager and continued
on as an employee with the Company) hit the back of the
net on six occasions.

At last things took a definite turn for the better
during the 1955/56 season. A 3-1 home victory over Bath
City augured well for the coming months, and the win over
Barry in the final of the South Wales and Monmouthshire
Cup (held over from the previous season), confirmed the
thought that there was going to be a better future.

Lovell's Athletic.

This optimism was borne out with a final 8th in the League, the best position for a number of years. But the real excitement came in the F.A.Cup where a run was made through to the first round proper. Qualifying round victories were gained at Cheltenham (2-1), 3-1 at Barry and an exciting 2-0 success over neighbours Merthyr Tydfil. The latter match produced a rare good attendance, aided in large part by the many supporters of the visitors, many of whom arrived in six coaches; a noisy crowd complete with many bells and rattles.

The draw for the Cup was not kind to the Club, for they had to make the long, and as it turned out, fruitless journey to London to play Leyton Orient. The match was over to all intents and purposes after 20 minutes, by which time the Toffeemen trailed by three goals, although a consolation effort made it 1-3 at half-time. But the final scoreline read as a 1-7 defeat. (There was some consolation as Newport County lost 1-8 at Brighton on the same day!)

But the saddest event of the year (1956), was the death of the Club's founder and greatest supporter, Harold Lovell. There is no doubt whatsoever that, but for his devotion and enthusiasm, coupled with the large financial contributions made to the Club, the football team would never had risen to the heights during the 1940's nor continued at the highest level in the non-League World. The role of Patron was taken over by the Founder's Son, John, who maintained the spirit and standards for a number of years before the Club's eventual, and inevitable, oblivion.

Helped in no small part by an exceptionally good home record - where they were undefeated until the first of April - the improvement in performances continued for the 1956/57 season to give an eventual 6th placing in the table for the Toffeemen. But there was to be no repeat run in the major Cup Competition, for they were despatched by three unopposed goals at Cheltenham. Although there had been a definite improvement now for two years, there was little affect at the gate, where the Club still struggled on with lamentably low figures, which by now had led to the Club operating with a near total amateur playing staff.

Lovell's Athletic.

A poor start to the 1957/58 season saw an improvement towards Christmas, but it was insufficient to prevent a return to a final lowly position in the Southern League. In the F.A.Cup it looked as if things would be better with victories over Merthyr, again, and a 'revenge' beating of Cheltenham (after two replays). But they finally bowed out to Llanelly with a 2-4 scoreline.

The 1958/59 season heralded a large influx of Clubs into the Southern League, and two separate zones, consisting of 17 'South Eastern' Clubs and 18 from the 'North-West'. It was also to be the last for the Toffeemen in this Competition. The crippling costs of running in the past a part-professional team, coupled with heavy travelling expenses and regular low attendances - which by this time had sunk to a pathetic 200 average at home matches - forced the Club into taking the decision to resign from the League, in April 1959. With a final place in their zone of 15th, there was little doubt that this was the best course of action. Yet, for the first time for eleven years, the team reached the final of the Welsh Senior Cup. Although they lost the final to Cardiff (played at Newport's Somerton Park), it was no disgrace since their opponents were obliged to field a First Team in the competition.

With the prospect of drastically reduced running costs, and frequent local matches, the 1959/60 season - with the First Team now in the Welsh League - was looked upon with a fair degree of optimism. The First Team took over the place of the Reserves in the National League, whilst the second eleven dropped down into the Monmouth Senior League Second Division. The first game of the season got off to a good start with a visit of newly promoted Tredomen, who were duly beaten 5-1, after a two goal interval lead - despite the Toffeemen playing with only ten men (due to an injury) for much of the second half. But this good start was not maintained, and as well as being knocked out of the F.A.Cup at the first attempt (by a single goal at Cheltenham), they could only manage a mid-table League placing by Christmas. This mediocre form continued to the season's end, with a final tenth placing of twenty teams. Apart from progress through to the 5th round of the Welsh Senior Cup - when a 0-2 defeat was sustained to Cardiff City - there was nothing to enthuse over. The final, first team, record produced only 12 victories and 6 draws from thirty-eight matches.

As ever support was the greatest disadvantage to the Club:

" Lovell's Athletic have never received the support that their performances have warranted, apart from the War period, but it has become even worse since the Club's departure from the Southern League.... "

...Was the comment from a local scribe. But a degree of blame could also be levelled at the same local Press, who - except for those rare wartime seasons - did little to promote or generate interest in the Club.

Ironically the Reserves, admittedly in a lower standard of football, were promoted in their League.

The 1960/61 season saw the departure of Secretary/ Manager Roy Macdonald after 23 years service, with Glyn Morgan taking over. However, the campaign started disast- rously with three straight defeats, but was then followed by a complete turn around in form which led to eleven consecutive unbeaten games (from the 1st of October). An interesting draw in the F.A.Cup had brought the Llanelly team, with several ex-Toffeemen in their line-up, to Rexville. But along with the result (a 2-3 defeat), it was disappointing to see such a small crowd at the match.

That season, together with the next, produced little in the way of honours, and mid-table League placings. It then looked as if the Club may have been on the way 'back', when they finished fourth in the League at the end of the 1962/63 season, although a full twenty points behind runaway Champions Swansea Town Reserves. But this was but a brief respite, for a year later it was back to a mid-table finish, with even worse to follow.

Towards the end of the 1964/65 season, things had become so bad that the very threat of relegation hung over the Work's team, and it was only a late flourish that lifted the team to a final eleventh place, with five Clubs below them.

By now, although of course they were unaware of it, the Club had come close to their final demise, but before the end, the 1965/66 season was to prove to be the best for many a long year. The team quickly surged to the top of the League, and by Christmas had obtained more points than for the complete previous campaign.

Lovell's Athletic.

They finished as proud League Champions, with a tremendous final tally of 24 wins, five draws and only one defeat. With nine points clear of their neighbours and Runners-up Newport County Reserves, it really looked as if they were in a position to become a sustained force to be reckoned with once again; yet the reverse was soon to unfold. In such a good season, it was strange that more success did not come in the various Cups. After beating Barry by 6-1 in the F.A.Cup, they then lost 1-2 to Gloucester City, and in their National Cup they made an early exit at home to Llanelli.

This success was not repeated one year later, and although the 1967/68 season was not a disaster, with a final League placing of only 7th of 16, it was clearly a great disappointment to the Company team, and their tiny band of supporters. The Club never really recovered from a poor start, which included four successive defeats in October. Earlier, another early F.A.Cup exit was made to frequent opponents Cheltenham Town. With the score at 0-1 after 63 minutes, a minor scuffle resulted in the Referee sending off the homester, Wilkins, and Cheltenham's Ferns, much to the surprise of the small group of fans that were present, and the final result was a 0-3 defeat. The local Press once again criticised stay-away fans, and blamed much of their absence on the necessity of the menfolk to help their wives with the shopping on a Saturday afternoon!

Gamely the Club struggled on with crowds rarely reaching three figures, which had dropped even further to between twenty to thirty by the, final, 1968/69 season. As ever this last campaign produced no honours, although the quarter-final stage of the Welsh Cup was reached, when the team were heavily defeated by 1-5 to 'foreigners' Chester. An exit was made at the same stage - relatively early for the Club that had in the past so dominated the Competition - in the Monmouthshire Senior Cup, a 1-4 defeat to Switchgear. In the F.A.Cup the usual early removal came, at the hands of Cheltenham - yet again!

Ironically this last campaign was quite a successful one in the League, and by mid-April there had been only one occasion when the team had not scored, and with Merthyr's Reserve team being beaten 6-5. The season ran on into May, and on the 10th, the last match was played at Rexville when Bridgend came to Newport. One week later the last game ever for the Club took place at Pembroke Borough. The final League position was a very reasonable fourth, with 17 victories, 11 drawn games and 6 defeats, with a goal difference of 80-45.

With no indication that the Club were to fold, in March they were invited to enter for the F.A.Trophy (one of sixteen Welsh Clubs), a competition that had been devised for Senior non-League teams to compete for, starting with the 1969/70 season. But the new campaign started with the notable absence of the Factory team that represented the Lovell's Company.

The folding of the football Club must have been particularly hard on Selwyn Kemp, a man who had started with the Club seventeen years earlier as a Player, and finished up as Secretary and Manager. He moved on to become the Manager of Chepstow Town, but he proved to be a loyal employee of the Sweet Company, with his continued service with them.

The Club's absence barely raised a ripple in Football, indeed there was scant mention even locally of their demise. The South Wales Argus of Thursday May the 8th briefly announced that Newport were to lose a soccer Club as Lovell's had decided to disband. With the Club financed almost entirely by the hard pressed Supporters Club, the lack of reasonable gates made it impossible to carry on. But this was not the only reason for the Club's extinction, for, as the Newspaper related, the Ground was needed for Development purposes (this was true but it didn't come to pass for nearly twenty years!). In addition, it must have been more than just coincidence that around this time there was a large change in the Management of the Lovell's Company. Harold Lovell, was without doubt the financial provider and greatest supporter, and had for years kept the Club afloat. But the founder's death in 1956 must have been a sad and enormous blow to the football team, and it was only the enthusiasm of his Son that ensured their survival for the next thirteen years. But with a Corporate buy-in to the Company, and the inevitable changes, there was surely no incentive and precious little interest in maintaining the operations of the Football Club. The team, in all honesty, would only have been a financial millstone around the neck of the 'new look'Company image. With the lifeblood and heart removed, the (Football) body immediately perished.

Lovell's Athletic.

PROGRAMMES:

During the Club's Southern League days and Wartime exploits, programmes were regularly issued for both First and Reserve team matches. With the drop down into the Welsh League the issues became a more moderate production - and then only for occasional games, such as important cup-ties. Perpetual low gates, and hence small production runs, coupled with a certain fascination for collectors, has led to surviving copies being much sort after, and are only occasionally seen offered by Dealers. It is very likely that programmes were issued during at least part of the pre-war period, and if so, can only be extremely rare.

REXVILLE:

The name 'Rexville' related to the area of the town in which the Company was situated. The Ground was conveniently located opposite the Lovell's Factory, at the junction of Albany and Alderney Streets in Newport, Gwent, and before it's use as a Football Ground (from 1918), the plot was no more than a flat piece of land. Initially the venue consisted of nothing more than an enclosed football pitch with uncovered standing areas to all sides. But in the Summer of 1922, 'extensive alterations and improvements' were made to the Ground - the exact nature of these was not specified. However, the Ground was now 'well equipped for both Players and spectators', and suitable for the good Gates that were hoped for. Except for the short period during the early 1940's large attendances never materialised. Also during the early 1920's, another pitch was obtained nearby. With the financial circumstances prevalent at this time, particularly in South Wales, the facilities were far better than probably all of the Club's opponents. Many teams were not only impoverished, but used only park pitches as their home venues, where paying Gates could not be taken.

In 1924, more Ground improvements were undertaken, and a modern shower bath was added for the Players comfort. During those heyday War years, further improvements were made to the Ground, and although the nature of these was also not specified, no doubt they were very limited due to the materials that were required for the war effort. Whatever form these improvements took, they maintained the ground capacity to an estimated 10,000.

Lovell's Athletic.

By the time that the Club entered the post-war
Southern League, the Club had a Ground - if not
attendances - to be proud of. Parallel to the Alderney
Street side, there was a timber Grandstand that seated
approximately 200 and stretched about one quarter the
pitch length. Parallel with, but well set back from
Albany Street, a half pitch width standing enclosure was
provided. Elsewhere, and including to each side of the
seated Stand, there were soil embankments. Between
Alderney Street and the Stand, there was a large Social
Club which also contained the Works Canteen and probably
the Football Players Dressing Rooms. The Ground was
completely enclosed by means of walls on two sides and
the factory's boundaries elsewhere. Natural 'sight'
barriers from trees in the area were also present.
Entrances were located at the Albany Street side, and
from Alderney Street, the latter immediately opposite the
Factory entrance. In the South-west corner of the ground
there was a Tea-bar.

It is probable that at least most of the features at
the Ground remained until the Club's demise, and even
some fifteen years later a few remnants could still be
seen. The 3 metre high brick wall, complete with two
turnstile huts and exit gates were still present (until
the late 1980's) off of the Alderney Street end.

Some grass banking still
remained, and although the
enclosed area was generally
overgrown, laying amongst
the vegetation lay several
timber roof trusses, probably the remains of the
former Grandstand.

With the area, together
with the Factory, earmarked
for development, it was
inevitable that these few
traces would not remain for
long, for the Ground has
now become a new housing
estate. The Lovell's Company still exist, but are
now located in a new Building on the other side of
town.

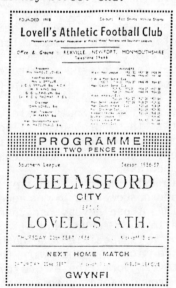

Lovell's Athletic.

(Photo: Dave Twydell)

The sole remains of the Ground in 1984:
The Turnstile and Exit enclosures in Albany Road.

Lovell's Athletic.

REXVILLE c. 1955.

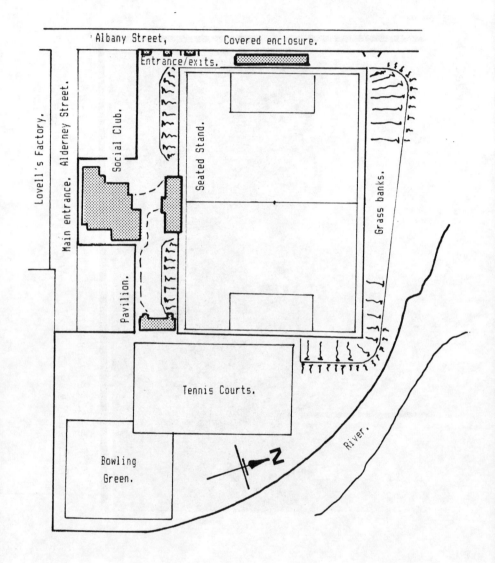

Lovell's Athletic.

LOVELL'S ATHLETIC F.C. Winners, Welsh Amateur Cup. 1953/54

Ground Location.

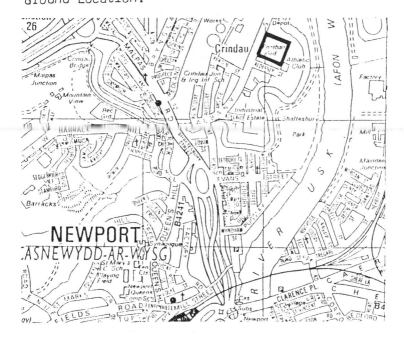

-69-

Romford.

ESSEX SENIOR CUP WON IN THIRD SEASON—1931-32

Final on April 9th, 1932, at Ilford. Romford 3, Clapton 0.

(Back row) Glyn Richards, S. G. Tansley, A. Groome (Reserve), G. Burchell, A. Anderson,
W. Pearl, F. Adams, S. Asater, F. H. Jones, A. J. Smith.

(Front row) M. Brazier, C. Rance (Trainer), G. Patterson, H. Reynolds, G. Webb (Captain),
J. Lumm, A. Skinner, T. Macpherson (President), F. Newling

Southern League Champions: 1966/67 season.

Romford's Team with Southern League Championship Shield.

Back Row, L. to R. : Mike Gcvaux, John Read (Capt.), Alan Reed, Derek Gibbs, Andy Smith, Bobby Fowler, Tom barnett Bobb, King, Harry Clarke (Manager).

Front Row, L. to R. : Harry Johnson (Trainer/Coach), Roy Sanders, Dennis Sorrell, Roy Aggio, Harry Obeney, Brian Taylor, Terry Topping. (Bill White the other member of the first team squad is missing from the picture).

Romford.

(1929 - 1978)

::

1929/30	-	1930/31.	London League.
1931/32	-	1938/39.	Athenian League.
1939/40	-		Isthmian League. *
1939/40	-		South Essex Combination. **
1940/41	-	1944/45.	Ceased Activities.
1945/46	-	1958/59.	Isthmian League.
1959/60	-		Southern League Div.1.
1960/61	-	1974/75.	Southern League Premier Div.
1975/76	-	1977/78.	Southern League Div.1 (South).

* Competition suspended after 1 game, due to War.
** Wartime Competition. Completed by end of 1939.

::

Summary of Main Facts.

Ground: Brooklands Sports Ground, Romford, Essex.

Colours: Various forms of Blue and Gold.

Nickname: Boro'.

Record Attendance:
18,237. 28th February 1953.
Versus Southall. F.A. Amateur Cup 4th round replay.

Major Honours:

Southern League Premier Div. Champions: 1966/67
                    Division 1. Runners-up: 1959/60.
                    Cup - Beaten Finalists: 1969/70.

Athenian League Champions: 1935/36. 1936/37.
                    Runners-up: 1933/34. 1938/39.

F.A.Cup :
3nd Round: 1960/61. 1961/62. 1971/72.
1st Round: 1932/33. 1935/36. 1945/46. 1948/49.
1964/65. 1965/66. 1967/68. 1974/75. 1975/76.

F.A. Amateur Cup:
Beaten Finalists: 1948/49.
Semi-Finalists -: 1937/38.

Essex Senior Cup. Winners: 1931/32. 1933/34.
                               1937/38. 1946/47.

Essex Thameside Trophy Winners: 1951/52. 1955/56.
                                1957/58.

Notable Players (joined from Football League Clubs):

Les Bennett (1959).   Ted Ditchburn (1959).
Malcolm Allison (1960).   Trevor Ford (1960).
Len Wills (1962).   Len Duquemin (1962).
Peter Brabrook (1971).   Ray Harford (1975).

The poster that

resulted in the

new creation of

Romford F.C. in

March 1929 ....

ROMFORD
FOOTBALL CLUB
v
ASTON VILLA

If you wish this to be a possibility turn
up at the Mass Meeting which will be
held at THE CORN EXCHANGE on

MONDAY, MARCH 18th

at 8 p.m.

and hear all about it.

We have a suggested Ground.
We shall have a Team.
We have the Ideas.

All we want is YOUR support.

Full information from—Hon. Sec. S. H. SMITH.

11, KINGSTON ROAD

Romford.

Although Romford F.C. were formed in 1929, they were
preceded by another team that bore the Essex town's name,
some 53 years earlier (a longer period than the total
'life' of the later Club).

The first 'Romford F.C.' were founded in 1876, and
played their matches at Great Mawneys. They had their
headquarters and dressing rooms in the White Hart Hotel.
In those far off days, at the birth of modern football,
many Clubs were springing up countrywide. But in the
South - and for some years - it was played on a strictly
amateur basis, unlike the developments in the Midlands
and North. At this time there was not of course any
League football, and the highlight of the season, for the
more prominent Clubs, was the F.A.Cup. The relative
status of the first Romford Club can be judged by their
entry into the 1878/79 competition. After beating the
'Ramblers' in the first round, the Essex team succumbed
to the 'Swifts' (who were situated in Slough) in a close
1-3 scoreline; the Swifts were hardly novices in the Cup,
for in 1874, and two years later, they reached the
semi-finals.

But not to be deterred, Romford continued to enter the
competition, and just two years later reached no less
than the 5th round (the Quarter-finals). This notable run
included a bye in the first round, followed by two
victories over powerful teams - Reading Abbey and Great
Marlow (the latter having been original entrants in
1871). However they were out of their depth in the final
game, for they lost by a 15-0 'cricket score' to Darwen.
But this was hardly a disgrace, for Darwen staggered the
football world of the day by becoming the first team from
the North of England to reach this far in the competition; a portant of the future for the all conquering
professional teams from afar. Romford caused no more
sensations in the competition, but they met on their
travels a number of mighty teams of the day, the most
famous being Blackburn Rovers in the 1884/85 season. This
match was played in Lancashire, and the result went to
form - an eight goal hammering; the Rovers were on the
way to their third successive Cup capture!

The South Essex League was formed in 1895, just seven
years after the first Football League in the World
commenced, and in these somewhat humble surroundings,
Romford F.C. competed. But their prowess appears to have
somewhat diminished, for during much of the 1899/1900

season they languished at the bottom of the League, and
in contrast to their much earlier exploits in the F.A.Cup
they bowed out of the competition with a six goal defeat
to Ilford. The Club had by now built up something of an
unsavoury reputation, for a South Essex League match with
Leytonstone was abandoned 25 minutes before the end for
fighting on the field! At this time 'another' Romford
team, by the name of Romford Victoria, were playing their
home matches at Brooklands; a Ground that was not to
become properly developed into a football arena for
another thirty years or so.

It wasn't until 1903 that any major honour in the
League competition was won by Romford F.C., and that
being only the Championship of the Second Division
Section 'A'! Although in 1890 and 1893 they were beaten
finalists in the Essex Senior Cup (Ilford and Chelmsford
respectively being the victors). However, in 1909 they
(presumably the same Romford) made a great stride upward
when they entered the predominatly Professional Southern
League, Second Division Section 'B'. The season was an
unmitigated disaster - they didn't even complete their
fixtures - for they finished bottom of the League, with
an horrendous record; nine games were played (they only
met the Champions Hastings & St. Leonards once), all were
lost, and with a goal difference of 7-33.

It is very likely that around this time the original
Club became defunct, for by 1909/10 there were two major
Clubs in the town, namely Romford Town and Romford
United. The 'Town', the more Senior of the two, competed
in the Athenian League for two seasons - upto 1914 - when
they moved on to the London League for the 1914/15
campaign. No major honours were won during this brief
period except the capture of the Essex Senior Cup in 1912
(a single goal win in the final over South Weald), and
lost at the last hurdle to Ilford one year later. But
after the intervention of the First World War they faded
from the scene. Romford United probably competed in the
South Essex League around this period of time, and
although it's name does not appear to relate to a
competition of great standing, the rules included the
necessity of member Clubs to have 'Private and enclosed
Grounds. The United, like the Town, also faded from the
scene after the Great War.

The mantle of 'Senior Club' in the town fell upon the
G.E.R. Romford team, from the 1919/20 season playing in

Romford.

the Spartan League that had been formed in 1907. This was
in essence a Works Club, being the Great Eastern Railways
team. For a few years the Club met with a reasonable
degree of success, and included the League Championship
in 1926, plus the runners-up spot at the end of their
first season and in 1924 and 1925. This Club faded away
in the early 1930's, following their departure from the
Spartan League in 1931 and also their move away from
Romford, to Loughton.

These early Romford Clubs played on a variety of
Grounds, in and close to the town. The 1876 team's
original Great Mawneys Ground, may have been one and the
same as the later named Victoria Road venue, or could
also have been the later Brooklands. The Victoria Road
Ground was located opposite the West end of this road
(just South of Romford Station), and later became a coal
yard. The Club then moved onto Church Lane, (probably one
of the fields to the North of, or at the end of, the
lane) but it is doubtful if either of these venues were
any more developed than partially enclosed fields.
Romford Town were based at the 'Shoulder of Mutton'
Ground (so named because of it's shape). This venue was
at least an enclosed venue, albeit the facilites were
nearly non-existant, with just a Pavilion on the East
side of the pitch. The Ground access was via a footpath
between the houses on the South side of Victoria Road.
The 'Shoulder of Mutton' was located behind the Victoria
Road houses, and just to the East of the, then,
Hornchurch Road. The Romford United Ground was situated
on the other side of the Hornchurch Road (probably one of
several fields but possibly in part of the current
Oldchurch Park) the thoroughfare has since been
redeveloped and renamed South Street. The last of the
town's Senior Clubs that were situated in the Town, the
G.E.R. Club, played on the earlier Victoria Ground of the
original Romford F.C. - which by 1920 was designated a
Recreation Ground and included a large pavilion on one
side - and later the Cricket Ground.

. . . .

By 1929, Romford had been without a Senior Football Club
for about fifteen years (the G.E.R. Club was never
recognised as a true representative of the town), despite

a rapidly expanding population. In 1800 the town was
little more than a large village of 3,000 inhabitants,
which had swelled to over 13,000 a century later, and by
1963 numbered nearly ten times this last total. It was
almost inevitable that a campaign for the formation of a
'Town' Football Club would be started.

The ball got rolling with a certain Mr. J. Gurney who
wrote to the local newspaper, calling Romford the 'Town
without a team', and urging the local sportsmen to do
something about remedying this situation. Mr. B.G.
Weevers took up the challenge and managed to interest
Messrs. C.W. Durrant, G.Richards (Editor of the local
newspaper), A.J. Smith and T.F. Collett - the latter a
prominent Fruiterer in the District. An initial meeting
was held in the back of Mr. Collett's shop in February
1929, when it was agreed that a more formal meeting of
those that were seriously interested should be held at
Wykeham Hall. The second meeting drew around sixty
enthusiasts, at which Mr. Smith was elected the pro-tem.
Secretary, and all were in agreement that a Public
Meeting, with a view to forming a new Football Club,
should be held.

An ingenious piece of publicity ensured that this
meeting, at 8.00 p.m. on March the 18th, was well
attended (at the Corn Exchange); so well that the crowd
overflowed into the Street causing an obstruction which
was not looked upon favourably by the Police! The
crowd-puller consisted of a simple leaflet that was dist-
-ributed around the town, prior to the meeting, with the
same notice being repeated on the front page of the
Romford Recorder newspaper. In large capital letters the
notice announced: 'Romford v. Aston Villa', and in
smaller type went on to explain the objectives of the
meeting to form a new Club, which one day might include
the headlined fixture! This eye-catcher produced the
desired effect under the principal leadership of - the
future M.P., eventual Club Chairman and later Lord - Tom
Macpherson. A lively meeting ensured that the seeds of
the new Club took root.

Enquiries regarding obtaining a suitable Ground had
already been made, the choice being Brooklands, a field
adjacent to a farm, on the Mawneys Estate. Membership of
the London League (Divisions 1 and 2) was granted, and it
was agreed to issue £1 shares in the fledgling Club. By
late April, the appeal for supporters to take up shares

Romford.

was reported as being successful, and a sub-committee was
appointed to deal with arranging a lease at Brooklands
plus the aquisition of a Stand and Dressing Rooms. The
subscription rates for membership of the Club were
decided upon at 7/6d. (37p) to include Ground entry at
all matches, which was increased to 10/6d. for the
enclosure and 17/6d. for a reserved Stand seat. By this
time many playing members had applied to join the Club.

On August the 14th, 'Romford Town's' (they never
officially had the 'Town' suffix appended to their name
despite frequent references), first practice match was
held at the Brooklands Sports Club Ltd. Ground. The big
strides that the Committee had taken in such a short time
were rewarded with a good attendance, and the occasion
also saw the opening of the new Pavilion. On the 31st of
August the first proper game for Romford F.C. was played
at Brentwood and Warley, which although lost (by 2-3) was
considered a good effort, by the many travelling
supporters. Two days later the first competitive fixture
took place, an Ilford Charity Cup-tie at Barking. Despite
going one goal behind after 10 minutes, Romford recovered
well to record a victory, by 4-2.

The first London League match was played, once again
away from home, at Bostall Heath. Generally the team was
adjudged to have played well, albeit they were slow to
recover after the surprise of conceding a goal after only
three mintutes. The new team were further shocked when
they went two goals down, but fought back well to go in
at half-time with a 1-2 scoreline. The second half was an
even contest, but the score remained at 1-2 by the full
time whistle. The Club were represented by: C. Bignall,
A.G. Taylor, S.B. Rose, W. Mynott, S.E. Lowe, W.H.
Palmer, C.E. Austin, F.J. Chapman, W.H. Barrett, S. King
and W. Durrant, with Chapman the goalscorer. On the same
day the Reserve eleven lost by four unopposed goals at
Park Royal, the Club who played at the large Ground that
had been formerly occupied by Queens Park Rangers.

It was to be several weeks before the team made their
first home appearance, and during the ensuing period,
they met with poor results. On the 21st of September they
made their debut in the F.A.Cup, where after a one goal
half-time lead at Grays Athletic they eventually lost by
1-4. Two days later they were crushed by 1-7 at Ilford in
a Hospital Shield game, where, although there were

several good individual performances, they did not play well as a team. On the 28th of September several team changes were made for another visit to Grays, this time in the F.A. Amateur Cup, which turned out to be something of a nightmare, with a 0-7 reverse.

At last the long awaited opening home match was played on October the 12th, and although it was a better team effort, the rot could not be stopped when Romford lost by a single last minute goal. One week later things were no better, for the second home match - against Beckenham - produced another defeat, by 2-3, in a contest that should have been won by the homesters. The crowd were incensed with some of the decisions of the Referee, which produced an unseemly half-time demonstration!

It was to be over a month before the next League game was completed, for on November the 13th, in the rain and with a cold wind blowing, the home match with Tooting Town was abandoned after 80 minutes, with the homesters leading 6-1. The replayed game a month later ended in a 3-5 defeat! Between times, a Friendly was played with Tottenham Hotspur, followed on November the 2nd, when the Chairman of the Club - Sir John Smith - formerly declared open the 'large and commodious' Grandstand. The team duly played their part by beating Shoeburyness Garrison (6-4), in the 2nd round of the Essex Senior Cup. But the Club's overall unhappy start continued and on the 7th of December, during the 2-1 (Friendly) victory over Barnet, the high wind demolished the Grandstand roof! This was a bitter blow for the Club, for although they had achieved much in such a short time, they were not endowed with money; in fact it was only the generosity of Mr. S.G. Tansley (on the Management Committee) which guaranteed £50 for the earlier 'Spurs visit.

The Club, for a while were nicknamed 'Blareum'. A strange nomlicature, but possibly adopted from the fact that Romford - that was once a Garrison town - was, at that time, said to be filled with the 'blaring of bugles and trumpets'. But whatever the reason they hardly made a noise in the football world, for the first eight League games (in 1929), all ended in defeat. The first victory came on the 4th of January with an encouraging 5-1 home win over Walthamstow Grange. This heralded an excellent recovery, for in the final 18 games - in 1930 - only six more defeats, and two draws, placed the Club in 10th position in a League table of 14 teams.

Romford.

It was at least overall an encouraging start for a new team that had to compete with the likes of Grays Athletic, Chelmsford, Mitcham Wanderers and Carshalton Athletic. Around the turn of the year, the local Siemans Electrical Company offered to provide floodlights at the Ground! Although this was not a novelty, (many Clubs had played under 'lights' - of a sort - in the 1800's) the offer had to be declined due to the strong opposition by the Football Association against such an innovation!

The second season was altogether a more successful time, aided in no small way with the Club's capture of Charlie Rance - the ex 'Spurs and England player - in the role of Coach and Trainer. The team started off with a 4-1 away win over Bostall Heath, and after two defeats, recorded a 10-0 home victory in the return with the Bostall team. The Club did not enter for the F.A. Cup, but in the Senior Amateur competition, they achieved some excellent victories. Their run took them through to the 3rd round proper (the last sixteen), an exceptional performance for a Club only two years old, and equalled only by the Universities Club, Pegasus, (one year later) The eight games, resulted in wins over Great Eastern Railway, Dagenham, Crittall Athletic, Brentwood and Warley, Tilbury, Egham, Kingstonian (by 5-1), with defeat coming at the hands of Wycombe Wanderers - eventual finalists. Highly creditable performances for a Club of Romford's status. This was the first season with centre-forward George Webb in the team, who scored a total of 48 goals (37 in the League); Webb was to stay with the Club another five seasons, when in each he figured prominently in the goal-scoring charts.

With some more notable League victories (7-0 over Epsom Town and 9-1 versus Carshalton), the Club fought their way to a final third in the League, with Chapman and Conley ever presents in the team. The up and coming team's abilities were sufficient for them to be accepted into the Athenian League for the 1931/32 season, but at a cost; it required a £20 fine for their late resignation from the London League! And so in only two years, the Club had reached the unofficial 'Second Division' of Amateur teams in the South. A satisfactory start was made at this higher level with a midtable final League position from 10 wins, 6 draws and 10 defeats, and with Webb again leading the League goalscorers - but with only 16 this time.

The only real blot on the Club's copybook was their worst to date defeat - of 1-10 at mediocre Enfield - but the balance was virtually restored with a 10-2 home victory over lowly Bromley. The double was completed over the Kent team, together with an unwanted double that was accomplished by Skinner of Bromley, for he scored an 'own goal' in each game!

In the Amateur Cup, a 3-1 victory over fellow-Leaguers Southall, was followed by a 1-5 home ('revenge') defeat by the 'Giants' Kingstonian, in the 2nd round proper. A re-entry into the F.A.Cup produced nothing more than an initial win over Jurgens followed by defeat at the hands of Barking. However, for the first time in their short existance, the Club captured the Essex Senior Cup, following a 3-0 win in the Final, over Clapton.

The season had been quite rewarding, and had provided the Club with a platform from which they were soon to become a dominant force in Southern Amateur football.

The 1932/33 season started well enough with a 4-1 home defeat of Enfield, but this was followed by a very lean period, that started with three draws and three defeats, and sent the team plunging down the table. Fortunately things picked up from Christmas onwards, to result in a final, perhaps somewhat disappointing 7th of 14 Clubs in the League. Webb was the only ever-present, and also the leading League goalscorer with 18. But the real attention was drawn to the premier Cup Competition, when a run was made from preliminary round through to the first round proper for the first time, that required a total of seven games. Victories were recorded over Dagenham, Grays Athletic, Jurgens and Walthamstow Grange (after a 2-2 draw) in the early rounds. The Jurgens match - at Purfleet - came close to a farce and disaster, for although the team arrived, the playing kit didn't! Only a frantic telephone call to a local sports dealer, in Grays, produced a complete set of shirts and shorts, and allowed the match to take place, albeit somewhat late! The final qualifying round produced a giant-killing 3-1 home win over the Professionals of Bedford Town, and earnt the Romford team a visit to Football League Club Bristol City. The active Supporters Club ensured that the team were well supported by the many fans who made the trip West by train.

But at this point the run came to an expected end with
a four goal defeat, although the Amateurs were described
as playing like Professionals.
The Club, and Brooklands, were honoured with the
staging of an Athenian League versus Isthmian League
match, when a large crowd saw two of their favourites,
Patterson and Reynolds, play in a 3-2 victory over the
Amateur 'cream'.
The next campaign was to be the Club's best ever in
their short life to date. Although the first game was
lost at Barking, in the weeks up to Christmas, just two
more losses were sustained in the League. But Christmas
itself was to be a bleak period, with two defeats, one by
1-5 at Golders Green (the later named 'Hendon F.C.'). But
this was to prove to be no more than a temporary
'hiccup', for the team then embarked on an incredibly
successful run which saw them gradually rise up the
League. Eleven successive victories were recorded, followed by a draw in the last game at Hayes. Of those
winning matches, one was by 7-0 (at home to Southall),
while others included two by four unopposed goals, and
two by 3-0. From a lowly team at the turn of the year,
the team was transformed into Championship challengers,
and although at the end, they were five points adrift of
table toppers Walthamstow Avenue, Romford achieved a very
satisfactory Runners-up placing. As so often happens, a
winning team usually contains a settled one, and although
23 players were used in League matches, eight members
played in 21 (of 26) games or more. Despite these
results, the team made little impression on the two major
Cup competitions, losing at the first attempt in the
F.A.Cup, and only reaching the 4th qualifying stage of
the Amateur. The Club's defeat in the latter competition
(by Bromley), ended an unbeaten home run, in all
competitions, that extended over thirteen months. But to
compensate, the Essex Senior Cup was won, when the
favourites - Walthamstow Avenue - were beaten by 3-0.
The Club could not capitalise in the League the next
season, and finished in a disappointing fifth position.
But this was no more than a temporary set-back, for in
the next few years upto the Second World War, the Club
proved themselves to have the strongest outfit in the
Athenian League.
After three League matches in the 1935/36 season, the
Club hardly looked like Championship contenders, with two

Romford.

A Pre-war Aerial View of the Ground at Brooklands.

Romford.

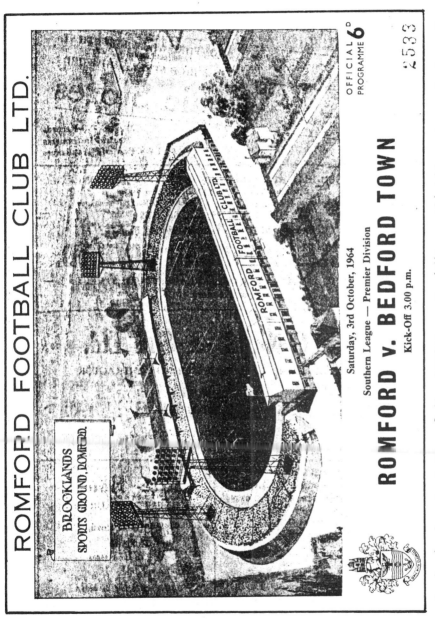

ROMFORD FOOTBALL CLUB LTD.

BROOKLANDS
SPORTS GROUND, ROMFORD.

OFFICIAL
PROGRAMME **6**ᴰ

2533

Saturday, 3rd October, 1964

Southern League — Premier Division

ROMFORD v. BEDFORD TOWN

Kick-Off 3.00 p.m.

A typical programme of the 1960's – providing a slightly enhanced view of the Ground!

-83-

defeats (to Leyton) and one home win. However, they then
embarked on an incredible run which produced just one
more defeat (to lowly Wealdstone) upto the end of the
season! High scoring victories included 6-1 over eventual
third placed Walthamstow, 5-0 over Sutton United and four
goal wins without reply versus both Golders Green and
Uxbridge Town. The only stumble in the Club's bid for
honours occurred on the 4th of April, when they missed a
penalty and lost 3-4 at Wealdstone. Then a Good Friday
win at Redhill (4-1) was followed by the two goals shared
draw at Barnet before a crowd in excess of 3,000. Four
victories and one draw, led upto the last game of the
season on April the 30th, and could not have produced a
more fitting climax - home to Bromley, the Championship
decider.

This home gate, before a (unspecified) 'large' attendance, saw the homesters score two goals with none in
reply. So for the first time, Romford were the Champions,
but only one point in front of their nearest challengers.
Once again a reliable and consistant team helped, when,
although no player appeared in every League encounter,
there was an unchanged team for 18 of the 26 matches.

But the season was memorable for more than the League
success. In the Amateur Cup, the team first beat Barnet
by 6-2, followed by their - away - seven goal thrashing
of Maidstone. The Club were in fact fortunate to only
sustain a fine of £60 for playing an ineligible player in
the match! The 3rd Round brought Dulwich Hamlet to
Brooklands, and attracted 5,500 fans (which would have
been considerably more had it not been for the poor
weather). There had been so much rain prior to the game,
that it was a doubtful starter, but it was played,
complete with three 'ponds' on the pitch! The homesters
ran out 4-2 winners in a thrilling game. By reaching the
4th round (the quarter-finals), the Club had exceeded any
other run, and another home game was their prize.

A new record attendance of 7,500 was present for
Sutton United's visit, a game which was remembered
particularly for it's good sportsmanship. After going
behind by one goal, Romford pulled back to a 2-1 interval
lead. They added two more goals in the second period, a
somewhat flattering scoreline, to progress on to the
Semi-finals. This round required a short journey across
London - accompanied by many cars, coaches and trains -
to Dulwich Hamlet's Champion Hill Ground.

Romford.

Their opponents were the renowned Casuals team, and
over 18,000 were present to see a close fought contest.
All seemed lost at half-time when the Essex team went in
for the break two goals behind, but a spirited fight back
brought them level, only for the Casuals to score the
winner just five minutes before time. The Casuals went on
to win the Cup in a replay over Ilford at Upton Park.
    To cap an incredibly good season, the team even
reached the first round proper of the F.A. Cup once
again. Straight wins were first achieved over Harwich &
Parkeston (their victors one year earlier), Barking,
Leyton, Dagenham and Guildford City before meeting
Folkestone, and a defeat was only conceded at the second
attempt. Individual honours also were bestowed upon three
of the Club's Players. 'Homegrown' George Burchell gained
an England Cap, as did Jack Anderson and George Patterson
- the latter for Scotland.
    The only failure in a season that would be difficult
to ever surpass, was an early exit in the Essex Senior
Cup. At Ilford, in the second round, before an attendance
of over 10,000 (receipts of £304), the team lost by the
odd goal in three.

    With the Club now financially stable, plans were
considered during the summer of 1936 for the Club to buy
Shortlands, as the time could never be better, especially
since the Cricket Club were playing their last season on
the combined Ground. The start of the season gave the
team a rare chance to travel abroad, when they played in
Ostende and recorded a 2-1 victory. There appeared little
that the Club could not achieve as they swung in to their
winning ways. By the season's end, the situation was
nearly as good as a year earlier. The Athenian League
Championship was again won, but this time by a full ten
points over Walthamstow Avenue. The campaign produced an
incredible record of only one defeat (the second match at
Leyton) and one draw, plus 24 straight victories, during
all of which the team scored 102 goals while only
conceding 35. In ten matches five goals or more were
scored, with the 6-0 home win over Sutton United being
the best. Howlett, Wingfield and Walker were all
ever-presents, and Osborne led the goalscorers with 32 in
22 outings.
    The Cup competitions were, however, relatively
disappointing with defeat at home to Sutton United in the

Romford.

Premier Amateur Competition at the third round stage, and
defeat to, yet again, Harwich, in the 2nd qualifying
round of the F.A.Cup (after a replay which attracted a
4,000 home attendance). One year later however, an
earlier exit was made in the F.A.Cup, whereas the
semi-final stage was again reached in the Amateur Cup. On
this latter occasion, Chesham United, Walthamstow Avenue,
Leyton, and Harwich & Parkeston were first overcome.

The team had an excellent chance of reaching the
Final, when they led Erith & Belvedere by two goals at
Clapton Orient. But they let their lead slip, and a
replay became necessary. Once again the Essex team were
ahead (2-1 at half-time), only for the Kent side to fight
back again, and Romford eventually lost by 4-2 after
extra time. But at least this season, the 1937/38, they
won one cup, the Essex Senior. The final was played at
Ilford (attendance 9,100) when the team were held to a
goalless draw by Eton Manor, but won the replay.

Back in November, a significant step was taken, when
the old Club was wound up, at an Extraordinary General
Meeting, and a new one - "Romford Football Club Limited"
- was immediately formed. 80,000 shares at 2/6d. (12.5p)
were issued with the former shareholders having the
option of exchanging on a 'nine new for one old' (£1)
basis. The main aims were the purchase of the Ground and
an upgrading of the facilities within. This action by the
Club, in forming a Limited Company, was the first ever
taken by an Amateur team.

On recent past performances, the League showings were
almost bad, for the team 'only' finished in third place!
The Club lost touch in the second half of the season,
after losing three consecutive games. Three excellent
seasons should have earnt the Club a 'promotion' to the
Isthmian League, but the powers that be in this renowned
competition thought otherwise, although the invitation
was exended to them one year later.

During the 1938/39 season, the Club showed their
undoubted talents, although the Championship once again
eluded them, and they had to settle for the Runners-up
position, ending five points behind Walthamstow Avenue -
another team that had demonstrated their prowess. Two
notable victories were the 8-1 win at Southall, and
incredibly eight goals without reply - at home to
Walthamstow!

Romford.

But yet again the Club's endeavours in the Cups were
disappointing. It was a first time exit in the Amateur
Competition (to Leyton) where they were three goals
behind after 35 minutes, and achieved only three wins in
the National Competition, although the first was by 12-1
at home to the Purfleet based Stork Club. The only really
bad result was a semi-final exit in the Essex Senior Cup,
when the team lost by five unopposed goals before a 9,000
crowd at Ilford, to familiar adversaries, Walthamstow
Avenue.
Although they undoubtedly deserved it, the Club were
surprised when they were invited to join the Isthmian
League for the forthcoming 1939/40 season; this reaction
was not so surprising in view of the 'Closed shop'
attitude of this Premier Amateur Competition. Such a move
it was hoped would attract bigger crowds and plans were
made for further improvements to the Ground. Meanwhile
the Supporters Club were disappointed that their
membership hadn't quite reached 1,000! Eight seasons of
successful Athenian League football had come to an end,
as did many careers, with Wartime hostilities fast
approaching. During these years, Jack Anderson and George
Burchell headed the appearances chart for the Club with
162 each (both between 1931 and 1938), whilst Johnny
Osborne had hit the back of the net on 108 occasions.
And so the 1939/40 season started with Romford
entertaining Ilford on the 27th of August before a near
3,000 crowd. The game ended in a 2-0 win, and five days
later the team travelled to the familiar Ilford Ground,
but this time to play the home team in a South Essex
Charity Cup-tie - which was lost 1-2. All the hopes and
expectations of the football team were then cut short as
the Second World War commenced, and normal football
ceased. The 3rd of September fixture versus Nunhead was
cancelled, and the Essex team was never able to meet
those opponents from South London, as the end of the War
resulted in the folding of this old established Club.
There was only a 'small crowd' present for a Friendly
match with Dartford on the 16th of September. Two more
meaningless games were played (versus Wimbledon and
Leytonstone), before the war-time South-Essex Combination
got underway. The opposition included Leyton, Ilford,
Clapton and Tilbury, and the latter team was played at
home in the first game. A 2-2 draw ensued, but the low
attendance proved that the fans were either at war or not

interested. The Competition finished around Christmas, at
which point Romford F.C. announced their intentions to
close down until the end of hostilities; for over five
years in the event.

The first game at Brooklands, and also the first for a
Romford team, in 1945, was a somewhat insignificant
Reserve fixture. On August the 25th a South Essex league
game was played before a crowd of only 300. But one week
later the Club was able to continue with it's long
interupted Isthmian League programme. The attendance
however, was considerably more than for the earlier
Reserve's game. But with a team that had not played
together before, the homesters went down by 1-2, to
Kingstonian, who scored the winner in the 80th minute.
This unhappy start continued with a 2-6 defeat to
Walthamstow Avenue on the 8th of September. But the team
soon got on to a more confident wave, and two home
victories followed. Upto Christmas things were quite
reasonable, but from then onwards, the team really took
off and gradually climbed the table. During this latter
period only two defeats were sustained, at Wimbledon and
Dulwich, and this string of victories put the team into a
final third in the table. A notable feature of the season
was the plethora of goals. Tufnell Park were beaten 8-0,
another eight were recorded in the eleven goal bonanza at
home to Corinthian Casuals, plus four victories where six
goals were recorded. Despite their high position, on the
debit side, a 0-6 defeat at Oxford City followed a 0-5
thrashing at Leytonstone a week earlier. But there were
constantly changing team members, as Players gradually
returned to the Club after the War, such that 49
different men were used in the 26 League games.
      However, the real excitement was reserved for the
F.A.Cup. Eton Manor (after a surprise draw), Crittall
Atheltic (by 7-1), Leyton and Dulwich were all beaten to
take the Club through to the first round proper again.
The team were rewarded with the visit of a Football
League Club for the first time. This season, and from
this round onwards, matches were played on a two legged
basis, and the first was played at Brighton and Hove
Albion. A crowd of only 7,425 attended, and saw the
non-Leaguers go down 1-3 in a match in which the defence
earned the honours.

One week later, on November the 24th, the Club were not disappointed with the huge crowd of around 8,000, but the deficit proved to be too much. Despite taking a one goal interval lead, with a 25 yard goal from Olton, a final 1-1 draw was insufficient for progress onto the next round. The season was an overall success, for the crowds were high, (even in excess of 3,000 for Barking's visit in the Thameside Cup) and a 750 membership within the reformed Supporters Association often saw six coaches packed with fans for away games.

Things continued the next season in much the same vein, and the League Officials were shown to be fully justified in including Romford F.C. within the League, for a third final placing was again reached. The only blot on the season was a 2-7 defeat at Dulwich in December, in which five goals were conceded in 25 minutes! But there was little joy to be had from the two major Cup Competitions.

There then followed three seasons of indifferent League performances when 6th, 8th and 9th positions were realised in the 14 team table. During this period the first round of the F.A.Cup was reached in 1948, when six straight victories led to a visit to Yeovil, and a 0-4 defeat was the outcome.

But it was this same season that the Club's greatest achievement occurred, in the Amateur Cup. The team won right through to the Final, following five outright victories. But in the second game, the first round, the austerity of the post-War years was apparent when the team travelled to Hitchin Town. With clothing coupons still in force, only the barest minimum of playing kit was available, and with only one set of shorts, the Players were unable to change at half-time after a first half period of driving rain and thick mud!

The next round brought Briggs Sports to Brooklands, but due to fog and a heavy frost it was necessary for a late inspection by the Referee. His positive decision led to chaos outside the Ground, where large crowds had gathered, for the gates were not open until 2.15 p.m. - the original kick-off time. Despite the start being delayed for 30 minutes, the impatient fans broke a gate down, but there were no injuries, and the game got underway before an estimated 6,000 crowd. The homesters leaving it until the 88th minute before finally scoring a deserved goal, the only one of the match.

The luck of the draw once again favoured Romford, and
before a crowd of 8,070 they entertained Moor Green from
the Midlands, in the fourth round. This game was an easy
victory, for after scoring straight from the kick-off,
they went on to win 5-1. Their reward was then a long
trip upto the North-east to play Billingham in a
quarter-final game, along with many chartered coaches, in
which the fans paid £1-30p. or as an alternative, £2-40
for the special train. On the same day, the Reserves
played at home to one of the best ever attended second
team games - a telephone link-up to the Ground relayed
frequent reports from the North! In the Cup, the visitors
fell behind to an early goal, but a spirited fight back
finished with them winning the tie by 2-1.

The Club, team and supporters were dismayed when the
venue for the semi-final with Crook Colliery (later
'Town') was deemed to be played at Roker Park, Sunderland
- another long trip for those concerned. In front of an
attendance of 24,215 (receipts of £2443), including 1,000
from Essex, a thrilling game finished at 2-2. This draw
meant at least a Southern replay, and before 25,284 at
Upton Park, Romford ran out easy three goal winners.

And so for the first time ever, not only would the
team be playing in the Final, but also at Wembley
Stadium. The occasion produced unprecedented excitement
in the town, with enormous crowds wishing their team well
when the coach left at 11.30 a.m. for the short journey
across London. A large crowd of those who didn't make the
journey, waited outside the Radio Shops in the partly
deserted town, hoping to hear the B.B.C. broadcast of the
game. But they were disappointed, for the Dealers were
not inclined to relay the progress, fearing that they
would be charged by the Police for causing an
obstruction! 95,000 paid £20,250 at the Stadium (with
each Club receiving £6,000), to see a closely fought game
that resulted in a single goal victory to the Kent Club,
Bromley.

The match was a personal triumph for the evergreen
Scottish Amateur International George Patterson. The 40
year old left-winger had joined Romford from Queens Park
for the 1931/32 season, and went on to play a total of
212 Athenian and Isthmian League games for the Club; a
period that of course included the less active War years.
The award of an Amateur Cup finalist medal was a fitting
end to a long career. The event also provided the Club

Trainer (since 1937) with a return to the Stadium, for he won a medal there in 1930, as part of the Arsenal F.A.Cup winning team.

After such a finale, the first match of the next season (1949/50) attracted a large crowd, at home to St.Albans. But the match was a big anti-climax as many fans left well before the end, as Romford slumped to a surprise 1-5 defeat.

After several indifferent years in respect of the Club's League match showings, the position improved for the 1950/51 season. After a second game (first home) match ended in a 1-4 reverse, the team set about their winning ways. Six straight end of season victories, resulted in a final 3rd place in the table. Yet despite such a notable position, the match away to Corinthian Casuals on the 24th of February was lost by 1-7, and the return game resulted in a 0-3 defeat. Seven games were played in the F.A.Cup, but with a start in the preliminary round plus three draws, only the third qualifying round was reached. A marathon tie required three games before Woodford Town edged through with a final 2-1 scoreline.

The next few seasons in the League were little short of disastrous. Gradual slips down the final tables (4th, 7th and 10th respectively) led to the final humiliation of bottom in 1955. It was a desperate campaign from the start with the first victory not coming until the 15th League game (which included ten defeats) - an incredible 7-3 home win over Wycombe Wanderers. But any hopes of a permanent recovery were immediately dashed when another four defeats and just one drawn game followed - the last match being an even more remarkable scoreline of 6-9 to Woking! But although the last eight games ended with only one defeat (including a 1-7 defeat to Champions-elect Walthamstow Avenue), it was insufficient for the Club to avoid finishing in the wooden spoon position for the first time. However, high scoring games were rare, for only 43 were scored in League games, with the leading marksman being Rubery with just eight successes.

The early fifties depression extended to the major Cup competitions, apart from reaching the last qualifying round of the F.A. Cup in 1951, and the 3rd round of the Amateur Competition in 1953. Although the Club's League

form was going through an indifferent period, this was
the era of large attendances, and for the 'right' games,
big crowds could be expected. In the 1950/51 season, the
team travelled to Moor Green for an Amateur Cup encounter. Four goals were shared before a post-war record
attendance of over 4,000, and although the Essex team
lost the replay, by two second half goals, the crowd at
Brooklands totalled around 10,000. Two years later, in
the third round stage of the competition, on Feburary the
28th, an all-time record attendance of 18,237 packed into
the Ground to see the replay versus Southall. This match
followed two goals shared at the Western Road enclosure
(watched by over 10,000), but at the second attempt,
Romford bowed out by 1-2 after a 1-1 half-time scoreline.

In League competition there was little improvement,
with second and third from bottom placings following the
disastrous year of 1954. During the latter season, a
humiliating defeat by 1-10 at Oxford City was experienced
- and this after an encouraging start to the season of
two victories. The final years of the 1950's, and those
for the Club as Amateurs in the Isthlian League continued
in this bleak fashion. With just one victory in their
last thirteen games, the team slumped to finish bottom in
the 1957/58 season, and only an improvement over the same
period one year later lifted the Club one place higher at
the finish.

There was still little to enthuse over in respect of
Cup Competitions, and during the whole of the post-war
period (to 1959), the Essex Senior Cup was lifted only
once, despite the Club being recognised as one of the
foremost in non-League football.

Drastic action had to be taken to pull the Club out of
it's long term slump. No more drastic than them
relinquishing their Amateur status, to become Professional for the forthcoming 1959/60 season. They were
fortunate in being elected into the revamped Southern
League in view of their recent lamentable performances in
the Isthmian competition.

There are a number of Clubs over the years that lived
to regret the decision to turn professional, for they no
longer exist! Invariably a faction within a Club will try
to veto such a move, and then have the shallow
satisfaction of knowing that their objection to change
was probably right. But it has to be said that although
Romford F.C. eventually became defunct, it was only after

eighteen years in their changed status, and their progress and achievements during this time make it difficult to criticise this move alone. Most of the Club's (amateur) Players left, but the addition of Ted Ditchburn who joined the Club in June 1959 was a most welcome addition to a virtually new team.

The aquisition of the famous Tottenham goalkeeper was a coup, and despite his 38 years he was still capable of holding a first team place for five more years. He was not the only ex-Spurs Player to join the Club, for Les Bennett (via West Ham) also made the move around this time, followed by Charlie Withers and Les Duquemin two years later. Romford F.C. were typical of a Southern League team of around this period, when teams would blend together a selection of youthful hopefuls with unkindly labelled 'has-been' personalities from the Football League, who could nonetheless contibute to the part-professional scene.

Romford were one of nine additional teams that were recruited to form the revised Southern League set-up, with their entry into the new First Division. After a shaky start that only produced two points in their first four games, they gradually improved to record a total of eight victories and six defeats in the 21 games upto the end of 1959. The first home match had been attended by an excellent crowd of around 5,000, and an exciting tussle with Burton Albion finished with six goals shared; all three Romford successes came from Harry Bennett.

At the turn of the year, the team lay seventh in the League, and although defeat came at Folkestone, there was only one more reverse to the end of the campaign. A highly creditable runners-up position was the final result, and it was only their goalscoring which was seriously at fault; Cappi headed the lists with just 14. Conversely the defense had a very good record, with only 40 conceded League goals, during which on only two occasions did they let in three, one of which was the thriller with Burton Albion.

A disappointing and early exit from the F.A.Cup was made at home to Finchley when Ditchburn made two, rare, disastrous mistakes, and in the Southern League Cup the last eight were reached. But these were relatively unimportant compared to their League performances, which earned the Club promotion at the first attempt.

Promotion was confirmed after their 1-1 draw at Ramsgate, and hence another milestone was reached in the Club's history. The Club were reasonably happy with the support at the gate (3,750 versus Cambridge United and 250 less for Clacton's visit, being amongst the best), but on their travels it was often a different story; at Corby and Gloucester there were only 600 spectators at each, and several other Clubs did not normally reach four figures in their home games. But despite their success under Manager Jack Chisolm, the extra costs of running a professional team were felt with a £2,000 running loss on the season.

A bold move was made with a fruitless application for Football League status. No fewer than 22 Clubs were up for election (or re-election), and although Romford's two votes were better than some, this was far below Peterborough's total of 39 that deservedly gave that Club membership.

A moderate start was made to the 1960/61 season at the peak of non-League football - the Premier Division of the Southern League - but a slump from mid-November to March required some action. Trevor Ford the former Welsh International joined the Club from Newport County, and despite his high wages of £30 per week, after only ten appearances (and four goals) he walked out at the end of the season! But at least a good recovery was made during the last two months to ensure a respectable mid-table League placing.

The 1961/62 season proved an unremarkable one in League competition, with inconsistancy throughout leading to a similar final position in the League as one year earlier. The only highlights were the five goal thrashing of lowly Wisbech, and a ten goal - equally shared - thriller at Bedford Town. The excitement was saved for an appearance in the final rounds of the F.A.Cup, the team's first for twelve years. Wembley were first cast aside by 7-0, followed by a 3-1 victory over Leytonstone. In early October, Hornchurch were the visitors to Brooklands, and before a crowd of 3,293 (receipts of £330), another victory ensued. The luck continued with the Club, for the final qualifying round produced another home tie, this time with Enfield, and in front of 4,843 fans, a close fought match resulted in a 2-1 win to the homesters.

Romford.

There was disappoinment when it was announced that the
first round proper would require a visit to Surrey to
meet Sutton United. But aided by 16 coaches and hundreds
more who travelled from Romford by car, a crowd of 3,918
saw four goals shared between the two teams. The midweek
(pre-floodlight) replay attracted only 3,835 to Brooklands, where a demolition of the visitors by five
unopposed goals was the result.

The second round draw could not have been better, a
home game with high flying Northampton Town from the
Football League Division Four. The interest in the town
came close to matching that aroused when the local team
went to Wembley Stadium, and following the gates being
opened at midday, the final attendance was the second
highest ever, 11,073. The match receipts of £1,587 helped
to swell the total in the cup run to £3,852. With
additional excitement being provided by the B.B.C. TV
cameras, the match was a flop from Romford's point of
view for they were easily overcome by five goals to one.

Another season came to an end. one that had had it's
highlights, but in the 'bread and butter' existance had
perhaps not fulfilled the hopes of the Club's Oficials
and supporters. Ever rising costs required average home
gates of 3,500, a figure that was seldom reached, but the
lucrative F.A.Cup run at least saw the Club safely
through for another year. Boxing Day saw the debut of
Malcolm Allison, a treat that attracted a healthy 3,300
to Brooklands for the encounter with Dartford, and 4,000
were present for the match in January versus Guildford.
But generally the Club were unable to maintain the
break-even figure, 2,010 for the Boston United match and
2,205 for the penultimate home game with Folkestone being
more typical.

Around this time there were the first rumours of a
proposal to sell the Brooklands Ground for housing, and
move the Club just South of the Town centre to Oldchurch
Park. This plan was partially fulfilled but only some
fifteen years later! An even more unlikely rumour spread,
that was firmly denied by the Club Secretary, of a
proposed merger of the Romford and the Charlton Athletic
Clubs. Charlton did once move, to Catford, as well as
their more prolonged stay at Selhurst Park, and it was
also once suggested that they would move across London to
Slough!

ROMFORD FOOTBALL CLUB

SOUVENIR PROGRAMME

SERVE WITH GLADNESS

ROMFORD
v
SALISBURY

SOUTHERN LEAGUE FIRST DIVISION (SOUTH)

TUESDAY, 19th APRIL, 1977   Kick-Off 7.30 p.m.

Official Programme 20p   Lucky Programme No. 151

ROMFORD (Blue and Gold)		SALISBURY (White and Black)	
Steve Biggs		1	Steve Tilley
Ray Pettit		2	Peter Syrett
Paul Gilbert		3	Barry Fitch
Kevin Handelaar		4	David Lock
Joe Peck		5	David Hibberd
Ian Hamilton		6	David Verity
John Arnold		7	Alan Green
Graham Parker		8	Paul Christopher
Les Cobb		9	Coln Guy
Pat Ferry		10	David Selby
Mickey Hanson		11	Eric Welsh
Frankie Bishop		12	Bob Andrews

Romford's last match at Brooklands....
.... and the last goal,
scored by Mick Hanson.

Romford.

ROMFORD FOOTBALL CLUB

ROMFORD
v
FOLKESTONE and SHEPWAY

SOUTHERN LEAGUE FIRST DIVISION (South)

Monday 1st May 1978   Kick-Off 3.00 p.m.

Official Programme 10p

Played at Rainham Football Club

ROMFORD (Blue and Gold)		FOLKESTONE	
Steve Biggs		1	M. Goodburn
Roger Dent		2	J. Smith
Paul Gilbert		3	C. Plum
Bill Bailey		4	K. Robinson
Joe Peck		5	J. Keirs
Ian Hamilton		6	B. Irvine
Johnny Arnold		7	N. Sparks
Frank Bishop		8	A. Wilks
Kevin Walsh		9	P. Westgarth
Les Cobb		10	J. Stone
Micky Hanson		11	F. Ovard
Graham Parker		12	P. Prior

Referee:

A. L. BARRELLS (Westcliff-on-Sea)

Linesmen:

(Celtic Flag)
P. HEALY (Colchester)

(Orange Flag)
R. A. HEWITT (Colchester)

The Romford Press Ltd., Romford. Essex

The last programme for the last match, that never was!
Several cancellations resulted in the game being played at Folkestone.

-97-

Only 13 Players from a large squad were retained under the new leadership of Ditchburn in the role of Player/Manager. By now it was recognised that floodlights were a near necessity, but the Club could ill afford the estimated £25,000 outlay.

The 1961/62 season started as often had happened, in poor to indifferent fashion, with only two wins in the Club's first nine games, and it was left to the F.A.Cup to provide the main interest and extra revenue once again. After victories over Wembley, Leytonstone and Dagenham, the fourth qualifying round brought fellow-Leaguers Cambridge United to Romford. A close fought match was won with an indirect free-kick which was deflected off a player, to record a 2-1 margin to the homesters; a well above average attendance of 5,323 were present. Once again the team had reached the first round proper, and at this stage the Club beat Walthamstow Avenue 3-2. The second round draw built up the excitement amongst the fans once more, for on this occasion they were due to meet Watford of the Football League, Third Division.

In this match the team were given little chance, as they lay fourth from bottom of their League at this time. But the match for the first 65 minutes was a very even affair, then Allison gave away a penalty. Scoring from the resultant kick, Watford from then on never looked like losing, and eventually ended up as 3-1 winners.

But at least Romford F.C. received a healthy boost from the share of the 1,850 gate, which represented 12,250 spectators.

Whilst avoiding relegation, the final 11th place in the League had been insufficient to attract good attendances, and by the season's end the Club had a large overdraft at the Bank. It had been decided to raise £40,000 from a new Share issue back in December 1961. But the innovations regarding the Club were somewhat overshadowed with the death of former Chairman, Lord MacPherson, a founder-member of the Club.

These early years of Southern League football had produced some memorable moments, if not a high degree of success in the day-to-day League games. There then followed four seasons of mediocrity, where little of note was achieved not even in the F.A.Cup. A mid-table place in the table at the end of the 1962/63 season, was followed by a far more encouraging fifth in 1964.

The story could have been so much better after an excellent start had seen the Club lead the League, following an incredible run of the first 24 games without defeat, and included only six draws. While there was nothing spectacular in the scorelines, the team could be happy with the consistently good form which took them upto mid-January before their first League defeat. After losing by the only goal at home to Guildford City, the rest of the campaign was as bad as the first part was good. These last eighteen games produced only 8 points from two victories and four draws.

It must have been most demoralising for the team, Manager Ditchburn (who only made 10 League appearances), and the supporters. There wasn't even a good Cup run to look back on, for early exits were made in both the Southern League and F.A.Cups.

The poor run continued into the next season, and it was only a reasonable recovery from the New Year that saved them from relegation, to a low mid-table safety area. The 1965/66 season produced a definite improvement that was generally spread throughout the campaign, despite the loss of the first two games, both away from home. With exemption through to the last qualifying round of the F.A.Cup, the team beat local rivals Chelmsford City before entertaining Luton Town in the first round. 10,500 were present to see the locals hold their Football League opponents to a 1-1 draw, before the Club bowed out at Kenilworth Road by a solitary goal.

There was a consistancy in the team that led to three Players being ever present in League matches, and a final placing of 7th out of 22. Just fourteen different Players were used in League games, although occasioned more by economic reasons, but several changes were made in the team that led to quite unexpected success in the 1966/67 season.

The campaign got off to a far from good start, with a 4-1 defeat at Kings Lynn. The first victory didn't come until the fourth match (the second home game) when Burton Albion were overcome. This far from exciting start continued in a similar vein, and over Christmas a dismal record produced just one point from three games. The end of the year marked the midway point in League matches, during which 8 were won, 4 drawn and 9 lost, resulting in a mid-table placing. Although the first match of 1967 was lost at Burton Albion, the next encounter - a 2-0 home

win over Bath City - signalled the start of a run through
to the end of the season, during which the team gradually
climbed the table. As May approached it became apparent
that Romford were in with a chance of the Championship,
especially from February the 25th, when a single goal
victory over Chelmsford City saw the start of a 12 match
sequence without defeat. Easter passed with a 100%
record, starting with the Good Friday Brooklands match
with fellow title aspirants Wimbledon. The 4,361
attendance represented the best in the League that
season, and a two goal win resulted. Another top of the
table clash saw the Essex team overcome Nuneaton Borough,
and finally a four day double was completed over the
Surrey 'Dons'.

There was a slight slip when Hillingdon Borough held
the Club to a 1-1 draw, in front of 3,445 fans at
Brooklands, and with three games left the team were only
in third place, albeit just one point behind the leaders.
After beating Hereford United by 2-0 at home - before a
disappointing crowd of only 3,895 - Cheltenham were
overcome by the odd goal in five. This left Romford on
equal points with the leaders Weymouth, but second on
goal average. 300 supporters were at Worcester for the
final match; the Championship decider, from which two
points were almost certainly required. The 2-0 victory
was enough to edge the team into top place - and
Champions - at the crucial time, with Nuneaton one point
behind and Weymouth two in arrears. Even the Reserves
were not to be outdone for they finished in the
Runners-up position in their League, attracting a
season's best crowd of 2,845 for their last home game.

The season came to an entertaining end with a Benefit
match for Bill Seddon. The Arsenal first team did the
honours and although a 1-3 defeat for Romford resulted, a
crowd of 5,000 spectators was present. Ironically during
the past year, there was little to enthuse over in other
competitions, with an exit in the F.A.Cup to Bedford Town
(the replay at Brooklands attracting the season's best
gate of 5,226) and an embarrassing 2-7 defeat to
Folkestone in the League Cup.

But all things considered it was an outstanding
achievement by Manager Harry Clarke, with a squad of only
16 Players and on a small budget. The average attendance
at home games was 2,779 (varying from 1,842 to 4,361) a
discouraging drop compared to one year earlier; but such

was the lot of most Southern League Clubs, Hillingdon
only recorded a 1,133 average - over 150% lower than for
the 1965/66 season. Although nothing was freely
expressed, the first real signs of financial problems
must already have been occuring, but even so the Club
made an application for election to the Football League,
and received 5 votes, as did Wigan Athletic - the best of
the 'also rans'. This was the Club's eighth consecutive
application, and although they had led the pack on two
previous occasions, the number of votes was always
woefully short for a successful bid. They made no
application in 1968, and although two further attempts
were made, the best of these later three, was just two
votes in 1969.

After winning their first match, at home, the next
season, the second was lost at Cambridge United, the
latter bringing to an end their unbeaten run of 15 games.
The team could not maintain the necessary form to retain
the Championship, and as results were indifferent, so
were the attendances. On December the 23rd there were
only 2,000 present for the United's visit from Cambridge,
and the season's best for the local derby match with
Chelmsford attracted less than 4,000. The final League
place of 6th, was no disaster, but was obviously
considered not good enough for the stay away fans. As the
1960's drew to a close, and with the dawn of a new
decade, things got gradually worse, both on the field and
from a financial standpoint.

After another 6th placing at the end of the 1968/69
season, a long drop to 17th of 22 was the Club's lot one
year later. A spirited rise to third in 1971 was but a
brief respite, for the following season saw another
downward move, this time to eleventh. The only real
excitement during the latter campaign was an appearance
in the later rounds of the F.A.Cup, the first since 1967
(a three goal defeat in the first round proper, at
Wimbledon). But on this occasion the first round was
easily negotiated, when Witney Town were beaten in
Oxfordshire, and the next game required a visit from the
Gillingham team. This time there was no hope of a five
figure attendance, as had happened with the last Cup
visit from a Football League team. A close fought game
ended with just a one goal defeat by the visitors. It was
not known at the time, but the Kent team were to be the
last Football League visitors in the F.A.Cup.

By now a new Cup had been introduced for the more
Senior non-League Clubs, the F.A.Trophy, and although the
third round was reached in the inaugural season of
1969/70, this was never bettered in the following eight
seasons of entry for the team. Meanwhile another
Competition in which the Club had not fared well, the
Southern League Cup, at long last produced some results
which took them to the Final in 1970. The team had only
once reached the last eight before, but two defeats to
Wimbledon this time, put paid to any glory in this
direction.

The finances took another blow when the Romford
Bombers Speedway team vacated their joint share of
Brooklands, since for a while the extra rent money had
helped to keep the Club going. But by now it had become
common knowledge of the Club's intention to sell the
Ground, although the hoped for help from the local
Havering Council was not forthcoming.

The Club was destined to never appear in the top half
of the Premier Division of the Southern League again, and
the next four years saw them gradually drop lower in the
table by each season's end. 11th in 1972, 14th one year
later, then 16th, and finally fourth from bottom - and
relegation - in April 1975. By early 1975 things were
becoming desperate in every direction.

Following the departure of Harry Clarke, a stalwart
with Romford for 13 years, the Club was left Managerless.
Arrangements had already been made for the sale of the
Ground, which had by now become a necessity, and this
became apparent three years later. By the dawn of 1975,
the team had won only three League games - a better
second half did eventually lift them off the bottom of
the table, but not high enough! The Directors could not
get an agreement with the local Council with regard to
another Ground, and perhaps the most significant point in
this tale of woe were the attendances which had slumped
to their lowest level since the Club had turned
Professional; the home win in March raised the Club one
place above bottom, but only 707 diehards were there.

When the new Manager, Ray Freeman, arrived, he was
given the near impossible task of pulling the Club around
- on the field - while the Directors meanwhile were still
struggling to keep the Club in a financially viable
position.

Romford.

In May, a possible Ground share with neighbours
Hornchurch was declined.
The 1975/76 season started in a dejected and
demoralised fashion, caused not least by the relegation
to the Division 1 South of the Southern League after so
many reasonably successful years in the top flight. It
was also expected to be the last campaign fought from
Brooklands.
As things turned out, the start of the season got off
on a high note. The first game produced some good
football, and a 2-1 win over Salisbury. This was followed
by six victories and one draw, which lifted the morale
around the Club. There was a temporary halt when they
lost at home to Bexley United, but five more points out
of a possible eight left them still in an excellent
position at Christmas. With only four defeats in the
League upto mid-March they looked good bets for promotion
- even if they were to have no future home venue! Then
their chances were more or less dashed when the total
number of reverses was doubled in the next four matches.
On April the 19th, when what should have been the last
game at Brooklands was played, they took a point off of
runaway leaders Minehead, followed nine days later with
four goals shared at Guildford and Dorking. Perhaps this
last game was a bad omen, for it was to be the last time
that Romford would play the resurrected 'Guildford City'
team, for the Surrey Club became defunct just a few
months later.
The Ground problems were put aside for another year,
for in the final event they were able to play the 1976/77
home games at Brooklands. There were hopes of sufficient
finance to bring the squad upto 17 Players (even this
figure was scarcely sufficient), under Manager Dave
Bickles. But the near promotion of the last campaign -
third in the League (only two promoted) - was obviously
not going to be improved upon, when they lost their first
four matches. In fact there was little improvement until
December, from whence they recorded four victories. The
second half of the season produced a good run, with only
five defeats in their last twenty games, but it was all
too late for promotion, and they finished sixth in the
League. The last home match, at Brooklands was played
against Salisbury, and a 2 goal victory ensued, in
something of a cup-tie atmosphere. The attendance for
this sad occasion was 1,508, way above the norm., for the

season's average gate was even less than the 800
experienced during the previous campaign.
Even then after all these years Romford F.C. did not
have the satisfaction of playing the last football match
at Brooklands, for this honour went to Hornchurch F.C.
who staged their game with Chesham United at the Stadium
on April the 30th, as their normal venue was unusable due
to the laying of a new Athletics track.

The 1977/78 season started in a farcical situation,
with the first eight League games all being played away,
although during this disadvantaged time some creditable
results were obtained. Only two defeats were recorded,
but the last was a 0-6 thrashing at Margate on the 22nd
of October. Despite the many promises and reassurances,
the new Ground - which had finally been agreed upon at
Oldchurch Park - was far from ready. Objections and
delays came from all quarters! The residents near to
Oldchurch Park were outraged at the thought of a Football
Stadium on their doorstep, but to counteract this, the
Club had presented the Council in April 1977 with a 2,000
signature petition supporting the Club's intention of
staying within the Borough. A Plan was submitted for a
modest 2,000 capacity Stadium at Oldfield Park, but
progress was frustrated with interminable revisions and
refusals from the Council.
The barest minimum had been achieved at Oldchurch
Park by the start of the new season, with little more
than some excavation work, and a flimsy perimeter fence.
The Club therefore now had no option but to make a
request to play their initial games away from home. The
Southern League approved this measure, but only until
October the 1st. But this date came and went, and still
nothing was happening at Oldchurch Park. On October the
28th, the latest Oldchurch Park proposals were turned
down, at which point the Club Chairman, Vic. Nichols
conceded that the latest occupation date of November the
5th was impossible. A few days earlier the team in a
severely depressed state were defeated in the game at
Margate, and no doubt out of sheer frustration a Director
resigned!
By now it had become apparent that all 'home' fixtures
would have to be played at a variety of other Club's
locations; Deri Park, the home of Rainham Town, Dartford,
Dagenham Barking, Chelmsford and most frequently at the

Aveley F.C. Ground. It was little wonder that this once well supported Club could now only attract poor crowds, with attendances varying between 200 and 460. There were 650 present for the 'home' tie with Hendon in the F.A.Trophy, but the Clubs had agreed to switch venues, and the 'home' was Claremont Road! Even so it said much for these keenest of fans, for some Clubs were having an even greater struggle to attract reasonable crowds; the Romford games at Trowbridge produced a figure of 154, and Andover could only provide an attendance of 199.

In November, the Oldchurch Park never ending saga continued with the Council's refusal for work to start on re-erecting the excellent Brooklands seated Stand due to ground bearing problems at the new site. Now at the end of their tether, the Directors drew up revised plans for a more modest covered enclosure, with the forlorn hope that the revised plans would be speedily passed by the local Authority. But suitable alternative Dressing rooms and Clubhouse ideas were not sanctioned, and even the rapidly dwindling resources were not improved with the hoped for sale of the Brooklands Stand to Dagenham F.C. which did not materialise.

By Christmas the Club were fifth in the League, then another body blow was dealt the Club, when Vic. Nichols died on Boxing Day, his passing no doubt accelerated by the ever increasing worries for the Club. Geoff Welton accepted the thankless task of Club Chairman.

In all the circumstances, the season was quite successful so far as League games were concerned, and if it had not been for an excessive number of draws - 15 in all - then more victories and the extra points would have led to a promotion position. By the turn of the year the Club had risen to third in the table, and in April they had improved this position by one place, but the final run-in of three draws and two defeats put paid to any hopes of finishing in glory. On the 8th of March, the 5-1 'home' victory over Tonbridge, saw Hanson score three times, the first Romford hat-trick for five years!

The final match ever played by the Club became something of a farce. Initially this home game was due to be played on May the 1st, it was then postponed until the 5th, and then finally the 11th. The problem being to try to find a suitable 'home' venue when other Clubs were frequently using their own Grounds for their last games. At last agreement was reached to play the fixture at

Dartford's Watling Street enclosure, but when this then became unavailable at the last minute, there was little option to play out what was to become a meaningless game, at the Stadium of their opponents, Folkestone and Shepway.

This last game was to be far from a noble exit. Romford could only raise a team of ten Players, and this included the Manager, and against the odds they took a shock lead after only two minutes. But by half-time the demoralised and depleted team trailed by 1-3. Although Gilbert reduced the deficit by scoring from the penalty spot in the second period, the final result was a 2-4 defeat.

With probably the lowest paid footballers in the League, the team achieved a very respectable fifth place in their Division, although there was nothing of merit in the Cup competitions. An early exit was made in the F.A.Cup with a defeat - in a replay - to Walthamstow, the F.A.Trophy run came to an end at Hendon (after beating Chelmsford City at the second attempt), and Waterlooville soon put paid to any hopes in the League Cup.

It was not until early July that some of the facts, and the deplorable state in which the Club now found itself, were made Public.

The sale of Brooklands in 1975, realised the enormous - at that time - figure of £600,000; a sum that would appear to have been ample for providing a non-League Club with a suitable new Stadium. But why should the Club wish to sell to Developers a Ground that was considered one of the best outside of the Football League? Inevitably the sale of valuable building land would provide the funds for the building of a new Stadium on a less expensive site, and, as is usually the case, allow the Club to wipe off it's inevitable debts, and perhaps leave some money in the 'kitty'. But for Romford things were vastly different, for their own debts amounted to a staggering £350,000! From the residue it was revealed that £210,000 was owing in Tax, leaving the paltry sum of £40,000 to build and equip a new Ground. It was revealed that in 1976, there was £200,000 left from the sale, but the 1976/77 season had seen losses of £91,000 incurred. These earlier losses together with a further large shortfall from the last season, all added upto the final enormous figure.

Naturally there were many accusations and bitterness felt towards the Directors, particularly from Jim Parrish, the former Club Chairman who had been associated with the Club for forty years, and who had been asked at the eleventh hour to advise the Club on it's next course of action. The only sensible move was to close the Club for a year, and then hope to make a fresh new start. But this type of action has rarely - if ever- been successfully accomplished.

What went wrong? The immediate thought would be that over the years dishonest dealings had been made to account for the enormous cash shortfall, but since the Club was a Limited Company - and responsible to it's Shareholders - it is doubtful that such figures could have been concealed. In addition no action was taken against any member of the Board, either publicly or by any individuals.

The root of the problem probably went back to the summer of 1961, when the Club - already with a large overdraft - found it necessary to try to increase their capital to £50,000 with a new share issue, and it is doubtful if this was completely successful. Four years later a large sum was spent on the fine new Grandstand, (valued at that time at £50,000) and earlier in 1962 when £15,000 had been used to provide the Club with their excellent floodlight system. For Romford F.C. it would have been quite easy to borrow the money, for being the owners of Brooklands, the site would have been sufficient to offer as collateral. At this time the Club were fairly successful on the field, and this was reflected by their reasonable crowds. This, together with their avowed intention of being elevated to the Football League - which could have become a reality - no doubt led to continuous expenditure for further progress. At the time, this would have, not unreasonably, seemed to be the best course of action. However, it was but a short time before the team slumped, coupled with a drastic nosedive in attendances - due to the football 'climate' and the Club's own inabilities. And so the Directors were left with a large Ground, excellent facilities and a large Bank loan! The interest on the loan quite possibly exceeded the much reduced income generated through the gate, and there was probably great difficulty in meeting these repayments, quite apart from reducing the capital sum. Indeed it is possible that further loans may have been necessary just to repay the outstanding interest payments - and quite possible so long as the Club still owned the valuable Brooklands site. The vicious circle had to end, and it did when the Club sold Brooklands.

The Directors, over the years, could justifiably have been accused of naivety and poor management, and later a degree of deception in not admitting to the hopeless state that the Club was in. Obviously, even in 1975, most of the proceeds of the Ground sale would not be available for a new Ground, and the Club looked towards the local Council for some help. Should a local Authority be expected to use ratepayers' money to bale out an independ- antly run Limited Company (i.e. the Club)? Probably not, but it would seem that the Council made little effort to help Romford F.C. even in a non-financial capacity. Havering Council did provide the Club with a suitable site for leasing, i.e. Oldchurch Park, but the lack of progress would seem to be a joint failing by both the Club - who obviously had insufficient funds (which they only admitted to when it was to all intents and purposes, too late) - and the Council who, probably aware of the Club's financial plight, were generally obstructive towards the development. Inevitably the plans for a new Ground met with opposition from local residents, but there was obviously a sizeable number of supporters who expressed their hopes of progress. The continuance of a Senior Football Club in a town can be regarded, surely, as an amenity to the community, and any successes be reflected towards that town.

The team never kicked a football again, but the name of the Club lived on for some years (and the Supporters Club even longer), but when Havering Council finally terminated the proposed useage of Oldchurch Park, in January 1981, that was, in effect, the final end of Romford F.C.

The demise of the likes of Bedford Town F.C. (in 1982) was caused due to their lack of ownership of a Ground, and hence little in the way of capital assets. But the grim lesson learnt by Romford F.C. was that even with sufficient collateral, unless it is used wisely, the same fate can still befall a Club.

Brooklands:

The 'modern' Romford Club were formed and started
playing at Brooklands in 1929, but the site had already
hosted a number of different sports, notably hockey,
cricket and tennis. Even at this time serious thought was
given to converting the area into houses, and was nearly
sold to a builder, but it was only the inter- vention of
the town's sportsmen that thwarted this plan. The Ground,
at this time, was little more than a field within
farmland, with a Farmhouse in the South-east corner. Part
of the area was leased to the Football Club from the
Romford Sports Ground Limited, with cricket and football
now being the principal users. At this time the areas for
the two sports lay side by side, and at right angles
(approximately North to South) to the eventual Football
Ground of later years. The facilities initially were very
limited, with just £50 being spent to create an enclosed
Ground and a small seated Stand on the North-east side;
despite the description of this "large and commodious
Grandstand"! Elsewhere spectators had just flat standing
areas, with one side encroaching onto the Cricket pitch
outfield.

As early as 1931 the desire to turn the pitch at right
angles and use the enclosure solely for football,
complete with new embankments, was first mooted. But it
was not until 1937, one year after the outright purchase
of Brooklands, that this progressive step was taken. The
overall planning of the dramatic changes was undertaken
by the Architect Archibald Leitch, the football Ground
specialist who had designed countless other Stadiums, and
it was not long before the final dream was completed.
Even if the fans had to wait for an excellent enclosure
of concrete terracing all round, plus both seated and
standing enclosures, at least the players were able to
benefit immediately from the new spaciousness, rather
than pitch barriers that had been no more than a few feet
from the touchlines.

In the summer of 1944 willing volunteers were called
upon to clear the Ground of obstructions, remove the
weeds, and to cut and roll the grass. After several years
of non-use, and some vandalism, substantial renovations
required electrical re-wiring and the refurbishment of
the Dressing Rooms. The one third pitch length seated
stand, was located on the South-east side, with double

this length of standing enclosure opposite, but as early as 1939 the ambitious Club drew up plans for a substantial increase in the seating capacity.

A new Stand to seat 1,500 at a cost of £7,000 had been envisaged, but the War delayed any moves in this direction. Even in the early post-war years the capacity of Brooklands was estimated at 20,000, and it was voiced (somewhat ambitiously) that this figure would be increased to 50,000 once the original Leitch design was completed. In fact it was not until 1965 that the new Stand became a reality, with a capacity of 2,000, and by now at a cost of approximately £30,000. Earlier, four large Pylon floodlights (an ambitious and expensive installation for a non-League Club) were erected at a cost of around £15,000. With an excellent pitch - in the summer of 1959 it had been ploughed up, re-levelled and re-seeded, the Club - as a non-League outfit - were now the proud owners of a Ground second to none. In fact Brooklands was better than a number of venues used by Football League Clubs, even if the 50,000 capacity was something of an overstatement; only about half this number were able to be comfortably accommodated.

It was a great tragedy that the Stadium was demolished in 1977 to make way for a housing estate, and now little remains, except for some of the original Ground enclosure walls. The entrance to the estate, through an opening between re-built pillars at the end of Brooklands Road, was also the main access to the Ground, and to the rear of the seated Stand.

Programmes:

Whereas pre-war programmes are hard to find, Romford F.C. were prolific issuers, especially during the 1960's, and unlike many defunct non-League Clubs, examples from this era are plentiful. During the 1965/66 season, the front covers proudly (albeit somewhat exageratedly), displayed an artist's impression of the fully developed Brooklands Stadium. The Club's progammes over the years were always one of the best in non-League circles. This standard remained right up until the final season, when a very respectable, properly printed 12 pager was issued, despite the Club's frequent changes of 'home' Ground.

Romford.

Despite the poor
quality, a sign-
ificant photograph.

The original
Romford F.C.
in 1886.

-111-

Romford.

ROMFORD EXPRESS

Week ending July 8, 1978

INCORPORATING THE ROMFORD TIMES

7ₚ

RED CARD FOR BORO

ROMFORD Football Club is to close down for the 1978-79 season.

The shock announcement to disband the team was made by Boro chairman Geoff Welton at a meeting of the club's board of directors.

But the decision was only taken after long talks with former club chairman Jim Parrish.

By EILEEN GREEN

This week Mr Parrish associated with the club for 40 years called for a full inquiry into the handling of the club's finances.

"The club received £600,000 by selling Brooklands. The shareholders will want to know — and I am a shareholder—exactly where this money has gone.

"It is up to the board to call the Annual General Meeting to show us the accounts.

"The directors called me in to advise them and get them out of trouble, and closing down the club for a season seemed to be the only solution.

"I am terribly disappointed. The directors

chose to do it their way and they got it wrong.

"If I had been in the driving seat I would have certainly done things differently."

But now they need new directors — young and enthusiastic people to breathe new life into the club.

Mr Parrish, former President of the Southern League and a present member of its management committee is one of the most influential men in non-league football.

But doubts are already being raised by supporters and players alike that the club — which just failed to clinch election to the

Penniless club to close next season

Football League in 1967 — will open again.

An official club statement said the decision had been taken "to secure the future of the football club."

The Directors have asked the Southern League to excuse them from participation in the 1978-79 season to also give the necessary amount of time to complete the facilities at Oldchurch Park.

"We believe that this action, although difficult will ensure the long term future of the Romford Football Club," said the chairman.

Work on the multi-thousand pound club stadium at Oldchurch Park was expected to be completed for the forthcoming season — but there is now no possibility of the new ground meeting Southern League standards.

The club moved out of its old home, Brooklands in Romford at the end of the 1976-77 season. The ground was sold for a staggering £600,000 to a housing development firm and properties are now being built on the soccer site.

Mr Welton, who took over the chairmanship of the club following the death of Mr Vic Nicholls late last year says that of the £600,000, almost nothing is left.

"£350,000 of the amount we received for Brooklands went to pay off club debts, and another £210,000 was eaten up in tax," said Mr Welton.

"This left us with just £40,000 to cover the cost of running the club last year and pay the bills.

"As we played all our games away from home we had no income coming in

from gate receipts. We hope to save £15-20,000 this season by not running the team.

Club manager Dave Bickles still has a year's contract to run and the club will honour this by holding weekly training sessions "to develop the skills of local youth and to give local players the opportunity to be included in the future plans of Boro."

The end for Romford F.C.

-112-

1966: Captain Brian Kelly in action. (With the covered enclosure opposite the Stand in the background).

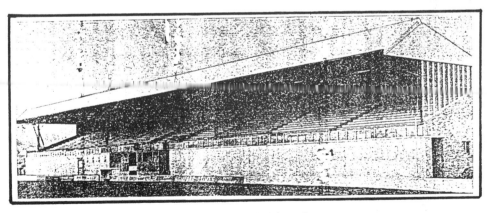

1965: The excellent new Seated Stand.

HAVERING RECORDER APRIL 1965

Romford.

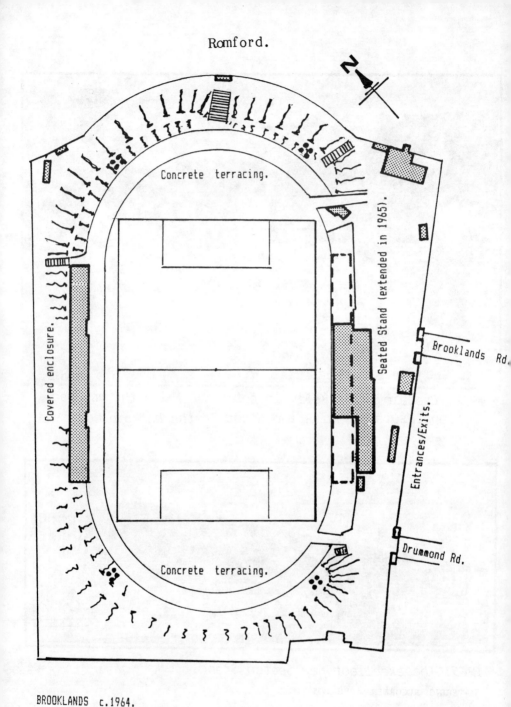

Concrete terracing.

Covered enclosure.

Seated Stand (extended in 1965).

Brooklands Rd.

Entrances/Exits.

Drummond Rd.

Concrete terracing.

BROOKLANDS c.1964.

Romford.

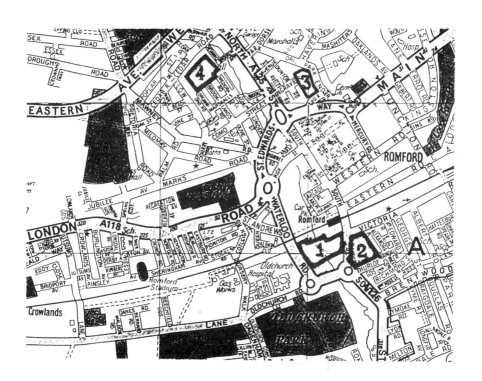

Ground Locations:

1. Victoria Road Ground.   2. Shoulder of Mutton Ground.

3. Church Road Ground.   4. Brooklands.

(Plus a Ground in or close to Oldchurch Park).

Rugby Town.

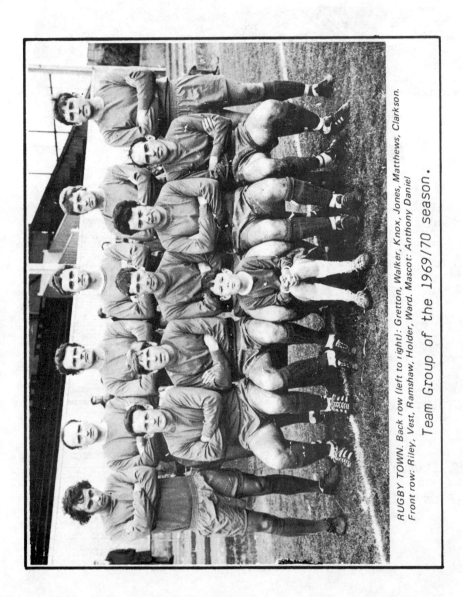

RUGBY TOWN. Back row (left to right): Gretton, Walker, Knox, Jones, Matthews, Clarkson.
Front row: Riley, Vest, Ramshaw, Holder, Ward. Mascot: Anthony Daniel

Team Group of the 1969/70 season.

Rugby Town.

Rugby Central: 1904 - 1914.
Rugby Town: 1919 - 1934.
Rugby Town Amateurs: 1946 - 1950.
Rugby Town: 1950 - 1973.

::

1904/05	-	Rugby & District League Div.2.
1905/06	- 1906/07.	Rugby & District League Div.1.
1907/08	- 1913/14.	Coventry & Nth.Warwicks Lge.Div.1
1914/15	- 1918/19.	Ceased Activities.
1919/20	- 1933/34.	Birmingham Combination.
1934/35	-	Birmingham Combination. *
1946/47	- 1947/48.	Central Amateur League.
1948/49	- 1949/50.	United Counties League.
1950/51	- 1953/54.	Birmingham Combination.
1954/55	-	Birmingham League. South Division.
1955/56	- 1957/58.	Birmingham League. Division 1.
1958/59	-	Southern League. North-west zone.
1959/60	- 1961/62.	Southern League. Division 1.
1962/63	- 1965/66.	Southern League. Premier Div.
1966/67	- 1967/68.	Southern League. Division 1.
1968/69	-	Southern League. Premier Div.
1969/70	- 1970/71.	Southern League. Division 1.
1971/72	- 1972/73.	Southern League. Div.1. North.

* Did not complete season.

::

Summary of Main Facts.

Grounds:
1904 - 1920: Lower Hillmorton Road (1), Rugby,
             Warwicks.
1920 - 1922: Brown's Farm, Hillmorton Road.
1922 - 1926: Lower Hillmorton Road (2).
1926 - 1927: Sidney Road.
1927 - 1934: Hillmorton Road.
1934.   : Tower Ground, Southfields Estate.

1946 - 1950: Thornfield Recreation Ground.
1950 - 1973: Oakfield, Bilton Road.

Rugby Town.

Colours: (Latter Club):
White Shirts, Black Shorts, followed by:
Black and White striped Shirts.
(Latterly) Tangerine Shirts, White Shorts.

Nickname: 'Town'.

Record Attendance:
4,013. 6th October 1962.
Versus Nuneaton Borough. F.A.Cup 4th qual. round.
Also: 7,500. 25th September 1946.
Versus Derby County (Friendly).
(Exhibition game at English Electric Co,
Willans Works, Newbold Rd., Rugby)

Major Honours:
Rugby & District League 1st Div.Champs: 1906/07.
                               2nd Div.Champs: 1905/06.
Coventry & North Warwicks. Lge. Champs: 1912/13.
Birmingham Combination Runners-up: 1921/22. 1925/26.

Central Amateur League Champs.: 1947/48.
Birmingham Combination Champs.: 1953/54.
Southern Lge.1st Div.(4th-Promoted): 1961/62. 1967/68.
Birmingham Senior Cup Winners: 1970/71.

Well known Players.

S.Crowther (Previously incl. Aston V. & Man. Utd.)
C.Thomson (Previously Nottingham Forest)
J.Walsh   (Previously Leicester City)
D.Hines   (previously Leicester City)

RUGBY TOWN finished fourth, only two places away from promotion, in the First Division North of the Southern League last season.

They were fourth in 1971-72. So it ought to have been all systems go for a drive towards the Premier Division next year.

It won't happen. The dream is shattered. The players are dispersed among neighbouring soccer clubs eager to snap up their talents. By July 19, Rugby Town will be dead and buried.

The only activity at Oakfield next season will be breeze stirring the weeds and rattling the cracked and creaking fences. The only visitor, the occasional creditor looking hopefully for a return on his outlay.

Rugby Town has died for a lack of support, lack of money, lack of interest. A hobby has become a nightmare this past year for the four man board of directors thankfully keeping things going from week to week and now sadly winding it all up.

The collapse of the club is a sad reflection on the town. More than that, it's a sad tribute to the efforts of the people who put so much time, effort, and cash, into it, and to the memory of the chairman who died a year before his club did.

ROCK BOTTOM

Each fortnight, when the committee met to discuss the latest financial crisis, Jack Wilkins dug into his own pocket so that the club could survive. Now he is gone—and Rugby Town has followed him.

"I don't know how he would have done it. But somehow he would have kept this club going. The amount of money and enthusiasm he poured into Rugby Town can never be properly expressed. With 20 men like him, we would be alive and kicking today."

The words are those of Peter Lutkin, one of the dwindling band of directors mournfully preparing to throw the first clod of earth on the coffin when the final shareholders meeting is held on July 18 and the creditors gather the following day.

Rugby Town Epitaph.

(Rugby Advertiser)

-118-

Rugby Town.

In a town that has been dominated by the 'other' form of football, it had finally taken nearly a Century before a Senior Club was able to firmly establish itself. The first 'Rugby Town', lasted 30 years (including the First World War period), and the second only 27 years. The latest of the 'Town' Clubs - V.S.Rugby - has exceeded both in longevity. Following notable F.A.Cup runs and reasonably secure membership of the Southern League Premier Division, it looks at last as if the town of Rugby has a permanent Football team!

The town gave it's name to the Rugby version of football, which originated at the famous Public School, and in the 1830's one of the first attempts at playing 'Football' with organised rules was made. Principally in the North of the Country, but also in the near vicinity of Rugby - notably in Birmingham and the Nottinghamshire area - the round ball version of the game gained popularity. The influences of the Public Schools on all forms of Football in the mid to late 18th century was most marked, and in the town of Rugby it was the oval ball version of the game that won the day.

Against this background it was always going to be a struggle to establish a Senior (Soccer) Football team, even though the population of the town by the turn of the Century was sufficient to support such a venture. Since the inception of the Football League in 1888, other Regional, County and 'Town' Leagues had quickly sprung up around the Country, and it was rare to find any town - or even village - without at least one football team worthy of support. In Rugby things were somewhat different! When it came to a Winter sport, the town was dominated by Rugby Football teams, and in the early years of the Twentieth Century, the 'Rugby and District Association Football League' could only boast of a handful of teams that were split into two divisions. Even then, some of the teams were not based in the town itself, with Daventry as a notable exception. In 1903, the only two town teams of any note were Rugby Rovers and the bizarre sounding 'Rugby Martians'; the name of the latter team would seem to have recognised the alien nature of the round ball game!

No records appear to exist with regard to the formation of the Rugby Central (later Rugby Town) Club, but they first put in an appearance at the start of the

Rugby Town.

1904/05 season, playing in the Rugby and District League
Division 2. The first competitive game was probably
played on the 10th of September 1904, and a more
insignificant start could scarcely have been made, when
the team played against the might of the Rugby Martians
Reserve Eleven! The match, played at the Martians home
base, ended in a 2-2 draw, with Armstrong scoring the
first goal for the Central team. With only eleven teams
in the Division, League matches were not played every
week, and the second match was not until October the 1st,
which was won, at home, by 3-2 over North Kilworth.

Four victories followed, and despite dropping just one
point, in that opening match, the Central could only
attain second place in the table by Christmas, after
playing six matches and recording a notable goal
difference of 24 - 7. But the new Club had made their
mark in the League, and by the end of the season their
record was sufficient for promotion to the First Division
of the League.

The Club were now to be in contention with the likes
of Daventry, Eydon, Volunteers, St.Matthews and, no less
than, the first team of the Martians outfit! But sweeping
all before them, the Championship of the League was the
Central's lot by the end of the season. The Club at this
time were playing at a Ground on Lower Hillmorton Road,
within the Eastlands Estate, at which gate money was not
allowed. But for competing in the local Hospital
Challenge Cup, permission was granted to use the Recreation Ground (many years later this venue was to become
the home Ground of the second 'Town' team), where a small
admission charge was permitted. An attendance of 1,200
(probably a record for a soccer match in the town, at
this time) assembled to watch the game versus the local
Martian team. Rugby Central triumphed over these
unworldly opponents, with a 2-1 scoreline.

The 1906/07 season kicked off with a home match versus
St.Andrews and in front of between one and two hundred
spectators. But either due to lack of interest or the
establishment of other Leagues in the locality, the Rugby
Competition (First Division) now contained only five
teams, and many Friendly games had to be arranged
throughout the season.

The Club's prowess led to acceptance to the more
senior, Coventry and North Warwickshire League, for the
1907/08 season. The Central remained within this League

until the outbreak of the First World War, and along the
way became Champions at the end of the 1912/13 season.
The Club disbanded during the War years, only to
re-emerge in 1919 in a more Senior capacity.

The reformation of the Club in 1919, was not only
under a new name, that of 'Rugby Town', but also as a
Professional Club. For the first time there would be a
Football Club, that it was hoped would truly represent
the town and bring the alternative form of football to
the area, at a high level. For this brave move, the
Directors of the Club, perhaps to their surprise, found
that (initially) there was a great deal of support from
the townspeople.

The Club were immediately accepted into the Birmingham
Combination, a competition that was first founded in 1892
under the title of the Birmingham Junior League, as
distinct from the Birmingham and District League that had
been formed three years earlier. Until 1908, the
'Combination' was hardly in competition with the
'League', for it's membership was composed of very much
Junior teams as opposed to the more professional
competition. But after that year, the name change from
'Junior', attracted more Senior - and Professional -
Clubs, such as Atherstone Town (in 1911), Bournville
Athletic, Halesowen and Hednesford Towns, Redditch United
and Stafford Rangers. For Rugby Town remembrance of the
local matches against the likes of Rugby Martians must
have seemed light years away!

But the Club, aided by good - paying - support were
far from overawed, and finished their first season in a
very creditable fourth place in the table of sixteen
teams. In this first promotime season since the War,
Cradley Heath St.Lukes - members since 1908 - were the
Champions with Stafford Rangers taking the runners-up
spot. For this one season, the Town Club had used the
same Ground as in the pre-war days - in Lower Hillmorton
Road - where gate money had now been allowed. But for
some undefined reason (probably for development of the
land), it was necessary for the Club to move a short
distance to a new Ground known as Brown's Farm.

The 1920/21 was to prove to be another good one as far
as results were concerned. The League now contained 18
teams, Dudley Bean and Oakengates Town being the
newcomers, and for much of the campaign, the Town looked
very likely Championship contenders.

Rugby Town.

The locals were willing to support a winning team, and attendances increased dramatically to, generally, between two and three thousand at each home game. But their hopes were dashed in the penultimate match, when a defeat to Redditch United, decreed that they would 'miss the boat'. Even so, their third place in the League was very creditable; they finished just three points behind the Champions Cannock Town.

Despite the good support, it was obvious that the Club was operating in an uneconomic fashion, since there was a loss of £200 on the season. The Town formed themselves into a Limited Company during the summer of 1921, and with the formation of an enthusiastic Supporters Club, they set out on the next season with renewed hope.

The 1921/22 season saw many changes within the Birmingham Combination, with a number of Clubs moving on to fresh fields, including the reigning Champions plus the runners-up, Walsall Talbot Stead. In their places, five new Clubs joined; Leamington Town, Newhall Swifts, Round Oak, West Birmingham (for just one season) and Wolseley Athletic. In a generally weakened competition, the Town did even better than a year earlier, and finished in the runners-up spot, although nothing could stop the runaway new Champions, Cradley Heath St.Lukes - their last season in the Combination. Even so the Town recorded only five defeats and seven draws in their thirty Combination matches.

But all was still not well on the money front. Despite the good support, the over expenditure on running a professional team was proving to be a financial drain. The Club's problems were not eased with the necessity of moving to another Ground, to make way for a housing development on the Brown's Farm Ground. A move was made back to Lower Hillmorton Road, but this time to a different field, and to where they would remain for four years. The financial situation meant that a number of players had to be released and replaced with Amateurs. This in turn affected the team's performances, the crowds dwindled, and by the season's end, despite the economy cuts, the Club was struggling. In fact at one point, around mid-season, serious doubts were expressed on whether they could continue. The impoverished Club finished a dismal 10th in the Combination out of fifteen teams.

In such a short period they had risen to a state of euphoria, only to be followed by a plunge down to a doubtful survival level.

For the 1923/24 season, there were once again changes in the composition of the Combination. Although only two Clubs moved on to new pastures, there was an influx of fresh blood, including Walsall (of the Football League) Reserves, such that the numbers were made up to 18 teams once again. But for the Town Club it was to be another year of struggle. Despite even more financial cuts on the playing front, the savings were once again balanced by ever decreasing attendances - which seldom rose above 500 (receipts of £10). Another poor playing season resulted in a final 14th in the table.

The Club however carried on with a spirit of determination, and reduced the admission charges, in the hope that this would lead to substantially increased attendances. But the gamble was not successful, and although the position in the Combination improved - to 9th of 18 teams - the Club were once again faced with a large loss by the season's end.

Although an improvement to 9th in the Combination - with a good goal difference of 73-36 - was the final position at the end of the next season, the financial situation was still bad, and another loss was made.

Another gamble was made before the start of the 1925/26 season, after two years of austerity, in which there had been little success and dwindling support. Despite the financial risks involved, further Players were signed on which of course resulted in a heavier wages bill. On the field this policy was a great success, for the Club's best ever season was enjoyed and it was not until the final game that the Championship issue was decided, for upto then the Town were in with a very real chance of the top spot. But it was not to be, and the runners-up position had to be accepted. 23 Combination games were won (far more than in any previous or subsequent seasons) and a record number of goals were scored - 97. Leamington Town became the new Champions, with Rugby Town just two points behind them.

Whilst the Directors could look back with satisfaction on these performances, the serious financial situation was not alleviated. The gates had barely improved, and there was a substantial loss on the season of over £300, although this was fortunately balanced out by the money

Rugby Town.

raised from weekly competitions and other fund-raising schemes. Less than two months into the 1926/27 season, the Club were informed that they would have to vacate their Ground. Such news, at short notice, presented great difficulties, and it was necessary for them to move further South to a field off of Sidney Road as the only option. The lack of facilities and distance from the town, coupled with the difficulty of access, depleted the attendances even further. This situation was not helped by indifferent results and a disappointing final table position of 11th. It came as no surprise at the season's end, when another heavy loss on the year was announced.

Although the Sidney Road site was far from ideal, the Club had no sooner settled there, than during the close season they were informed that once again they would have to move on. These constant changes did not help the morale - or the Bank balance - and this time the move was made back to the Lower Hillmorton Road; but this time further East than the earlier Ground. But this was still not an ideal situation due once again to the distance from the town centre. The Club had enough problems, and these were added to when the simple Stand that had been erected blew down during the Autumn, and was so badly damaged that it was beyond repair. The parlous state of the finances made it impossible for this enclosure to be replaced for several months. But eventually, during the summer of 1928, a more substantial replacement was built that could accommodate over 200 seated spectators.

Things were far from good on the field, for the 1927/28 season ended in 16th place (third from bottom), and with 131 goals conceded, this represented an average of almost four per match. One year later a climb was made to ninth in the table of seventeen, and for a period the team looked like serious contenders for the Championship. But most rewarding of all was the increase in attendances, the best for several years, that were no doubt influenced by the re-forming of the Supporters Club during the season.

The start of the 1929/30 season began with a great deal of optimism, and these hopes appeared to be justified when the team soon put themselves in with a very real chance of the Combination Championship. But, just like a year earlier, they fell away towards the end of the season, and after the Club's earlier hopes, it was

Rugby Town.

a great disappointment to finish in only 7th place at the
end. But the previous three years of extra expenditure,
principally on employing more Professionals, had taken
their toll. Although the team had been moderately
successful on the pitch, the overall picture was of more
financial gloom. Three years of losses could not be added
to, and once again the Directors decided that they would
have to rely more on promising local Amateur players.

The match results took a disastrous turn for the
worse, the gates yet again dwindled, and at one time
during the early months of 1931 it looked as if the Club
would not survive to the end of the campaign. But as
always, tenaciously they struggled through, although
finishing in the Combination table just one place off the
bottom. Everything had worked against the Club, for in
addition to their poor performances, they were hampered
by generally poor weather at home games and aided by a
trade depression, that all contributed to reduced
support.

By a substantial majority, the Club was re-elected
into the Birmingham Combination, but could hardly have
looked forward to the impending season with much hope. A
poor start led to the Club's Officials calling a Public
Meeting in November, in the hope that something could be
done to ensure continued survival. The Meeting, in Benns
Buildings, was surprisingly well attended, and the
radical decision was taken to go into voluntary liquid-
ation and refloat the Club on an entirely new basis.

The Club passed into the hands of a Committee composed
solely of townspeople, and hence true supporters. Several
ideas were put forward, amongst them the formation of a
Ladies Supporters Association. This brave, fresh start,
had immediate benefits for support increased, but not
enough to encourage a pull away from the depths of the
Combination table. At the season's end, the team finished
as wooden-spoonists with only eight victories and a goal
difference of 51-103.

Once again the Club were re-elected, and sweeping
changes were made in the team for the 1932/33 season. The
outcome was quite spectacular, and the early season
results saw the team at the head of the table on more
than one occasion. But as had happened in the past, this
new found form was not maintained, and a poor second half
of the campaign produced a slide down the table, with a
final finish of 11th (of 20 teams).

Rugby Town.

Although attendances had again risen slightly, it was
still a struggle to maintain a financial balance, and on
some occasions there was insufficient money to pay the
weekly wages!

The 1933/34 season - the last complete one - started
with renewed determination, and more frequent meetings of
the Committee were held in order to try to identify and
rectify problems before they became a crisis. In a
desperate attempt for success and increased support, a
near fully professional team was engaged again. But it
was all to no avail, and by February 1934, the Town were
in dire straits yet again. A 'No surrender' Scheme was
launched with the support of the local 'Rugby Advertiser'
Newspaper. But the monetary support was poor, as it was a
year earlier when a 'Guarantee Reserve Fund' produced
little financial benefit.

There was once again a disappointing showing in the
Combination games, and although the attendances averaged
a moderate 600 through the year, the last home game - on
April the 14th versus Bromsgrove Rovers - attracted only
425 to the Lower Hillmorton Ground. This fixture ended in
a two goal defeat - the previous home win having last
occured way back on the 20th of January! Even worse was
the last game of the season which finished as a five goal
defeat to the Birmingham 'A' team. The Combination had
consisted of 18 teams once again, and the Town ended up
in 14th place. The total expenditure on the year was £648
(£68 more than a year earlier). With total gate receipts
of only £358 (£50 down on the 1933/34 season - despite
the money from two well attended F.A.Cup ties) - which
represented another large loss on the season.

It was almost the last straw when yet another ground
move was necessary for the 1934/35 season. The new venue
had the benefit of it's location being nearer the town
centre, with the promise of Public Transport facilities,
but such was the financial plight, that the re-building
of any covered enclosure was out of the question at the
start of the season. The new Ground was known as the
Tower Ground, and was an eleven acre field adjacent to
Naseby Road, on the Southfield Estate. Despite the
absence of any spectator facilities, the Ground was
enclosed, for which admission charges of 7d. (3p) and 2d.
for boys was levied; for the Members enclosure the cost
was 7d. for Ladies and one shilling (5p) for men.

Rugby Town.

The new Ground was not ready at the start of the season, and all the early matches had to be played elsewhere. The season kicked off on August the 25th with an awful 0-7 defeat at Dudley Town. Next week the Club were due to play Atherstone Town at home in the F.A.Cup, and an alternative Ground in the town was found, at which the attendance was a healthy 940, but the result was far from good. After going in at half-time three goals down, the final result was a humiliating eight goal without reply hammering. Two more Combination losses followed (by 1-6 and 0-3), before the Club's long awaited home debut. With nothing in the kitty a rope to enclose the pitch had to be borrowed, and in pouring rain (and with no cover), a pathetic attendance of just 202 were present to witness another defeat, this time by 1-3 to Darlaston.

Despite the signing on of three new players, the season had started as the poorest ever, with five straight defeats. Worse was to come, on a different front, when the Club's A.G.M. was attended by only eight members!

Two more heavy defeats followed, by 0-6 at Redditch, and with the same scoreline at home to the Wolverhampton Third Eleven - the latter match producing a crowd of only 275. Two weeks later the West Bromwich team attracted only 8 more spectators to the Tower Ground, but on this occasion at least the defeat was a close one - by 3-4. Frank Blockley the former Norwich and Stockport County Player was signed on in time for the Birmingham Senior Cup-tie game at Cannock Town. The Rugby team had been drawn at home, but the inadequate Tower Ground facilities, meant that a reversal of the tie was necessary. It was all to no avail, as the team once again crashed, this time by 0-3.

The end of Rugby Town F.C. was very near, but at least in their final death throes the team's form improved. After losing at home to Bournville Athletic by only 2-3, the return match on the 17th of November, at the picturesque Recreation Ground, secured for the Town their first point in a 2-2 draw. Fourteen days later although another defeat was suffered (at home before only 365 fans), at the hands of Halesowen Town, the team at least played with spirit. But to all events the end came with a devastating eleven goal reverse at Walsall Reserves before an attendance of 1,837.

Rugby Town.

RUGBY TOWN F.C. DISBANDED

"UP AGAINST A BRICK WALL"

MR. F. QUARTLY EXPLAINS THE POSITION

Continuance Impossible Through Lack of Support

A UNANIMOUS DECISION

RUGBY Town Football Club, the leading Soccer organisation in the borough, is no more.

This was the outcome of a unanimous but reluctantly given decision at Monday night's public meeting convened to 'discuss the Town's position, that the club should be disbanded forthwith. After Mr. F. Quartly, chairman of the club for the past four seasons, had given a clear indication of the impossibility of continuing to run on its present lack of suggestions were a view to temp...

scheme might be evolved as time allowed, perhaps that would be the happiest way out.

Times had changed very much since the club entered the Birmingham Combination. The evil days did not commence straight away, and there used to be "gates" between 2,000 and 3,000.

That meeting must face whether it was going to the rest of the to do it. was

A CHEQUERED CAREER

UPS AND DOWNS OF THE TOWN

BY ASSOCIATE

MANY regrets will be felt in the sporting circles not only of Rugby but of other Midland towns at the untimely passing of a club which dates back to pre-war days under the title of Rugby Central.

At that time they figured in the Coventry and North Warwickshire League, of which they became champions in 1912-13, and a year or two before the outbreak of war they were admitted to the Northamptonshire League.

The entry of Rugby Town into the Birmingham Combination as soon as the cessation of hostilities enabled ordinary competitive football to be resumed co-incided with the start of the club's career as a sub-organisation. Its subsequent career has been a story of up chiefly down have mar all.

*The
end of
the original
Rugby Town F.C.
in December 1934.*

(Rugby Advertiser)

-128-

Rugby Town.

It was ironic that what became Rugby Town's last match should also be their best of the season. On the 15th of December, after losing by 1-2 at half-time to Evesham Town, the homesters fought back in the second period and equalised with Howe's second goal. But in front of only 280 faithfuls, the winner never came. The match receipts totalled a paltry £7-20p. The line-up for this match consisted of:
Hammond, Dyson, Burrows, E.J.Murphy, W.J.Hall, McLeish, Smith, Brayson, Howe, Grieve, MacGregor and Hinson.

On Monday the 17th of December 1934, a Public Meeting was held to discuss the future of Rugby Town F.C. The Chairman for the previous four years, Mr.F. Quartly assured those present that everything possible had been done to secure the future of the Club. But all financial schemes had produced little, the town as a whole were not interested in keeping alive a Senior Club; there was little option but to close down immediately. Approximately 50 Members attended the Meeting at the Victoria Inn, with two Members of the Committee missing. Mr.S.S.Reeve the Honorary Secretary for a number of years was seriously ill - and tribute was paid to him for his past efforts - and Mr.C.S. Bostridge who was also ill, and who sent his apologies for absence.
Gates had averaged less than 300, yet three times this number were necessary for any chance of survival, the Meeting was told. The Chairman stated that the Club had struggled throughout most of it's fifteen years, and although he had only been connected with the Club for the past four years, he was not prepared to carry the burden of worry any longer. Those present paid tribute to Mr.Quartly, and the rest of the Committee, all had come to the end of their tether and most of them intended to resign at the Meeting. After a long discussion, it was estimated that £200 was required to fulfil the Club's commitments for the rest of the season and the start of the next, but there were no suitable suggestions on where this money could come from. At the conclusion, it was reluctantly agreed that the Club should cease.

The Club's resignation from the Birmingham Combination was given the next day, and the Competition's Committee expressed their regrets and sympathy. Banbury Spencer F.C., the Football section of a Work's Sports Club

immediately took over the Town's fixtures -their Reserves
taking over the first team's games in the Oxfordshire
Senior League; Banbury Spencer claimed that they could
attract crowds of around 3,000 for their matches!

<<<<<<<<<<<<< : >>>>>>>>>>>>

There was a gap of ten years - which included the grim
years of the Second World War - before serious thoughts
were given towards the forming of another 'Town' team.
On the 8th of May 1946, a meeting was held at the
Victoria Inn, when two dozen football enthusiasts got
together to discuss the possibility of forming a Senior
football team in the town, again. Such an idea had been
informally mooted a few months earlier, but the main
stumbling block remained then, as before, the difficulty
of securing a suitable home Ground. The Council were
sympathetic towards the idea of a new Club, but were
unable to offer any tangible help.
There were a number of options, including the
Hillmorton Recreation Ground (the site of one of the
grounds of the former Town team), but in every case,
these new founders discovered that a 'gate', or even a
collection, would not be allowed at any of the venues; it
was expressed that in this respect the town was '50 years
behind the times'! But anxious to get a Club started, the
newly elected Committee decided to make use of the
Thornfield Recreation Ground (that was conveniently situated close to the town centre), and operate as a purely
Amateur Club, under the name of 'Rugby Town Amateurs
F.C.' The leading founders of the new Club included,
B.Clarke, F.Carvell, A.Haywood, H.Jones, B.Sykes and
J.Prime
With no football competition in the town at a Senior
level, the new Club were readily accepted into the
Central Amateur League. And so on the 25th of August
1946, the first appearance of the team was made at Rootes
(Coventry), where the newcomers lost 0-2. One week later
a second Friendly match was played at Southam, which was
also lost, this time by 2-6.
The big day arrived, on September the 7th, at
Thornfield Recreation Ground when Rugby Town Amateurs
played their first League match. The team consisted of:
Fincham, J.Scott, Gibbons, D.Holmes, Allen, Widdison,
Ginn, R.Scott, Harrison, Holman and Haywood.

Rugby Town.

It must have been most encouraging, but also very vexing, for the Club's Committee to find that a crowd of around 2,000 - unpaying spectators - were present. The match got off to a bad start when the team Captain, Gibbons, had to leave the field injured, after only 3 minutes of play. Outnumbered and outplayed, the homesters were three goals down at half-time. But the second half saw the new team storm back, to win the match in a manner that could not be equalled for spirit and determination, especially from a debut performance by a new Club. From a header, Holman had the honour of scoring the first goal, followed by two more shots on target, to bring the scores level at 3-3. Then to cap a memorable day, R.Scott scored the winner.

A few days later, the team played the R.A.F. in a Charity match at the Oakfield Ground in Bilton Road, a venue that was not available at that time on a regular basis, but a few years later was to become the team's regular Ground. Paid admission was allowed on this occasion, and an attendance of 1,200 was recorded. The second League game was played at The Butts, the home of Coventry Amateurs, where the full-back Gibbons (ex-Walsall and Shrewsbury) made his debut, and a two goal victory ensued. The third competitive game was at home, and before another crowd of approximately 2,000, when an exciting battle finished with the Town's 100% record intact, following a 4-1 victory over Smethwick Highfield. During the match three penalties were awarded, two of which were awarded to the homesters. The Club had entered for the F.A. Amateur Cup, and since it was obligatory to charge for admission, the Club managed to secure the English Electric Company's, Willan's Works Ground which was located off Newbold Road. An all ticket crowd of 2,200 saw the team triumph by 7-2 over Sheldon.

The enthusiasm for this new Town team surpassed anything that the Committee had dared hope for, and a plumb Friendly match was organised against Derby County (the F.A.Cup holders) on the 25th of September. A party of fifteen from the Football League Club spent the day in Rugby, and the hospitality included a round of golf, before the game in the evening. With a view to raising funds for the Club, this game was also played at the Willan's Works Ground, at which a staggering attendance of 7,500 were present; this figure was to remain as the Club's all time record attendance.

Rugby Town.

Early arrivals were greeted with 'amplified gramaphone
music', and although the match ended as a 2-8 defeat, the
venture had been an unqualified success.

The team's first League defeat came on the 5th of
October - a 2-3 reversal at Boldmere - and was followed
by an exit from the Amateur Cup, following a poor display
on a bad Walsall Wood pitch, by 1-3. But the team soon
bounced back, and won the next (League) game by 7-2 over
the Lye Town Club. Coventry Amateurs were next beaten,
before a home crowd of 1,900, in an A.F.A.Cup game, but
this in turn was followed with defeat in the Birmingham
Senior Cup, to Bournville, with a 3-6 scoreline - after
Rugby's 2-1 interval lead!

By the year end, the Club could look back with
satisfaction on their footballing debut. The Club's good
form continued to the end of the season, and although
they lost out on the honours, this was rectified one year
later when they became the League Champions. Boldmere
St.Michael's - the reigning Champions - were finally
pipped at the post in the final run-in, in the season
when this Midlands Club brought honour to the League with
their appearance in the F.A. Amateur Cup semi-finals.

The ambitious Rugby team saw the United Counties
League as the next stepping stone, into which they were
elected for the 1948/49 season; a wise move since the
Central Amateur League became defunct two years later.

The first match in this new competition got off to a
poor start with a 2-4 defeat at Rushden Town, but the
team, aided by the support of the newly formed Supporters
Club, soon got into their winning ways and were up
amongst the leaders by December. A lean month followed,
which ended with a 4-0 victory over Wellingborough, and a
handily placed 6th position in the League table at the
start of 1949. But they only flattered to deceive, and it
was to be another four weeks before the next League
victory, although during the interim a Birmingham City X1
were beaten 4-2 in a Friendly game. After a further poor
spell, Spalding United were overcome by the odd goal in
five, in early March. The team were normally still well
supported, but this game was played in attrocious weather
- a snowstorm for much of the time - and the sparse
facilities ensured that only a few hundred fans were
present.

The best win of the season was gained with a 9-0
demolition of Grantham, and with seven victories in the

final eight games, a creditable 8th in the League was realised. The last home match was won by 6-3 over Abbey United (the Club who later become Cambridge United), and on the 7th of May, March Town were beaten by the only goal of the game. Rugby Town Amateurs were the only entirely Amateur team in the League, but in 38 League games, 91 goals were scored, although 77 were conceded. The major Cup Competitions produced little with early exits in both the F.A.Amateur and Birmingham Senior.

The Club decided to remain in the United Counties League, but their desire and ability to progress was severely hampered by their home Ground, at which it was quite impossible to either develop or generate money. Particularly vexing was the situation where the team now had a rival Club in the town. Oakfield F.C. had managed to secure the Bilton Road Ground, and although only playing in the Leicestershire Senior League, they were able to attract paying customers (600 for an end of season friendly match versus the local Rugby and District League). Whilst Rugby Town Amateurs had the status, Oakfield had the most suitable Ground, a sensible amalgamation was soon to take place!

The two rival Rugby Clubs continued in their respective Leagues for the 1949/50 season. By now, the active Supporters Club was proving to be a financial benefit to the Parent Club, and before the season's start they donated £400 to the Football Club's funds. The season got underway against the Coventry City Third team, and before 1,700 Thornfield fans. An interesting early season Friendly was played when the Town hosted a match against their rivals from Oakfield. A 2-2 draw resulted before an excellent attendance of 1,900. Corby Town were the early pacesetters in the United Counties League, and their visit to Rugby, even on a wet afternoon, drew a crowd of 1,400 to Thornfield. As happened a year earlier, December produced little for the Town team, including the encounter on a windy and cold day, when there were no more than 500 present for the Northampton 'A' team match, which was lost by 2-4.

By the turn of the year, serious talks between the two leading teams in the town had resulted in the definite plan to amalgamate, and although this was still to be formalised, another Friendly encounter was played (with a view to choosing the best team members from the two Clubs), this time at Oakfield's enclosure.

Rugby Town.

On this occasion the United Counties eleven were humbled by a 1-5 defeat. This was a lean period for the Town Club, and although March Town were beaten by 4-2, in front of only 850 enthusiasts, the team could only attain a low mid-table position. In a Friendly match against Hillmorton Sports late in the season, some new Players were given a run-out, which finished as a 6-1 victory. But the League results were still indifferent, and there was only an attendance of 666 for Eynesbury Rovers visit to Thornfield.

Easter saw the Town enjoy a run of three victories, including the 3-2 success over Abbey United, in front of 1,500 Rugbyites. Meanwhile Oakfield produced a good, late run, when they played 14 games without defeat. The last League game for the Club, as Rugby Town Amateurs, was on the 29th of April, when Kettering Reserves were beaten in an exciting 6-4 thriller, followed by the last ever match under this name, a Friendly at home to Banbury Spencer (an irony since this was the team that filled in for the earlier Rugby Town on their demise) when an embarrassing 0-5 defeat resulted on the 9th of May before a crowd of 600. Oakfield won their last home game (2-0 over Barwell), before their final match, when they were beaten at Moira by 3-4.

On the 22nd of April the first match, as a combined team, produced a 2-2 draw with the Chelmsford City team. But of great significance was the attendance of over 2,000 at the Bilton Road Ground.

Rugby Town Amateurs finished 9th in the League, before the final amlagamation with the Oakfield team, when the respective Supporters Clubs also joined forces.

The obvious choice of home Ground was to be the Bilton Road enclosure, and a 1/- (5p) fund was immediately launched with the idea of providing a Stand. From the two former teams, professional terms were offered to several Players, and the Club had by now become 'Rugby Town F.C.', a Professional outfit.

The new Club, gained entry into the Birmingham Combination for their first season of 1950/51. This League was the one in which the earlier Town Club had seen out their days, and the coincidence stretched further when the first match was played, at home, once again versus Banbury Spencer. During the close season new rules for the combined Club were agreed, several new Players were signed on, and volunteers helped to prepare and level the area designated for the Stand. On the 19th of August, At Oakfield, Bilton Road (the new Ground), an excellent crowd of 2,400 was present to see the Oxfordshire team share two goals with Rugby.

In the next game things didn't go to plan, for a four goal reverse was suffered at Dudley! Hinckley then visited Rugby and fought out a 2-2 draw (after leading by two goals at one stage) before another crowd of over 2,000. The Club's first victory came with the visit of the West Bromwich 'A' team. After eight games an inauspicious start had been made for the team lay seventh from bottom in the table. But the enthusiasm was certainly there, for the Club were well represented in the 1,900 attendance at Stafford Rangers when they claimed their first (4-2) away win.

By early December things were not looking too bright, for they had now slipped to 3rd from bottom, but with four points from six over Christmas, it was hoped that a general move to the good was in store. But these hopes were not justified, and by the season's end 17th of 20 teams was the final table placing. The record read: 12 won, 8 drawn and 18 lost, with a goal difference of 57 - 87.

It was to be four years before the team fulfilled the hopes of it's supporters, for during the interim, little of note was accomplished either in the major Cups (the F.A. and Birmingham Senior) or the Birmingham Combination. But the team were well supported during this period and some of the Players were 'checked out' by Football League teams, which led to Geoff.Wright moving to Walsall in March 1952 for £250. This Player, who had previous spells with Bournemouth and Aston Villa, was to return to Rugby in 1955. But if the honours were not won, at least the Club was gradually consolidating itself into the Professional Football World, and at the end of the 1952/53 season they finished fourth in the Combination table (of 18 teams), with 16 victories - 8 draws and 10 defeats. Despite regular entries into the F.A.Cup the Club during this period, nor subsequently, was ever able to reach the first round proper.

The 1953/54 season was to prove to be the most successful in the Club's short history. After losing their first match, a consistant good run followed, which resulted in the team holding the third place in the Combination by the New Year.

Rugby Town.

On the 9th of January the Club played their first ever game under floodlights, when they won 3-2 at table-topping Bilston. Gradually the team continued to the top, and on March the 13th - supported by 200 fans - they were confirmed the Champions with the point obtained at Gresley Rovers. The last match of the season produced a single goal victory, at home to Atherstone, to complete a memorable season; just four defeats were suffered in the latter half.

Llewellyn and Smith were ever-presents in 46 first team games, with Awde's 31, leading the goal-scorers, the most since 1947, when Holman achieved 48. The Reserves also had a successful year for they finished fourth in the Leicestershire Senior League, before moving onto the - more geographically suitable - South Warwickshire League for the next campaign.

There were a number of developments made before the 1954/55 season. Bobby Davidson was appointed as the new Manager, William Browning became the new Club Chairman, and the Club were elected into the Birmingham Senior League. For many years the two Birmingham competitions ran together as virtual competitors - but always with the 'League' having the edge over the 'Combination' - until finally in 1954 when the Combination disbanded (after well over half a century) and most of the members Clubs were admitted to the enlarged Birmingham and District League. The recent successes led to an increase in season ticket sales, and improvement work at the Ground continued. Terracing behind the Bilton Road goal was completed, and half of the proposed narrow covered enclosure was made ready.

The team got off to a flying start, winning first at Brierley Hill by 2-0, and then beating Symington's at home, by the same scoreline. An excellent crowd of 2,584 were present for the latter match, a game in which the Town missed two penalties - a 'crime' that they were to be guilty of on several occasions during that season! But this start could not be maintained, and only a mid-table placing resulted by Christmas. With the influx of new Clubs, the League had been split into two sections with the Town in the Southern Division, and a good, late season run, culminated by them finishing in 5th of 20 teams.

Rugby Town.

The Club's praiseworthy showing in this generally recognised higher echelon earned them a place in the newly created First Division of the Birmingham League, where they were to meet more new teams. Included were neighbours Nuneaton Borough (reigning Northern Division Champions), Burton Albion, and the Reserve team of Shrewsbury Town. Without doubt the team were now playing in a higher standing Competition than ever before, and they did well to hold their own against such formidable opposition. By the end of the season, although only finishing below mid-table, it was hoped that this had been a time of consolidation. Such hopes were justified a year later when the Town finished in fifth place of twenty teams. Although nine points behind the Champions, Walsall Reserves, with 19 victories, 7 draws and 12 defeats, it had been a very satisfactory campaign, even if any real progress in Cup Competitions had once again eluded the Club.

The 1957/58 season caused no shocks, other than that of resignation (along with Burton Albion and Nuneaton Borough) at the end, and the joining of the Southern League! the Club's acceptance into this highest competition outside of the Football League itself, was all the more remarkable since the team could only finish third from bottom of the Birmingham League! This was without doubt a most ambitious move, since the Club would now not only be faced with long and expensive journeys, but would be competing with the likes of Hereford United, Kettering Town, Bath City and Merthyr Tydfil - each of whom were seasoned Southern League campaigners.

The League was re-organised for the 1958/59 season (the start of denegation for the Competition many would argue!), with the introduction of thirteen new outfits, into 'North-west' and 'South-east' zones. There were many who felt that the Club was overreaching itself, for gone were the days of regular four figure attendances for Rugby Town, and in common with most Clubs they were feeling the pinch. Well attended matches were now rare occurences. Even so, the season did produce for the Club their record attendance to that date! Near neighbours Nuneaton Borough were the visitors, and a massive 3,998 were present for this local derby game.

Misgivings were, to a degree, borne out, for although the quality of opposition had never been higher, the normal crowd figures did not rise appreciably.

Rugby Town.

Rugby Town

3p   Programme

1971/72 season Programme.
With view of seated Stand.

Rugby Town.

(Aerofilms Limited)

Aerial View of Oakfield – 1971.

Rugby Town.

The team maintained a lowly placing, and in what had been a bad season, it was some surprise for Tommy Crawley to head the Club's goalscorers with a very creditable 42, 30 of which were in League matches.

Finishing third from bottom did not require a re-election application, but it did destine the Club to the First Division (as opposed to the Premier) for the forthcoming 1959/60 campaign. Yet worse was to follow! The season was a disaster as the team finished bottom of the Division of twenty-two teams, although their 31 points were only five short of Hinckley Athletic, six places higher. This dour season had been one of falling gates - only 600 for Romford's visit - although this plight was shared with several other Clubs who also could not attract average gates of four figures. The season included a 1-7 thrashing at Folkestone in October.

The necessary re-election was successful, and the Town set out on the 1960/61 season with some apprehension. But any doubts were soon cast aside as the team maintained a reasonable placing in the table, and finished in 8th place. Upto Christmas, even promotion looked a distinct possibility, only for the team to fall away in the next few months. During November an exciting victory for the Town produced the unlikely score of 6-5, over Ahford Town. Significantly, of the promoted teams Cambridge United finished second, 10 points above Rugby. The Directors hoped that the Club had now risen above the grim performances of two years earlier, and the next campaign was to prove to be the case, it being one of the best ever.

The Town started off in a far from impressive manner, but some good results in early 1962, saw them rise to 5th in the League after an impressive home victory over Trowbridge. Their form was helped considerably by the goal-scoring of Daper, who's prowess included 9 successes in three games. As the season drew to a close, the Town were in with a very real chance of promotion, and a top of the table battle at Oakfield with Corby Town on the 23rd of April, drew a crowd of 3,100 - the biggest attendance since October 1953. The last League match produced a two goal win at Nuneaton, and was followed by the last game at home to Yiewsley. This game attracted a crowd of 1,800, and a fortunate one goal victory, was enough to assure the Club of fourth place (three points above Margate in 5th), and promotion the next season.

A rare, successful run, was made in one of the Cup
competitions when the Town reached the Final of the
Birmingham Senior. But before a crowd of 3,248 at
Coventry City's Ground they were to lose heavily to
Locheed Leamington with a 1-5 scoreline.
Much of the credit for this happy season was given to
Manager Eric Houghton, and a good understanding within a
largely settled team. The battles ahead were to prove to
be stern ones, amongst the cream of non-League football.
New Dressing rooms at Oakfield were completed in time
for the first Southern League Premier Division match in
August 1962, when Poole were the visitors. The attendance
numbered 1,836 (well above the previous year's average),
and a 1-1 draw was the result. In the next match however,
the team were way out of their depth when they were
defeated at Weymouth by four unopposed goals. After five
games things were far from good, with the team languishing near the bottom of the table following two
defeats, two draws and a single win - the latter by 3-1
at Bath. Although Hednesford were beaten in the F.A.Cup,
the League results continued to disappoint, including
defeat at Chelmsford before a tremendous crowd of 5,800.
All attention was diverted to the F.A.Cup when the 3rd
qualifying round draw was announced; a home game with
neighbours Nuneaton Borough. The game attracted a great
deal of interest in the town, and with over 20 bus-loads
of Borough Supporters making the short journey. The gates
were opened early, and a new record attendance was
confidently forecast for the game on the 6th of October.
The crowd numbered 4,013 on the day, beating by 15 the
earlier record of 1958, and by winning by the only goal
of the game, the Town entered the fourth, and final
qulaifying round, for the first time in their history.
The next game in the competition brought fellow-Leaguers
Wellington Town (the later named Telford United), to
Oakfield, where, before a disappointing attendance of
only 2,500, the homesters took the lead in the 20th
minute, only to eventually fall away. The final result
was a 1-1 draw, but in the replay, the Town were thrashed
by four goals; the prize for success would have been a
tie at Bristol City.
By Christmas, the team were third from bottom
(although having played less games than most), after
recording only three victories and four draws from the 14
games played. But the last two-thirds of the season

produced something of a recovery, and the team reasonably consolidated their place in this highest of Leagues (outside of the Football League itself), with 16th position in the final table.

By the skin of their teeth, the Town survived relegation at the end of the 1964/65 season, despite a 'goals against' tally of 98! With four teams destined for the First Division, Rugby Town finished fifth from bottom, just two points clear of the drop! But one year later it became clear that the team were out of their depth at this high level, and with a points tally of only 32, they finished just two places above tail-enders Margate. But of greater concern was the Club's financial position. Heavy losses, from high costs coupled with low crowds, brought the Club to the brink of extinction. In fact the Club actually resigned from the League at the season's end, although this was then hastily retracted, and the Club was reinstated!

One year later things continued to get worse, and a mediocre team ended up below halfway in the lower division of the Southern League. At this time the Club announced that they were £3,454 in the 'red'. Somehow the Club survived this poor period both on and off the pitch, and were now fortunately about to head for promotion.

By the New Year of 1968, the team were slightly off target from the fringe of the promotion positions (24 points from 21 games), but from then on a consistant run led to an upward move. Much credit was due to Player/Manager Billy Hails who during the previous Summer had started with virtually no Players! As promotion became a possibility the fans started supporting the team in increasing numbers, with 1,069 present for the single goal victory over Merthyr Tydfil, and 816 for the 4-1 thrashing of Trowbridge. But even so with gates now averaging 1,000 this was still insufficient for the current expenditure, and it was necessary to call a Public Meeting on the 23rd of April, when the Club's precarious financial position was announced.

The Club's deficit had now risen to £5,400, and it was reckoned that £3,000 would be needed to be raised by the end of the season to ensure their survival. These figures may seem to be fairly insignificant, but they were not the owners of the Oakfiled Ground, and therefore had no substantial assets.

Rugby Town.

An earlier offer of £15,000 for the Ground had been
turned down. £670 was owing in Tax, and the installments
on the Floodlights repayment plus the Ground rent were
both three months overdue! There were still 20,000 shares
at one shilling each available and those present, around
100, were encouraged to do all that they could to raise
some capital. The Club did survive that season, and a few
more besides, but from this time on they were living on a
knife edge.

But the Town were not the only Club to be having
financial problems. Lowly Barry Town attracted barely 200
for the Town's visit (a single goal win to the visitors),
and even the match versus fellow promotion aspirants
Crawley Town only drew 478 to the Sussex Club's Ground.

Champions-to-be, Brentwood recorded a crowd of 1,010,
near the season's end, and the 1-1 draw took the Town
team to third in the League. The three points taken over
the Easter matches meant that the team were still in with
a chance of promotion, but the question mark still hung
over the Club's continued existance. The last League
match was a real cliff-hanger, when Rugby travelled to
Dartford to contest the fourth - and promotion - place.
With a scoreless draw resulting, it was Rugby who went
up, on goal average only, in preference to the Kent team.

At the end of the season, under the leadership of new
Chairman Jack Wilkins, the Club were newly constituted
following the merger of the Supporters Club and the
fund-raising Tote Committee. The Club had avoided folding
up completely, but only for a few years!

The teams constituting the Premier Division of the
Southern League for the 1968/69 season make interesting
reading. Cambridge United, Wimbledon and Hereford United
were all present and awaiting their chance for Football
League status. While at the other end of the spectrum,
Hillingdon Borough (final runners-up that season),
Romford, Guildford City and Bedford Town - together with
Rugby Town - were all destined for oblivion in the not
too distant future!

The team started the season with a goalless drawn
match at Peterborough, followed by another friendly, a
1-6 thrashing at Kettering. This match was a foretaste of
things to come, although on this occasion the Players did
have the handicap of a goalkeeping injury. But their
promotion did attract better home attendances initially,

-143-

Rugby Town.

and there were 1,100 present for the first home game with Burton Albion, a Southern League Cup match. In League games a very creditable scoreless draw (attendance of 2,508) was achieved at Yeovil. After three games the Club lay third from bottom, and early games in which the scores finished level became a feature; Goalless at home to high-flying Wimbledon (attendance 1,298) followed, then 2-2 against Kings Lynn. By the season's end however, the team had recorded a total of only six draws!

Having gone unbeaten at home during the previous season, the sequence soon came to an end with the return game versus Yeovil, and defeats soon became the norm. An early exit was also made from the F.A.Cup when defeat came at home to Bedworth United, after sharing six goals in the first match. A two goal reverse at Oakfield one week later left the team floundering in third position from bottom. By Christmas the bottom spot was reached, after losing at home to Wellington in front of a, by now, much reduced attendance of 530. A brave fight was made towards the end of the campaign, but insufficient to avoid the drop once again. With only 25 points the team finished one off the bottom, while Bedford Town, one spot higher, finished with eight more points. Of the four demoted teams, three of these were Bedford Town, Rugby Town and Guildford City - a trio with limited futures.

Despite heavy expenditure cuts, Rugby Town came close to regaining their lost Premier Division status during the next two years, when they finished in 5th and 6th place respectively in the final League tables. But the 1971/72 season was to prove to be the Club's penultimate one.

Amongst the pre-season Friendly matches played, were two of particular interest. A Derby County X1 - a repeat of one of the first games played by the original (post-war) Club - were beaten 2-1, and fellow Rugby Club, Valley Sports - the team that were shortly to take over as the town's top representative - were easily overcome with a 5-1 scoreline. But the competitive matches did not get off to such a good start. Four of the five League Cup matches were lost, which soon put a halt to progress in that competition! In League matches things looked slightly better with two defeats and two victories in the first five games.

This form was improved upon as the season progressed, and at the end of the day a creditable 6th in the League

Rugby Town.

(the team missing out on promotion by goal average only) was achieved under Manager Jimmy Knox. But the end was in sight! The lease on the Ground was coming to an end, and no alternative venue had been found. With regular lowly support, there was little money (and perhaps insufficient enthusiasm) to surmount the final hurdle.

The 1972/73 season started in good fashion, and on beating Merthyr Tydfil in the opening game, the Oakfield crowd of 897 was most encouraging, both vocally and in numbers. Yet despite following this win up with a scoreless draw at Barry (an attendance of only 150), and a victory at Bedworth (before just 148), the next home game was seen by only 409 enthusiasts - a 1-2 defeat to Corby. And despite a second place in the League, after eleven games, the crowd of only 444 for the home encounter with Kings Lynn surely deserved more.

By the end of September, with regard to the future of the Club, things looked bleak indeed:

'TOWN GROUND PLAN IS REJECTED.'
This was the headline in the local newspaper. With the Club desperately short of money, they had hoped that the Local Council would be prepared to spend £35,000 on developing a Ground at Ashlawn Road - for both the Football Club and the local community's benefit. The one small ray of hope was the announcement that the lease on Oakfield had been extended until the following Spring, therefore giving the Club a few months to hope for a miracle!

The team's experience in the F.A.Cup lasted one game. The visit of Nuneaton, always a popular fixture, drew a crowd of 1,871 - the biggest attendance for many a long day - and defeat for the homesters by the only goal of the game. For once, a good run was made in one Cup competition, the four year old F.A. Challenge Trophy. Loughborough United - coincidentally another Club that were playing their last ever season - were easily beaten by 6-1 in the first game. This was followed with another trouncing, this time of March Town by six unopposed goals in front of 485 Oakfield fans. Next on the list were Boston United (by 3-1) and then the biggest shock of all. Aided by the vocal support of 100 travelling fans, the mighty Yeovil Town were humbled with a 3-2 scoreline in front of a 3,500 Somerset crowd.

Rugby Town.

Romford were the visitors to Rugby in the second round proper, where a 1-1 draw transpired. In the replay, the Town were to be beaten unluckily by the only goal of the game, which was scored by a Rugby player! The team meanwhile were maintaining a good position in the League, even though crowds only hovered around the 400 mark, until defeats in February led to a dent in their promotion hopes. After being defeated at both Cheltenham and Grantham (both Clubs were eventually promoted), there were only 358 faithfuls present for the next game, at home to Stourbridge, when a one goal defeat was suffered. The next month things began to look more favourable, yet after a good victory at Bromsgrove, the Town then lost by 1-5 at Stevenage Athletic. As the chances of promotion looked less likely, the gates inevitably fell even further. For Banbury United's visit (a 1-0 win), there were only 340 present, and in early April, Locheed Leamington's appearance (two goals shared) attracted only 309.

There then came the announcement that was to virtually sign the death warrant for the Club. On April the 16th, the Borough Arts, Libraries and Properties Committee irreversibly announced that they had not recommended the Grant that was necessary to keep the Club alive. There was also to be no possibility of an extension of the lease at Oakfield, Despite the Club expressing their intention of retaining all of the Players, it now looked as if the end of the road had been reached.

On Monday the 23rd of April, Kidderminster Harriers became the last visitors to Rugby Town in the League. The chances of promotion for either Club had by now disappeared, and the crowd numbered only a paltry 355. At least it was a fine last effort by the Town team for they comfortably beat their opponents by 2-0.

The Rugby team consisted of: D.Jones, Vanham, Brady, Thomas, Griffiths, Cassidy, Foster, Stewart, Armstrong, Goodfellow and Lee (Lines was the substitute).

The next day the team travelled to Wales, and caused a minor shock when they ended Merthyr Tydfil's long undefeated home record, with their 3-1 win. Foster was the last goalscorer for Rugby Town with his 63rd minute effort. The Club were to play just one more game before the final curtain came down. In a Benefit match for Bob Ward, the team's trainer for 15 years, 357 devoted fans saw a 'Past' team beat the 'Present' eleven by 5-4.

"TOWN F.C. TO WIND UP - AND THAT'S OFFICIAL."

This was the grim announcement that was made on the 1st of June. "The Club died an uncaring death at the Weekend", was the curt statement given by a Club spokesman and Director, Peter Lukin. The Club had no money, and now no Ground, but as a Limited Company the final decision to fold had to be verified by the Shareholders, this course of action was inevitable. The initial share issue of 20,000 at 5 shillings (25p) each, had never been fully taken up, and now, the Club with virtually no assets, made them worthless.

What went wrong? Blame could hardly be directed at the Co-op. Society (the owners of Oakfield), for they had generously extended the lease of the Ground, even though the Club owed money to them. Inevitably the indifference shown, by and large, from the locals in a basically non-Football (Soccer) orientated town did not help the cause. However, there were other Clubs (and still are) in a similar standing to Rugby Town, who manage to pull through each season, albeit they have somewhere to play! What of the Management? There is little doubt that the running of a non-League Football Club is a labour of love, with the only reward being some degree of satisfaction. There was never any suggestion of fraud or attempt at personal gain (which has not always been the case when a Football Club has folded!). But despite the debts that gradually mounted over the years, and the inevitability of the loss of Oakfield one day, a degree of blame had to be laid at the Directors feet for complacency, and wishful thinking.

Finally what of the attitude of the Local Council? There is always a conflict of interests, and the comment with regard to the misuse of Ratepayers money by funding a professional Club is, in some eyes, valid. But most poignant was the statement made by the Mayor at the Second Annual Meeting of the Club in 1948:

"The Corporation is really interested in your Club, and has nothing but praise for you for remaining Amateur. The Bilton Road Ground (Oakfield) will eventually become Council owned, and we will look sympathetically on any move for which the 'Town' asks for assistance." (!)

THE GROUNDS:

(1) Rugby Town (1904 - 1934).
In view of the many years long since past, and the
frequency of the original Club's moves, it has not always
been possible to identify the exact locations. In any
event in most, if not all cases, the 'Grounds' were
probably little more than marginally enclosed fields,
with generally a small seated Grandstand. The rapid
growth of Rugby during this period was probably the
principal contributor towards the frequent moves of the
Club, where a previous venue was generally soon developed
into housing.

Lower Hillmorton Road (1):
This was stated as being on the 'Eastlands Estate', and
was most probably the site now occupied by Eastlands and
Lawrence Roads, although the address given suggests that
the site may have been two or three hundred metres South
of here. The Football pitch probably ran East to West
within the large field that fronted Clifton Road,
opposite Winfield Street. (Not to be confused with the
adjacent Whinfield Park Recreation Ground that still
exists today). It is most likely that on the re-formation
of the Club in 1919, this same venue was used, for one
season.

Brown's Farm:
This was almost certainly a field that is now bisected by
Percival Road and is now the rear gardens to the houses
in Hillmorton, Percival, Bowen and Warren Roads (opposite
the large Recreation Ground to the North of Hillmorton
Road). Brown's Farm was located just to the South of this
field, and was demolished when Percival Road was built in
c.1924.

Lower Hillmorton Road (2):
After the brief stay at Brown's Farm, the move to the
second Ground in Lower Hillmorton Road lasted for four
years. This was a 6.9 acre, irregular shaped, field with
the pitch located near to the road. The Ground had a
small, narrow, Stand (about 20 metres long), and an
adjacent Members enclosure on the North-west side. Later
Developments resulted in the current Eastlands Road which

now runs through what was once the Football pitch. During the Club's tenure they suffered the misfortune of the Stand blowing down on one occasion!

Sidney Road:
This next move was forced upon the Club at short notice, was no more than a temporary one, and for less than one season. The exact site was probably the large field that still exists (South of Sidney Road, and now a school playing field). It is unlikely that during this brief stay there were any spectator facilities.

Hillmorton Road:
This Ground was probably within the current recreation ground, opposite the former Brown's Farm Ground. A small Stand was erected at the Ground, but it soon suffered the same misfortune as it's earlier predecessor. But on this occasion finances were so limited that it was not before the summer of 1928 that another, 200 seater (and more substantial) replacement could be built. The Club were to enjoy (or endure) the longest time at this venue - seven years - before yet another move was forced upon them. If the location is correct, then it is not obvious why this last move was necessary since the ground still remains today.

The Tower Ground:
Whilst this move was beneficial in view of it's closer location to the town, the impoverished Club were unable to provide any spectator facilities during their few months in occupation (although some cover may have been erected during the last few weeks of the Club's assistance). The Ground was located just to the North of Naseby Road, with the current Tower Road running through the former football pitch.

These locations should not be confused with a number of other denoted - 'Football Grounds' - since these were either large communal types or used for the Rugby football game.

(2) Rugby Town (1946 - 1973)

Thornfield Recreation Ground:
Although ideally placed, close to the town centre, its
limitations prevented any real progress by the Club. It
was ironic that during this period of occupation, when
attendances were often between two and three thousand,
the Club were unable to charge admission, although if
they had, perhaps those crowds would have been smaller!
With a complete lack of facilities, the Club moved to
Bilton Road in 1950, when they combined with the Oakfield
Football Club. Thornfield was located South of the
recreation ground which still fronts Hillmorton Road
(opposite Whitehall Road), and is now partially covered
by the Leisure Centre.

Oakfield, Bilton Road:
The Oakfield Club occupied this open Sports Ground
(whilst playing in the Leicestershire Senior League). But
the Club did not have the resources to develop the
Ground, and the very sensible amalgamation of the two
Clubs in 1950 made this possible. Oakfield, named after
the large house of the same name that once lay to the
East of the Ground, was built into an enclosed Ground
within a six acre Sports area. The Football Ground was
contained at the Western end, with the pitch running
North to South. During the close season in 1950,
volunteers from the newly amalgamated clubs started
preparing the groundwork for the eventual, near full
pitch length, Stand. This Stand consisted of a seated
area with concrete terracing in front.

Four years later a narrow covered enclosure
(non-terraced) was added behind the North end goal.
Initially half of the full length was built (in three
sections, with each section providing cover for
approximately sixty spectators). Also during 1954, the
open concrete terracing behind the opposite goal (the
Bilton Road end) was completed. The side opposite the
seated Stand remained as a flat uncovered standing area.
The floodlights that were to come later, consisted of
four slender towers each side of the pitch. The main
entrance to the ground was off Bilton Road and the Club
Offices were positioned behind the Stand, as were the
dressing rooms, which were rebuilt in 1962. The Ground,
confined to one side of Oakfield, formed a compact

enclosure, and with fairly narrow standing areas on three
sides, it is doubtful if it could have comfortably
exceeded the record attendance of 4,000 plus that was
achieved in 1963.

It is difficult to see why the owners of Oakfield were
not prepared to extend the lease - apart from the
outstanding non-payment of rent at the time (!) - since
after the Football Club vacated the venue, all structures
were demolished and a large single sports area was
recreated. This is still used for football, but now with
two pitches running East to West - a good facility for
Junior competition, but it would seem comparitively
unproductive in terms of revenue! One feature remains of
the former Rugby Town F.C. - the concrete terracing that
formed the paddock area to the Stand.

It is ironic that the current Ground of V.S.Rugby (who
have no connection with the former Town Club) - off
Butlin Road - is located next to a Cemetery, whilst
adjacent to Oakfield there is a large Funeral Directors
premises!

PROGRAMMES:
Since these were regularly issued by the later 'Town'
team, they are relatively easy to obtain. The earlier
Club no doubt issued during their post First World War
days, but any such copies remaining can be considered
very rare.

400 SUPPORT GROUND PROJECT

MORE than 400 supporters of Rugby Town Football Club are
urging that the Borough Council should carry out the Ashlawn
Road ground development project, now estimated to cost about
£50,000.

A club spokesman said last night that this was the number
of people who had so far completed petition-type forms, circu-
lated by the club, which would now be handed to the Borough
Council tonight.

The council, at tonight's meeting will be asked to approve a
Finance and General Purposes Committee recommendation,
urging that the scheme should not be carried out by the corporation. There will also be strong pressure from the Labour
group for the council to find alternative accommodation for the
club, who have to leave Oakfield, their present headquarters, at
the end of the season.

October 1972... A desperate attempt to keep the Club alive.

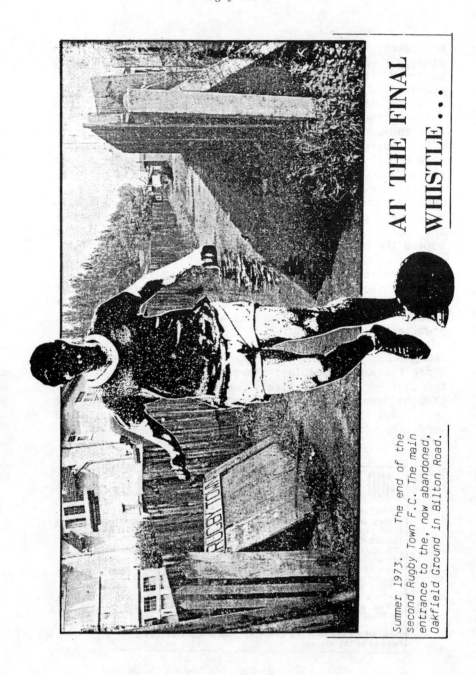

AT THE FINAL
WHISTLE ...

Summer 1973. The end of the
second Rugby Town F.C. The main
entrance to the, now abandoned,
Oakfield Ground in Bilton Road.

Rugby Town.

1984... All that remains of the Oakfield Ground is the Concrete Terrace to the Seated Stand. (Photo: Dave Twydell)

Rugby Town.

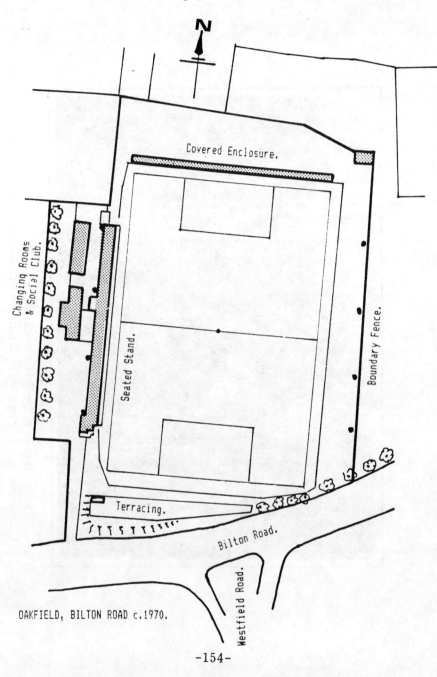

OAKFIELD, BILTON ROAD c.1970.

Rugby Town.

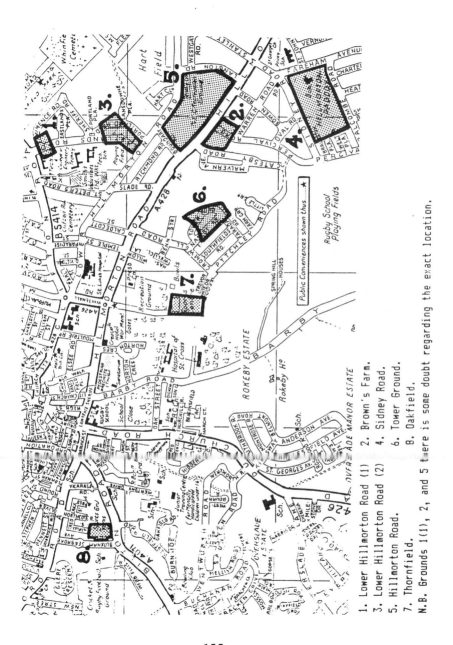

Rugby School Playing Fields

Public Conveniences shown thus ⭐

1. Lower Hillmorton Road (1)
2. Brown's Farm.
3. Lower Hillmorton Road (2)
4. Sidney Road.
5. Hillmorton Road.
6. Tower Ground.
7. Thornfield.
8. Oakfield.

N.B. Grounds 1(1), 2, and 5 there is some doubt regarding the exact location.

-155-

Slough Centre

A rare Team group – the 1954/55 season.

(Rear, L.to R.): Ashworth (Trainer), Platt, Alderman, Allsop, Day, Eyres, Evans (Coach).
(Front, L.to R.): Morley, Bradley, Rafferty, Stickland, Williams, Gillham.

Slough Centre.

(1937 - 1956)

Founded as 'The Centre F.C.(Slough)' in 1937.
Changed name to 'Slough Centre' in October 1942.
Amalgamated with Slough F.C. to become 'Slough United'
in June 1943.
Club split back into two Clubs as pre-1943, in June
1947. ('Slough F.C.' became 'Slough Town' in November
1947).
'Slough Centre' ceased as a Senior Club in April 1956,
although a Club of the same name continued in Minor
Football for several seasons.

::

League Record:

As The Centre/Slough Centre:

1937/38. - Windsor, Slough & District League Div.3.	-7th of 13
1938/39. - -Ditto-	-4th of 13
1939/40. - Windsor,Slough & Dist. Emergency League-North.	-7th of 11
1940/41. - -Ditto- -Section B.	-2nd of 9
1941/42. - -Ditto- -Division 1.	-8th of 9
1942/43. - Great Western Combination	-7th of 10

As Slough United:

1943/44. - Herts. & West Middx. League.	-2nd of 14
1944/45. - -ditto-	-3rd of 14
1945/46. - Corinthian League. (Founder-Members)	-2nd of 9
1946/47. - -ditto-	-2nd of 13

As Slough Centre.

1947/48. - Spartan League Div.1. (Western Section)	-3rd of 13
1948/49. - Spartan League Div.1.	-1st of 14
1949/50. - Spartan League Premier Division.	-7th of 14
1950/51. - -ditto-	-9th of 14
1951/52. - Delphian League. (Founder Members)	-8th of 14
1952/53. - -ditto-	-4th of 16
1953/54. - -ditto-	-5th of 15
1954/55. - -ditto-	-4th of 15
1955/56. - -ditto-	-18th of 20

Slough Centre.

Summary of Facts:

Ground Address:
The Centre Stadium, Belfast Avenue, Slough, Bucks.
(N.B. now Berkshire.)

Colours: White Shirts, Black Shorts.

Nickname: The Centre.

Club President: Sir A. Noel Mobbs O.B.E.

First Game:
27th August 1937: Dedworth 8. Slough Centre 0.
First Game as Senior Club:
4th September 1943: Slough United 7. St.Albans City 0.
(Attendance 1,500)

Last League Game:
7th April 1956: Woodford Town 6. Slough Centre 5.

Last Game (Friendly):
28th April 1956: Slough Centre 3. Pegasus 4.
(Attendance 200)

Record Attendances: (Each approximately 6,000)
As Slough United: April 1946 v. Grays Athletic.
(League match; 0-0)
As Slough Centre: April 30th 1948 v. Q.P.R.
(Friendly; 1-4)
Representative Game: May 1944.
Berks.& Bucks. F.A.   v.   F.A.X1.

Club Honours.
As Slough United:
Reached F.A. Cup 1st Round Proper — 1945/46.
Berks.& Bucks. Red Cross Cup — Winners: 1944.
Finalists: 1945.
Berks. & Bucks Benevolent Cup.
Joint Winners — 1945/46.

As Slough Centre:
Spartan League Division 1 (West) Champions — 1948/49.
(First Slough team to win a Senior League title)
Berks.& Bucks. Senior cup — Winners: 1952. 1953.
Finalists: 1954.
Berks.& Bucks. Benevolent Cup Finalists — 1954.

Slough Centre.

Few Clubs have had such a varied existance in only 19 footballing seasons. A name change, followed by an amalgamation, followed by a split back into it's earlier form... seven different Leagues (founder-members of two)... a Championship title, the first time in Senior Football for the town... a Ground which with modifications may well have become the home for a Football League Club... !

For nearly forty years the town of Slough had been host to a senior amateur football team, but Slough F.C. had led a fairly undistinguished - and not very well supported - life in the Spartan League during which the runners-up position on four occasions was the only real measure of success accorded to the team.

By the late 1930's, Slough, in Buckinghamshire (later 'relocated' to Berkshire) was rapidly increasing in size due to Industrial expansion; it was a virtual suburb of London. This rapid increase in population not unnaturally led to greater recreational facilities and the birth of the Slough Community Centre, said at one time to be the largest of it's type in Britain. One of the activities at the Centre was the formation of a Football Team in the Spring of 1937, which gained immediate election to the Windsor, Slough and District Junior League - Division 3, in June of that year.

The new Social Centre in Farnham Road made a public announcement on the 23rd July stating:

"The new Football Club, the 'Centre F.C.', does not wish to rob other Clubs of their Players, but can offer excellent accommodation at the Headquarters in Edinburgh Avenue."

A somewhat surreptitious way of attracting players !

One year later on the 17th of June plans were announced that, with a grant of £15,000 plus a donation of £2,000 from Slough Estates Limited, these 'excellent facilities' were going to be further enhanced; these sums of money, at this time, must have represented an unsurpassed boost to what was still a Junior Football Club. Edinburgh Avenue is today within a large Industrial Complex and no evidence of this original home Ground remains.

Slough Centre.

An inauspicious start was made by the team when on Saturday the 27th August 1937 The Centre F.C. played it's first match at Dedworth, and lost by eight unopposed goals! The Berks. and Bucks. Junior Cup was entered, but the preliminary round match was lost to Horlicks on the 18th of September by 1-5. High scoring matches were the norm, and the Club's poor start continued with a second away defeat in the League by twelve clear goals. The third League match, produced the team's first victory, of 10-5 over Slough Villa - a match that produced a good spirit of Sportsmanship from both teams.

By the end of November the Centre had attained a League placing of around mid-table, although more games had been played than most other teams, and this moderate form continued to produce a final 7th position in a League of 13 teams. The game at Horton in February was won, but the home team appealed against the result, and the match was ordered to be replayed - which subsequently became the last game of the season. This also resulted in a win by the 'away' team, on this occasion by four goals to one. Due to irregularities the Club had two points deducted from it's final record.

With over 2,000 players as members of Clubs in the five divisions, the League, not unreasonably, considered itself to be one of the most successful Junior organisations in the Southern Counties.

A big improvement was made the following season, for in competition with such Clubs as Gludex Sports, Windsor Argyle and Old Paludians Reserves a commendable 4th placing in the League with 14 wins, 6 draws and only 4 defeats was achieved.

The 1939/40 season in common with most other Leagues did not even get underway due to the intervention of the Second World War, and on the 8th of September the League announced the suspension of it's activities. Arrangements were quickly made for a new competition and just six weeks later on October the 21st the Slough, Windsor and District Emergency League came into being with The Centre entering the North section. The Club's opponents now included teams from higher Divisions of their previous League, such as Windsor Works, and High Duty Alloys. However, despite the higher standard, the team gave a good account of themselves and finished the season in seventh position in a table of eleven teams. The match in April versus Mc.Michaels was abandoned in the 80th minute

with the score at five each. The Centre's Captain
resented a decision by the Referee, and this resulted in
the Captain ordering his complete team off the pitch, and
his action was to have serious repercussions a few months
later.

On May the 11th, Miller Hydro were beaten 8-1 but the
result was declared invalid as the football pitch had not
been marked out correctly, however due to end of season
pressures to complete fixtures and an appeal by both The
Centre and (surprisingly), Miller's, the League allowed
the result to stand.

The Centre's Honorary Secretary, Mr. G.A.Clements, was
suspended by the League from Football and Football
Management - sine die - for failing to give any reason
why the team had left the field during the Mc.Michaels
match and for ignoring communications sent by the
League's Management Committee; the censorship went
further with suspension for the whole team until a 2/6d
(12.5p) fine per Player had been paid. These problems
were eventually settled and Mr. Burkhard took over the
reins as Sec- retary. A more professional approach was
taken with the appointment of the ex-Bolton and Watford
player, Yates, as Sports adviser to the Centre, which
appeared to produce the desired effect, with the Club
topping the table (now denoted 'Section B') by Christmas,
following an unbeaten eight match sequence, and a worthy
runners-up place as an end result.

The 1941/42 season was played for with another
divisional title change, this time with the Club playing
in Division 1, but it was an uphill battle and only
eighth position in the nine Club League table was
attained. In an unremarkable season the most embarrassing
result was in the second round of the League Cup. With
The Centre leading by a single goal and only three
minutes to the final whistle, Windsor Works equalised and
took the match into extra time. The final result was a
1-6 thrashing of the Slough team!

The 1942/43 season saw a large step up into Senior
Football when acceptance into the Great Western
Combination was achieved. The opposition consisting of
top peacetime Amateur Clubs - Wycombe Wanderers,
Maidenhead United, Uxbridge, Windsor & Eton, Marlow and
Oxford City plus former opponents Grenadier Guards,
Windsor Works, and Heavy Duty Alloys. The League had
included Reading 'A' and Chesham a year earlier but with

Slough Centre.

the resignation of these Clubs, Slough Centre and Windsor Works (Slough) - the latter formed in 1917 - were elected in their place.

The Works team put paid to the Centre's aspirations in the Berks and Bucks Senior Cup with a 2-5 defeat.

By the end of the year preparations were well under way for a move to a new Ground, and the venue was switched for the home match, with Heavy Duty Alloys plus another fixture, to the Windsor Works Ground. Successes were rare and after nine games the Club were only one rung off the bottom of the League. Such was the luck of the Club that with eight minutes remaining, the team were winning 3-2 in the game at Wycombe but finally succumbed 3-4. Nonetheless it had been a big upward step in status and with Billy Yates providing the main force behind the team, confidence was still high.

An inaugural friendly game was arranged with a Dutch Naval X1 at the new Ground in Belfast Avenue and the importance of the event was recognised with the attendance of Mr. (later 'Sir') S.R. Rous - Hon. Sec. of The F.A. It was a disappoinment that only a small crowd were present to see the Centre lead by four goals at half time and a final 9-2 victory in a very one-sided match. The first League encounter at the new Stadium produced a well merited seven goal victory over Maidenhead.

'Amber and Blue' writing in the Slough,Eton and Windsor Observer stated that:

" The immense possibilities of this Ground and the amenities of the Stadium are great...... when better times return, the Centre Club with such excellent facilities will make a big splash in Football Circles."

After a drawn game the Club lost by five unopposed goals at Oxford City in the Great Western Combination Subsidiary Cup, a match in which only ten players for the Centre were present, but where an eleventh was found from amongst the spectators! The final outcome in the League was a 7th in ten placing, with the Grenadier Guards as Champions.

A record attendance at the new Stadium was achieved when a F.A.X1 lost to Reading (1-3). Over 2,000 spectators paid £250, which went to Charity.

Meanwhile the 'other' Slough, i.e. Slough F.C., had been having a difficult time. This Club had used the

Slough Centre.

Dolphin Stadium for home Spartan League games, a venue it
shared with Greyhound Racing. At the start of hostilities
the Club continued playing, in the Herts. & Middx.
League, but were unable to use The Dolphin which had been
taken over for the War effort. The early days of the War
saw the Club using Slough Cricket Club in Chalvey Road
for home matches, but this was not satisfactory in the
long term. Not least was the difficulty of getting paying
customers into an unenclosed Ground. Maidenhead United's
ground was then shared, but this too was not the solution
as attendances were low for a Club that wasn't playing at
'home'. However on the 17th of June 1943 plans were
announced that Slough F.C. and Slough Centre F.C. would
amalgamate to form Slough United, an idea that was first
voiced two years earlier by The Centre's Bill Yates. The
Centre Stadium would obviously be used and the new
Committee would consist of equal representation from the
two former Clubs. The President - the Right Reverend Lord
Bishop of Buckingham - was to remain, as would the
colours of the former Slough F.C. For the next season
three teams were fielded, one in the Herts. & Middx., the
Reserves in the Great Western, whilst a third eleven
would play in the local Slough Wartime League. It was
generally agreed that with the excellent facilities at
the Stadium, coupled with the previous Senior level
football experience of Slough - despite being formed in
1880 they had never won a major honour - that come
peacetime, the foundations would be laid for a top grade
Amateur team.
   Many dignitaries were invited and attended the first
match of Slough United. Stanley Rous (again), The Mayor
of Slough, the Club President and Major-General Sir
Alfred Knox M.P. were amongst the personalities. The
visitors on the 4th of September were pre-war Isthmian
League members St. Albans City. A crowd of 1,200 paying
customers at 6d. (2.5p) per head and a total gate of
1,500 was present; the biggest Club match crowd in the
town since the 1930's. They saw a dream debut by the new
team which resulted in a seven goal without reply
victory. Exciting matches followed, accompanied by large
crowds; 5-0 at Tufnell Park and 2-0 versus Grays at home,
before nearly 2,500 spectators (a new record for the
Stadium). These results took the new United to the top of
the table. A 'hiccup' was experienced at Walthamstow but
further victories followed, including 7-0 over High Duty

-163-

Slough Centre.

Alloys in the Berks. & Bucks Senior (Emergency) Cup (attendance nearly 2,000), and 9-1 in the League at Wood Green. Despite a poor run-up to Christmas, by the turn of the year both first and reserve teams were in third positions in their respective Leagues, whilst the 'A' eleven were top in their's. The best game to date resulted in a 6-1 thrashing of Southall in Slough on Christmas Day, before a 2,000 attendance.

Surprisingly, Cup matches were fairly poorly supported with only 800 present for the first round match of the Berks. & Bucks Red Cross Competition and despite reaching the final of this Cup, only a small crowd was present for the home leg against Wycombe Wanderers. But the final outcome on the season was a very pleasing runners-up position for the First Team, mid-table for the Reserves (Champions were Windsor Works who existed on average crowds of around 200) and the winning of the Red Cross Cup. The final first team record (including Friendly matches) produced 23 wins, 4 draws and 9 defeats, with a goal difference of 113 - 57.

Thirty-seven players appeared in the three teams (with only two recognised Goalkeepers !) and top Goalscorer was Jimmy Ingram with 22.

At the A.G.M. in June 1944 it was confidently reported:

"The intention of the United Club - and those behind it - is to put Slough 'on the map' in the Football World, and provide a first class ground at the centre Stadium."

The 1944/45 season started in topsy turvy fashion, a seven goal defeat at Walthamstow, followed by the same score victory at home to Leyton - although the extent of this victory may have been influenced by the need of Leyton to borrow two Slough Players (one a goalkeeper)! On the 30th of September a large crowd were reported present for Walthamstow's return visit, which was in sharp contrast to the 100 or so who attended Leyton's matches. Leyton, in East London were having problems finding a permanent 'home'.

Entry for matches remained at 6d. (2.5p) and by now covering had been provided over part of the spectators' area. After eight games a mid-table position was held (whilst the Reserves held up the rest in their League), this had improved to second by Christmas; on December the

10th the second string obtained their first point in ten games! Wood Green's visit to Slough was a disaster for them. The visitors had won one game and lost fourteen, and on their arrival were three players short; the United obliged once again, and won the match 4-2 !

By this time Slough United were producing praiseworthy programmes. Surprising, since their contemporaries - the Football League Clubs - were generally only able to provide flimsy four page efforts at best; the Slough productions included several articles, including details of former Players in.....'the well compiled little booklet'.

By the end of March second place in the League was held, behind runaway leaders - by nine points - Walthamstow, but the final outcome was third, with 16 wins, 3 draws and 7 defeats.

The final of the Berks. and Bucks. Red Cross Cup was again reached but on this occasion the United were beaten by Windsor & Eton after beating Wycombe at the Wanderers Ground by 2-1. Despite this earlier victory, concern was expressed over the officiating at the game as the home team were clearly heard to call the Referee by his Christian name (Frank)!

"Easily the largest crowd ever seen at a match in Slough" - some 6,000, were reported to have attended an end of season Representative match. Berks. & Bucks. included Professional players and Brown from Slough United, whilst the F.A.X1 (who won 6-1) paraded Stanley Mortenson along with several other Internationals. The takings were £500, with seats costing a hefty 12.5p.

Although remaining bottom of the Great Western Combination for much of the season, a slight recovery by the Reserves transpired and they finished one place higher; Wycombe were top, nine points ahead of second placed Maidenhead United.

The 1945/46 Season saw a partial return to normality in respect of football, and Slough United became the founder-members of the new Corinthian League. This League for Amateur Clubs was regarded as being just 'one step' down from the Athenian League, which in turn was only a single level below the peak, the Isthmian League. The end of the War also meant the end of the Herts. and Middx. League, a competition with high standards that had flown the flag during those bleak years. In more normal times

Slough Centre.

the Corinthian League would have been in trouble with the F.A. for it was not sanctioned by the Association until after the start of the season!

The first League game saw the Kent team Erith & Belvedere - who had played in the South East Combination over the past few years - in opposition, and a good 3-2 win by Slough.

The season also saw the return of the F.A.Cup and a thrilling preliminary round match at Hounslow on September the 8th was the first game in an exciting cup run. The two teams shared eight goals after extra time, the score at 90 minutes being 3-3.

In the replay, Slough won 3-1. The next round meant another short journey this time to Yiewsley (later Hillingdon Borough) where a result of 2-2 ensued. However, no extra time was played since there had been no prior agreement between the teams, but once again the replay was won by Slough. Meanwhile an excellent start had been made in League matches, and after three games the United were top.

The second qualifying round in the F.A.Cup attracted a 2,000 gate to Belfast Avenue for the match with fellow Leaguers Walton & Hersham, and a comprehensive 4-0 victory was seen. In early October the biggest crowd for years - 3,000 - witnessed the United inflict a shock 5-2 win at Birmingham Combination club Banbury Spencer, and it was not until one week later that the United suffered their first League defeat - 0-1 at Maidenhead United.

The third qualifying, and divisional final, round in the Cup attracted 3,000 spectators to Belfast Avenue, and against the odds the home team beat Isthmian Leaguers Oxford City by three unopposed goals. Excitement was mounting when the last round before the Competition proper (when the entry of the 'big boys' would occur) got underway at Leytonstone. Several hundred 'Rebels' supporters were dismayed to see their favourites two goals down after only 20 minutes, but a thrilling recovery saw the Club earn a well deserved 4-4 draw. The replay was won by 3-1, and despite a Wednesday afternoon meeting the attendance was 2,000.

By now, matches had commenced in the later rounds of the F.A. Amateur Cup, and in the 4th qualifying round of this competition Marlow were beaten 4-2.

The first round proper of the F.A.Cup had never been reached by the former Slough F.C. and this feat generated

great interest in the town. Bromley were to provide the
opposition for the two-legged games but the first match
in Kent became a farce. The Slough team coach broke down
and the game commenced 40 minutes late despite the
efforts of the Club in securing Taxis - and a 1903 Car -
as alternative transport. With just 6 minutes remaining,
and the visitors only 2-1 in arrears, the match was
abandoned due to bad light; despite the late start it did
not stop a record attendance of 6,000 (£266) assembling
at Hayes Lane. The replayed game also finished in dispute
for on this occasion with 15 minutes remaining, and the
United all of 1-6 down, a thick fog descended, but this
time the Referee refused to abandon the game!
    Slough United could hardly expect to pull back this
deficit in the home second leg, nonetheless a record
attendance of 4,200 for a Club match were present. But
there was no sensational result, although the homesters
did win by a single goal.
    Not surprisingly the Rebels had, by Christmas, played
less League matches than their opponents but were still
in a useful third place.
    The attention now switched to the Amateur Cup where
wins were recorded at Chippenham Town by 5-1 (3,000 and a
£180 gate on a hard frozen pitch), and at Oxford City
(before nearly 7,000 fans including 500 from Slough) by
3-2. The end came at Moor Green (1-2) due to a disputed
goal eight minutes from time.
    The supporters had had plenty to shout about over the
previous few months, and plenty to read about:
    "The programmes which the United Club provide
    each week are beginning to become the talk of
    Amateur   Football   circles.....   lots   of
    Information..... news of old players.....of
    future games."
    It was also mooted at this time that perhaps Players
shirts should be numbered!
    The League campaign came to an exciting climax and
despite the United's excellent record it appeared that
Grays were unstoppable. The Essex team played at Slough
over Easter and a new Club record attendance of nearly
6,000 saw a goalless draw. The last league match was won
7-2 at Walton, but all to no avail for the Club had to be
content with the runners-up spot. With a record of
thirteen wins, one draw and only two defeats, this would
have been sufficient for the title in any other League,

(Above): March 1946, action from
match with Hilversun F.C. (Holland).
The first amateur team from the
Continent since the War.
(Note the seated Stand)

Peter Lund in action in the F.A. Amateur Cup game versus Slough Town.
September 1949.

SLOUGH UNITED FOOTBALL CLUB

Founded 1890

Souvenir Programme

CHIPPENHAM is an ancient borough on the River Avon, dating back to Saxon times, and King Alfred is reputed to have had a residence there. The town was noted in the country, having supplied King Alfred's retainers — and milling has been carried on over ages for upward of 1,100 years. Since the time of King Edward I it has returned members to Parliament. The Borough was incorporated in 1553 by a charter of Queen Mary. In 1885 it was merged into, and became head of, the North West Wilts Division of Wiltshire. The women of Wiltshire. Town Hall in the Market Place, the Bailiff; other and oak table at which the Burgesses sat can still be seen. The picturesque old town retains all its natural charm in spite of the development of new residential estates. The Parish Church of St. Andrew, in the Market Place is in the Norman style and the choice dates back to 1578. Residents have the choice of hunting with both the Duke of Beaufort's and the Avon Vale hounds, whilst the well equipped sports ground in Hardenhuish Park affords facilities for cricket, hockey, tennis, bowls, croquet—and football.

MAY 17th
1947

Following a friendly Cup match with Chippenham Town, a bond was struck between the two Clubs, with annual challenge games being played.

SLOUGH UNITED MAKES ITS DEBUT

Senior F.A. Officials Invited

Famous Club For First Opponents

TO-MORROW will be an outstanding day in the sporting life of Slough, for the newly-constituted Slough United F.C. starts its playing career with a match against St. Albans City in the Herts and Middlesex League at the Social Centre Stadium.

Club officials have done everything possible to ensure that the occasion is fittingly marked and invitations have been sent to the secretary of the Football Association (Mr. Stanley Rous) and the treasurer (Mr. E. Hubard), among others, to attend.

The suggestion that there should be an amalgamation between Slough F.C. and the Centre F.C. was first made by Mr. W. Yates (conced to the new club), when he was appointed games organiser at the Social Centre in 1941. Slough F.C. were finding difficulties in getting a ground, and in view of the fact that there was a fine pitch at the stadium worthy of senior football, Mr. Yates put forward his proposal, but later it was found that the stadium was not usable, with the result that the amalgamation was postponed until the present season.

A successful senior football team is an asset to any town, and the experience of the old Slough club ... with the enthusiasm and ...

... guised record, and ever since the days of the Miller brothers, one of whom Inter joined Chelsea, and W. H. Minter, they have been among the leading amateur clubs in the country.

The Team.

Slough's team will be: C. Wakefield; J. Douglas, J. Jones; J. O. Dickie, I. Williams, G. Cox; F. Fisher, J. Ingram, Lt. Walton, J. Thomson, G. Fussell.

Among others who have been invited to attend are the Mayor of Slough (Ald. A. E. Ward), Bishop of Buckingham (preside ... the club), Maj.-General Knox ... B ...

(Slough, Windsor & Eton Observer 3rd September 1943)

however, Grays amassed an amazing total of three more points to become the first Corinthian League Champions.

For all their efforts only one minor honour came the Club's way, when the Chippenham Hospital Cup was won in the Wiltshire town with a 4-0 victory. An invitation to return to this town was to be repeated for several years, and was all due to the sporting game played between the two teams in the Amateur Cup.

One distinction to come to Slough was the visit of Hilversum V.V. - the first amateur team to visit Britain since 1939 - when a near record crowd was present (over 5,000). The match receipts went towards the 'Help Holland Fund' and an excellent Souvenir Programme was produced.

Although there was a lack of trophies, the comeback into the postwar football scene was regarded as highly promising, and the next season was looked forward to with great interest. An insight into the forward thinking of the Club was provided by the 'Slough United Football School Coaching Scheme' that was begun in April 1946 and run in conjunction with local Leagues. The aims were self explanatory and also proved popular with the Football Association who organised a similar, but further reaching scheme. For an Amateur team, a rare pre-season tour was made to Holland, the goodwill was to the forefront even if the results were not; defeats of 1-3, 2-7 and 3-8!

Although the Centre Stadium in Belfast Avenue had undoubtedly the potential for an excellent Football Ground, the playing surface left a lot to be desired and work commenced on improving the condition of the pitch. Home games commenced at the former home of Slough F.C. - The Dolphin Stadium - the last match having been played there on the 26th August 1939. The previous season's glories however did not continue for in addition to losing the first League match at Carshalton (attendance 3,000 - the best there for several years) only the 2nd qualifying round of the F.A. Cup was reached and lost at Hayes by 3-6. Earlier Cup games had seen wins at home to Lyons Club before a 3,000 crowd, and a 4-2 replayed win at Windsor. Due to the pitch difficulties, the first game had also been played, away from home, before a bumper local derby gathering of over 4,000, although the midweek replay at the same venue was only seen by some 1,500. One highlight of a mediocre start was a 9-0 home victory over Edgware.

Slough Centre.

By late October there was public disquiet expressed over an apparent dissention between Officials from the 'Centre', and the original Slough F.C. representatives. A final, controversial, decision was made that first team games would continue at the Dolphin, 'for some years', whilst reserve games - in the Reading & District League - would be played at the now ready Centre Stadium. There was concern that this decision had been taken secretly, and the unease was highlighted by the sudden resignation of the Club Secretary.

The team were able to overcome the in-house squabbles and went from strength to strength which led to a third placing in the League by Christmas. There was no success in the Amateur Cup however, for defeat came in the first encounter at Enfield, by 2-4. High scoring League wins were frequent, 11-4 at Eastbourne before over 3,000 spectators, 7-1 at Bedford Avenue, 7-0 at home to Edgware (after that Cup win of 9-0) and a 7-6 home victory over Hounslow, the latter clinching the Runners-up spot for the Slough Club.

The season had been an overall success and though there was still no 'silverware' taken, the Berks. & Bucks. Senior Cup Final was reached, but lost, by 1-2 to Wycombe Wanderers at neutral Maidenhead before an enormous 8,267 attendance. This number beat the home Club's own Ground record of 7,901 that had been recorded in 1936. For the first time since the early 1900's a Slough player was selected for his Country at Amateur level, the Welshman Jimmy Jones.

The last few home matches had been played back at The Centre, and the last match by Slough United was played there on the 7th of June (a late finish to the fixtures due to the many earlier cancellations because of bad weather) when Uxbridge were the visitors.

The previous arguments again came to the fore, when the United announced that they would in future be playing permanently at the Dolphin. The idea was voiced that the former Slough Centre F.C. may be reformed again as an independant Club with home games at Belfast Avenue.

In late June 1947, the final parting of the ways occurred. In November 1947, Slough United - later to become Slough Town - continued in the Corinthian League. Whereas Slough Centre, the 'Junior' of the two original Clubs came into being once again, and were elected into the Western Division of the enlarged Spartan League.

Slough Centre.

It is ironic that 'The Centre' were to fold just nine years later whilst 'The Town' went onto greater glories, for the 1947/48 season was to prove a likely reversal of these eventual roles.

The first game of the season at The Centre Stadium was a 'Slough & District' team versus the F.A.Cup holders Charlton, where an entertaining match before a 2,500 crowd saw the professionals win 4-2. The first League game for the 'new' Slough Centre was won over Leighton United and this good start continued with the first defeat not coming until October - 3-4 at home to Yiewsley.

The Club had a unique experience in their F.A. Amateur Cup game, with their opponents being The Carpathians F.C., a new team that consisted of Polish Army players. They were the first and only foreign team to enter the Competition. At this time there was an influx of Poles into the Country, who had fought alongside Britain in the War, and although a team was formed they had no home ground. But they were able to travel to all their matches in a novel manner, by way of a captured German military vehicle! The match was lost by 'Britain' although revenge was taken with a Slough victory over the same opponents in the Berks. & Bucks. Senior Cup.

By early November the Club were in third place in the League, with one notable victory of 5-2 over Polytechnic despite at one stage being in arrears by two goals. The first away defeat of the season came on a quagmire of a pitch at Willesden at the end of the year, although good wins were achieved frequently - e.g. 5-0 at home to Marlow, 6-0 over Amersham and 3-0 over Wycombe Redfords (the latter considered to be the best match of the season). Before the largest crowd of the campaign, a one goal victory was achieved over the leaders Hemel Hempstead, but this result was reversed a few weeks later in the return match. Sandwiched between these games was a demolition of Henley Town with a final 10-1 scoreline, after being seven goals up at halftime.

A late challenge was made for the Championship, but eventually 3rd place had to be accepted. Two end of season friendlies were played. A three goal defeat to the Charlton Athletic 'A' team and a 1-4 reverse to Q.P.R. The latter was watched by a record crowd of 6,000. The Reserves, who had played in the Great Western Combination Division Two, finished fourth, with Harefield United as

Slough Centre.

Champions. Both Centre teams had fared well, and the Reserves were elected to the 1st Division of their League.

It was a different story over the other side of town at the Dolphin Stadium. Difficulties were met regarding the playing of home matches, and it was reported on the 8th of August that the Greyhounds may well kill the Slough United team. With Greyhound race meetings in the afternoons, a proposal was put that the Football team should play in the mornings, but this proved to be unacceptable. A compromise was reached with agreement to have 3.45 p.m. kick-offs until October, and home Saturday matches after this date to be arranged to avoid the Dog racing. The football team had a poor time of it and by October were placed second from bottom in the Corinthian League. In the final event the Club had to seek re-election to the League, and this hardly bode well for the reformed Club. Gate takings were a near financial disaster with a fall from £930 to £452 from the previous year when the Club was a combined outfit.

The start of the 1948/49 season started with a boost to Slough Centre with the news that a number of junior players from Q.P.R. would on occasions play for the Club, in order for them to gain experience. For a team who were still novices in Senior Amateur football this was a big, on the field, bonus. Improvements had been made to the Stadium, for now the Club could boast of seating for around 2,000 spectators - some under cover - and was rapidly developing into one of the better arenas in Amateur football.

The first match resulted in a home win by 8-2 over the Reserves of Headington United, followed by a six goal thrashing of Chelsea Mariners. Marlow were visited in the F.A. Cup and before only 200 spectators, with the majority from Slough, the Centre triumphed by 3 goals to 2. However, there was to be no glory in this competition for in the next round defeat came at home to Southall by two goals - a replayed match before one of the largest Club match crowds. A similar story was told in the Amateur Cup; a 6-1 victory over Morris Motors from Oxford, followed by defeat at Maidenhead United.

The League results could not have been bettered, and after six games all had been won giving a goal difference of 28 - 6, and two points clear at the top of the table. In the best game of the campaign, Marlow were beaten by

Slough Centre.

three goals. This was followed by the 2-1 away triumph at Leighton, which was marred by the sending off, due to retaliation, of centre half Trott (who had been keenly watched by Professional Scouts), and the foul language by the home 'fans' against The Centre.

Two more matches were played against - by now familiar Football League opponents; 0-1 to Q.P.R. in the 'All Good Causes Cup', and 2-3 to Charlton. This did not stop the League victories, and by late January, the Club were 3 points clear at the top. The first defeat did not come until the end of March when the main contenders for the title, Hemel Hempstead scored the only goal of the match. Before the return away match at Hemel, The Centre were just one point in front of the homesters, but a goal in the 87th minute clinched the title for the Slough team.

It had been an incredible League season which showed a final record of 20 wins, 5 draws, and only one defeat, with a goal difference of 81 - 19. For the first time ever a major League title had been won in Slough. In a Championship play-off the Club lost to Eastern section Champions Stevenage by two unopposed goals, but this did not stop them progressing into the Premier Division of the Spartan League.

In the Berks & Bucks. Senior Cup, the first date with Wycombe Wanderers was postponed due to Amateur Cup commitments of the latter. The re-match was abandoned after only 12 minutes, and then finally drawn by 4 goals each. Finally Slough Centre lost 3-4 - after being two goals up - the winner coming in the 87th minute!

With their differences apparently patched up a friendly with Slough Town was played at The Centre Stadium, and before 3,000 spectators the homesters lost 0-2.

The Spartan League Premier division was almost on a par with the Corinthian League, in which Slough Town were still playing, and this was soon borne out by the two Cup-ties that were played between the two. These resulted in a one goal F.A. Cup defeat suffered by the Centre at the Dolphin Stadium before a 3,000 crowd and a 2-1 home win over the Town in the Amateur Cup.

The League games for the 1949/50 season started in an excellent manner with successive wins over Letchworth Town (2-1), Cambridge Town - reigning Champions - and 3-0 over Huntley & Palmers at Kensington Road, Reading. Topping the League, the return with the 'Biscuitmen' was

disappointingly drawn 2-2. Following the F.A. Amateur Cup
win over the Town, the next round was drawn at home to
Windsor & Eton before over 2,000 spectators, in a bad
tempered game, and the replay was lost by four goals to
nil. A thrashing was received by 7-2 at Briggs Sports and
the earlier winning start was not maintained, for by
Christmas the Centre were only 7th of the 14 Clubs.

On the 6th of January it was reported in the press
that:

*"A lot of work has been done recently at the
Centre Stadium, and further stands are planned on
the side opposite to the Dressing Rooms...... The
Supporters Club have made considerable strides to
improve the comfort of the spectators."*

In fact a small covered enclosure opposite the dressing
rooms (which included a seated area) was the final extent
of any more improvements that were undertaken.

In January, following a four goal win at home to
Aylesbury United, the 'Town' were encountered for the
third time in a cup game - the Berks and Bucks. Before a
smaller crowd than expected, the Centre went down at the
Dolphin Ground by 1-3.

League match results continued in varied fashion, as
did attendances. A 5-2 home victory over Brentwood &
Warley before less than 500 fans, was followed shortly
after by the largest crowd of the season for the 3-0 win
at Slough over Champions elect Briggs Sports! The season
finished in a satisfactory mid-table placing.

Two further friendlies were played, a narrow one goal
defeat to Fulham and an entertaining 6-4 win (after being
1-4 in arrears at half-time) to Q.P.R. Reserves.

The 1950/51 season started with a spirit of optimism -
the covered enclosure on the popular side was completed
in August - and the team kicked-off with the same players
as those that finished the last campaign. The first two
League games, however, ended in defeats - 1-5 at both
Letchworth and Huntley & Palmers!

Conversely the F.A. Amateur Cup games produced several
victories; over Abingdon Town, Didcot Town and Pressed
Steel - at the latter game the covered enclosure which
held 400 spectators was officially opened but the total
attendance fell short of that which had been expected. In
the second qualifying round, Marlow were brushed aside by
six goals, and the next round involved the short trip to

the Dolphin yet again. The match was lost by the odd goal in three, in a game marred by rough play from The Centre, and poor refereeing.

By now the team had recovered to a mid-table placing in the League, a position that was held through to February. Some big defeats were experienced including 0-5 at Yiewsley, 2-5 at home to Chesham in the County Cup, and worst of all two defeats to Aylesbury over Easter with 0-8 and 0-5 scorelines; the latter team were ironically beaten later by Slough Town by 8-1 in the Berks. & Bucks. Benevolent Cup! Davies went off injured in the defeat at Yiewsley, and later signed as a professional with Q.P.R., as did England Youth International full back Richardson. In the Annual match with the Football League Club, this time versus their Colts, Slough centre were beaten by 4 goals, with Q.P.R. playing three ex-Centre players.

Despite winning their last League match by 3 goals over Berkhampsted, the final result was a poor 9th out of 14 teams. More dramatic was the turn around in the respective fortunes of the two Slough Clubs; The Centre had suffered with low attendances, due very much to indifferent performances, although the Supporters Club had donated over £200 during the season. Meanwhile Slough Town became the Corinthian League Champions, and conversely attracted a capacity attendance for their last and title- clinching League game.

It was to the Delphian League - in March 1951 - that The Centre pinned their hopes for the coming season, along with several other Spartan League teams who considered this new League to be of a higher standard.

The first two League games were lost, each by two goals, at Rainham and at home to ex-Metropolitan League Club Dagenham. After this poor start a good recovery was made. Willesden were beaten 'away' for the first time, and by the end of October, the Centre had climbed to third in the League; this was improved to top place following a 3-1 home win over Woodford, who had been undefeated to that date.

No sensations were caused in the Amateur Cup for following a close 5-4 win at Bicester, the Club's exit from the Competition came at Aylesbury by 1-2 before a 2,000 crowd - a poor, rough game in which The Centre had a player sent off for striking the Goalkeeper and where sub-standard refereeing was again reported. This match

marked the first victory of the season for Aylesbury! By
the Year's end the Centre were in third position, but
this was not held and eventually a disappointing 8th
placing of 14 Clubs ensued.

Aylesbury were met this season on no less than five
occasions! two League games (0-6 in the away match -
despite dominating the play for the first 20 minutes),
the Amateur Cup, the Berks & Bucks Senior Cup (a Centre
victory - by 5-1) and in the County Benevolent Cup - a
3-1 home victory.

Honours however did come the Club's way by virtue of a
surprise single goal win at Wycombe in the County Cup
over holders Chesham United, and an appearance in the
Final of the Benevolent Cup, which was lost by 1-4 - to
Chesham! Slough Town had been fined £5-25p for refusing
to play the replayed semi-final one week later with the
Centre, and the Delphian League Club were given a
walkover through to the Final of the Benevolent Cup
competition

The standards had declined with only 13 Clubs left in
the Spartan League, and there was talk of a new 'Berks. &
Bucks' League but this never materialised.

The start of the 1952/53 League season started well,
although the Amateur Cup was the most encouraging with
progress through to the final qualifying round - the last
before the 1st round proper - the furthest the Club had
ever reached. Bicester were first easily overcome by 6-1
at home followed by a two (late) goals victory, a replay
- over Chesham United. Spartan League leaders Huntley &
Palmers were then crushed 5-2 followed by an even more
emphatic six goal to nil win over Berkhamsted. The Centre
however met their match at Hitchin, where, cheered on by
hundreds of fans from Slough, they bowed out of the Cup
with a 1-3 scoreline.

Sandwiched between this Cup run the Club achieved a
morale boosting F.A.Cup win over Slough Town, but
progressed no further, for in the next round - due mainly
to their inept forwards - the Centre lost 1-2 at Edgware.
By Christmas, Slough Centre were in a deceptive, below
halfway, position in the League but due to the many Cup
games they lagged far behind the opposition in respect of
games played.

Rainham were beaten by 3-0, although the Centre did
score another 'goal' - but the ball that had been put in

Slough Centre.

the net was in fact a second one thrown onto the pitch by a spectator!

The early New Year matches produced two defeats, but during February and March they found their winning touch - including victories which led them onto the final of the County Cup Final again. The Final was played at Maidenhead versus Slough Town, and despite their past differences and inevitable close rivalry the match was played in a very sporting manner. A close fought encounter produced the sharing of four goals, and in the replay, to the delight of their supporters, the Centre won by two goals to one. The Town however achieved some revenge with a 3-1 win over The Centre in the County Benevolent Cup. League wins continued into April, and although there was no stopping Champions-to-be Dagenham, there was a real possibility of the runners-up spot. However, the final position was fourth, but it was, none the less, a satisfactory end to an exciting season.

Despite the achievements over the past year - which included a Cup win and the Amateur Cup run - plus the use of an excellent Stadium and talented young players, the one cloud on the horizon was the support at matches; attendances were poor, far less than those experienced across town at The Dolphin Stadium.

In the Summer of 1953, money was spent at the Ground by way of re-turfing the pitch, improving the dressing rooms and extending the covered seats to 800, yet only 'a handful of spectators' were present for the first home League match (when Bishop Stortford were beaten 4-1). Another good run was experienced in the Amateur Cup, which saw victories over the Town Club (4-1), Pressed Steel (Cowley) - at Oxford - and Wallingford (both by 4-2). The last victory came by 3-0 over Chesham United at Belfast Avenue. Defeat this season came at the hands of Chipping Norton by 2-4, despite a 1-0 half-time lead. In the F.A.Cup the Club lost to a 6th minute goal to St. Albans, a game that The Centre deserved to win. By mid-November only a mid-table place in the League was realised, but once again due to Cup matches, fewer games had been played than other teams. But by Christmas - following 4 straight wins - this position was improved to fourth. The team were without first team choice goalkeeper Yates who had broken an ankle in the first 45 minutes at Berkhampsted - a match that was nonetheless won by the only goal.

Slough Centre.

In the two local Cup competitions the Club recorded further victories over Slough Town, 2-1 at home in the Benevolent Cup where an expected large crowd was drastically reduced due to the intense cold, and by the same score in the Berks. & Bucks. Senior Cup at The Dolphin. Indifferent results came in the new year, and despite more matches to play than their rivals, the final outcome was only a 5th final position in the League table.

For the third successive year The Centre reached the final of the Senior Cup - a surprising feat considering their relative status alongside some others in the Competition. The final was again played at Maidenhead, and on this occasion two goals were shared with Wycombe Wanderers; in the replay the team were rather unlucky to lose - by 1-3. Before a large crowd the Benevolent Cup final was played, at Aylesbury United, but once again luck was against the Slough team for they lost by 2-3 to the homesters, who got the winner with a last minute penalty.

Slough Centre had proved their superiority once again over their close rivals - Slough Town - yet inexplicably they could not attract attendances worthy of their ability, unlike the Town who were generally well supported.

Before the end of the season a plan had been mooted to apply automatic promotion and relegation between the Isthmian, Athenian, Corinthian and Delphian Leagues, however the Isthmians - typical of their attitude at that time - quashed the idea.

The Slough Centre team had been watched during the previous season by a number of Senior Clubs, and it came as no surprise when the 1954/55 campaign started to find that three of the better players had moved on elsewhere.

Nonetheless the season started in good fashion, home League wins over fellow founder-members Woodford Town by 4-0, 5-0 over Leatherhead, and six games (but only two wins) in the qualifying rounds of the Amateur Cup. In the latter, Pressed Steel were again met, and again beaten, this time only after a replay. Despite being three goals down after 45 minutes at home to Chipping Norton in the next round, the Club fought back well to earn a replay with a 4-4 draw and went on to win the replay after extra time. The Centre met their match at Newbury Town for despite an initial 1-1 draw in Slough, they were soundly

beaten by four goals without reply in the replay.
There was no progress in the F.A.Cup, apart from a bye
in the preliminary round, for the first game was lost at
home to Wycombe Wanderers by 3-1. However, by
mid-November the team were handily placed in third
position in the League, which they held until the Year's
end, despite falling away somewhat, including a six goal
hammering at League leaders Dagenham. Aided by some good
away wins, but some slips at home, early April saw the
Club still in third place, with 3 games in hand - but 7
points behind leaders Bishop Stortford. However, the
leeway proved to much, and in a League of 15 teams the
Centre finished a final 4th.

After a 2-1 away win over Maidenhead United before a
large crowd in the Berks. & Bucks Senior Cup, the Club
succumbed to Wycombe by 1-5. There was one honour,
however, when the Benevolent Cup was won with victory
over Wolverton in the final by the odd goal in three.

Although once again the Club's performances on the
field were very reasonable, the sorry story of poor home
attendances remained.

For the purposes of training, a number of floodlights
had been erected down one side of the pitch, and these
were used unexpectedly when a home Reserve game with
Dagenham kicked-off over one hour late and the match was
finished with the aid of these floodlights. The
illumination must have been poor, since only two of the
four lights were used, and thirty-two would be required
for formal Floodlight matches!

The big talking point in January was the news that
Charlton Athletic were considering a move to Slough! It
was reasoned that with the ever increasing population of
the area, the South-east London Club could be better
supported. In addition the potential of the Belfast
Avenue Ground could ensure facilities for a Football
League Club. But the rumours were nothing more than that,
and it appears that no serious proposal was ever made.

There was no reason to suspect that the 1955/56 season
was to be the last for Slough Centre, although perhaps
the concern that had been expressed regarding the poor
support that the team received may have given a clue that
all was not well. In a growing town with a current
population of some 70,000 a total of only 2,000 on
average turned out to watch the two Senior teams in the

area - a fairly poor percentage considering that this was still within the era when football spectating was at its height. Depressing from The Centre's point of view was the fact that of those two thousand the Club only received some 25% of that figure. The Club had made steady progress since the splitting of the two Slough teams - when 4 to 5,000 would watch the one Club - winning the County Senior Cup Competition (competing with 'quality' sides) on two occasions, together with other notable achievements. The Stadium was undoubtedly of a high standard and the team had proved themselves superior to the Town Club in a number of competitive games. There was therefore no obvious reason why The Centre were very much the poor relations within the community.

A major signing was made when the Swedish Inter-national, Nielson, (who was temporarily working in Slough) agreed to play for the Club, although his expected first appearance in September was delayed until December. For no apparent reason the Club made a disastrous start losing five and drawing one of their opening six League games. The F.A. Amateur Cup provided no solace with a poorly played defeat at Aylesbury by 1-3 in the preliminary round. The first win eventually came with the 4-2 victory over Brentwood, but by now the team were languishing near the foot of the table, along with fellow strugglers Ware - who were later beaten 6-2 away from home. The poor performances inevitably reflected in the attendances with only 300 present for the four goals shared with Stevenage at Slough. This figure could be compared to the 2,500 who watched the Corinthian leaders, Slough Town, a few weeks later!

By mid-November there had been some improvement in performances, although the Club were still well down in the bottom half of the League table, which was not helped by the two Christmas matches which were both lost.

Little progress was made in the Berks. & Bucks. Cup apart from a 3-1 win over Windsor, for the next round was lost to The Town - after two replays. By now the two Clubs positions could be significantly compared; the Town, 3rd from top in their League, the Centre 3rd from bottom in the Delphian. The Benevolent Cup was lost by the Club - the holders - at Aylesbury in the semi-finals.

The last ever League game was played on the 7th of April 1956; ironically an exciting 6-5 victory at Woodford Town. Although Two goals down after 45 minutes,

Slough Centre.

the Centre were even at one time, losing by five goals to two. The team that day was composed of:
Brown, Goodhew, Gilham, Johnson, Simpson, Hayes Collier, Pascoe, Westcott, Hayman and Bradley.

On Tuesday April the 17th the shock news was announced:
" At a Committee Meeting of Slough Centre F.C. it was decided to disband the Club from the end of this season owing to lack of Support. "

The lack of support in effect meant lack of revenue, and the Club as part of the Slough Community Centre had, until this time enjoyed the Stadium's facilities free of charge. However, the new Rating and Valuation Acts that came into force at this time required only a fairly small contribution from the Community Centre in respect of Rates payable to the local Council (£387) providing that the Organisation was for ' Charitable, Educational or Religious' purposes, but 'Playing fields where charge for admission to the Ground is normally made' were excluded. The latter case pushed the Rates up to an incredible £5,000 plus per year. Not unreasonably the Community Centre was not prepared to pay this extra money unless it was forthcoming from The Centre Football Club, a sum far in excess of the Club's funds. In fact with gates seldom over 400 in the later years, the Social Fund of The Centre had been subsidising the Club to the tune of £700 per year!

The final match for Slough Centre provided a fitting end, a Friendly versus the renowned Universities Football Team, Pegasus. These illustrious opponents provided proof that the general public were not interested in the Club, for just 200 people attended the game.

At least it was a good competitive encounter, for the Centre 1-2 down at half-time fought back to share six goals, with only one minute to go. The referee however incensed the few spectators present when he awarded Pegasus a late penalty, and the visitors finished the game as 4-3 victors, and the man in the middle was booed off the pitch. The Centre's Captain at the end was Jim Platt, an ex-Pegasus player!

A last ditch effort to maintain a team was made at a meeting on May the 14th when most of the players vowed to try and continue playing. However, their resignation from the Berks. and Bucks. F.A. had already been accepted and any hopes of maintaining Senior status were lost. A Club was reformed as 'Community Centre F.C.', and entered into the Windsor, Slough & District League with their unfenced home Ground located in Farnham Park. But, to all intents and purposes, Slough Centre was dead.

There is really no obvious reason why the Club should have died through lack of interest, especially since smaller towns than Slough were able to command two Senior Football teams. Perhaps tradition comes into the reckoning, although despite a history dating back to 1889, the Town Club had never really made an impact in Amateur football and ironically it was not until their amalgamation with The Centre that they were able to attract support in any great numbers. Slough Centre had in a few Senior Football seasons achieved so much – Champions and respectable League placings, County Cup winners, connections with Football League Clubs, and in effect their own well appointed Ground. Who knows, perhaps if it hadn't have been for the formation of Slough United in 1943, the later Slough Town may never have risen to the status they later commanded. The short life of Slough Centre at least contributes to the history of a Club that is still in existance!

Slough Centre Stadium:

Few Clubs at even a semi-professional level had Grounds to match the potential of Slough Centre F.C. There was both covered and uncovered seating in several rows, which stretched along over half the length of the pitch. Behind the seated area was, and still is, a two storied 'Institution' looking Building housing the Administration, Changing Rooms facilities, etc. - space far in excess of that required for a Football Club, but used of course by other sections within the Community Centre. Opposite the seating area was a small covered sitting and standing enclosure, with a banked oval Cycle speedway track encircling the pitch. The Ground was fully enclosed with the Main Entrance in Belfast Avenue.

Until the Summer of 1986, the locations of the two enclosures could still be seen (although the structures themselves had been removed some years earlier), but various work at the ground, including the flattening of the cycle track, leaves little more than an enclosed Sports field and the large two-storied building.

Slough Centre.

Programmes.

It is unlikely that the pre-amalgamation Centre Club issued programmes, and even the wartime (and early post-war) 'Slough United' - much praised - issues are very much collectors' items. Slough Centre (from 1947) were generally poorly supported and shortlived, therefore, issues from this independent Club are only rarely available.

Slough Centre F.C. programme covers:

A typical example - one from the 1953/54 season....

.... And a representative match, which attracted one of the Ground attendance records.

Centre F.C. to disband to save £5,000

RATES BILL SHOCK FOR COMMUNITY CENTRE

By DEREK PRIGENT

IN the middle of the 19th Birthday Week celebrations, Slough Community Centre dropped a sensational bombshell. A statement issued in a five-minute interview late on Tuesday evening announced the end of the Slough Centre Football Club.

A statement came first from Slough Social Fund withdrawing the use of the Centre Stadium from the club and terminating financial support.

It was issued by the Centre warden, Mr. J. M. N. A. Nicholls.

Immediately the club announced it would disband at the end of the season.

Inquiries I have made indicate that —

SLOUGH CENTRE FOOT-BALL CLUB HAS BEEN DISBANDED TO SAVE THE COMMUNITY CENTRE.

If the football club continued would, under the new rating assessment, cost the Community Centre an additional £5,000 in rates a year.

This would result in the Centre being handed over to the County Council — with serious effects to the social facilities.

£5,000 UP, UNLESS . . .

Here are the facts and figures.

The Community Centre, and the swimming pool and stadium, are assessed as a whole.

The old assessment of £267 produced a rates bill of £387 3s.

The new assessment of £6,060 produces a bill of £5,573 19s. 4d.

But the Community Centre will not be liable for any more than the old rate of £387 3s. — providing it complies with Section 8 of the new Rating and Valuation Act.

This states that anything operated for educational, religious or charitable purposes or for social welfare should pay no more than last year.

But it also says — "Playing fields, where charge for admission is normally made, are not considered charitable or social objects."

And a charge is made for all Delphian League games at the Centre Stadium.

IN JEOPARDY

The Community Centre management feel that while this is so their appeal for relief under Section 8, already lodged with the Rating Authorities, is seriously jeopardised.

To safeguard the Centre's future, the management felt there was no option but to stop the club playing on the Centre Stadium — one of the finest amateur soccer grounds in the Home Counties.

There is a further consideration. Support for the club has been so poor that the Social Fund has been subsidising it to the tune of £700 a year. "Gates" are seldom over 400.

The move to close down the club was made with the utmost secrecy.

SWAN SONG

Slough Centre will play its last game at the Centre Stadium tomorrow week. The match is a friendly against the famous Pegasus side. It will be a fitting end to the club's career.

Even committee members called to the meeting on Tuesday evening did not know what was happening.

Players, circularised on Wednesday, were stunned when they heard the news.

STATEMENT

The statement issued by the Social Fund Council said it had decided to terminate the football club's use of the Centre Stadium, and to discontinue the financial support.

It mentioned the provisions of the Rating Act, and also the following points:—

The cost of running two teams bears too high a relationship in comparison with the many other recreational facilities at the Centre.

Mr. Percy Olding, the secretary, had notified his intention of retiring at the end of the season.

The statement ended by wishing the Town Club "every prosperity."

Sir Noel Mobbs, president of the Centre F.C., said: "I don't think I want to say anything."

Mr. H. G. Herrington, president of the Slough Social Fund — and President of Slough Town Football Club in succession to Lieut-Col. Leadbetter until Monday.

Mr. Jack Hales, secretary of of Slough Town F.C., refused to make any comment, but the Centre's secretary, Mr. Percy Olding, had something to say:

"It is a pity this had to happen. I am sorry for Slough Town. They will have to look farther afield now for their players."

PERCY OLDING.

(Slough Observer)
20th April 1956.

SLOUGH CENTRE F.C.

SATURDAY, APRIL 28th

1956.

CENTRE

Red Shirts

K.Brown

R.Goodhew
2

M.Pyatt
3

J.Platt
4

A.Gillham
5

G.Hayes
6

W.Pascoe
7

A.Johnson
8

A.Stewart
10

G.Westcott
11

J.Hayman
9

Referee: Mr.J.Burland ⚽

J.E.Howlett
9

J.H.Blythe
11

P.Hancock
10

J.W.Trimby
8

D.Miller
7

6

5

4

P.M.J.Walsh

K.A.Shearwood

D.F.Saunders

D.G.Harrison
3

G.H.McKinna
2

M.J.Pinner

White Shirts

PEGASUS

*The programme cover for the 'Centre's'
last match, against worthy opponents.*

Slough Centre

1985... The main building at Belfast Avenue. The raised perimeter track has now been removed, together with the seated Stand in front.

(Photo: Dave Twydell)

Slough Centre

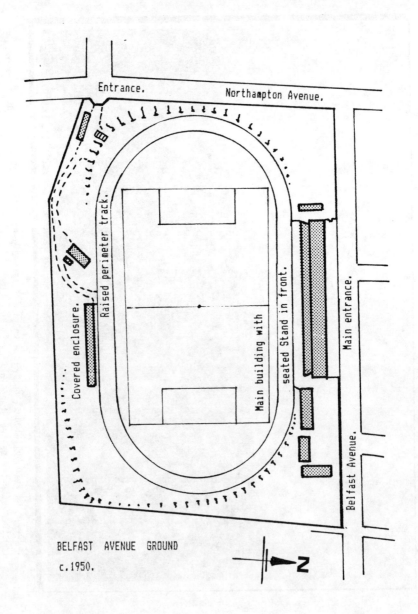

BELFAST AVENUE GROUND
c.1950.

Slough Centre

Ground Location.

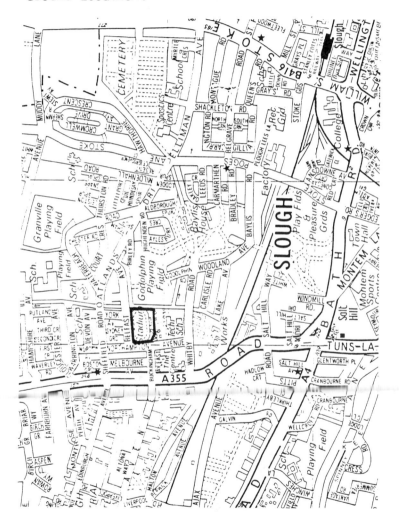

Team Group at Murray Park: 1920/21 season.

(Left to Right): A.Howgate, T.Pattison, E.Reed, A.Thompson, G.Hall,
A.Bell, E.Levitt, R.Waugh, R.Turnbull, R.Burton, J.Smith.

West Stanley.

(1889 -1959)

Founded as: Oakey's Lilywhites in 1889.
Changed name to: Stanley (1896)
Changed name to: West Stanley (1906)

::

Playing Record:

1889/90 - 1894/95.	Friendly Matches.
1895/96.	North-West Durham Alliance League.
1896/97 - 1905/06.	Northern Alliance.
1906/07 - 1914/15.	North Eastern League.
1915/16.	Northern Combination.
1916/17 - 1917/18.	Ceased Activity (Wartime).
1918/19.	Friendly Matches.
1919/20 - 1938/39.	North Eastern League.
1939/40.	North Eastern League *.
1939/40 - 1944/45.	Ceased Activity (Wartime).
1945/46 - 1957/58.	North Eastern League.
1958/59.	Northern Alliance.

* League season not completed due to Second World War.

****

Summary of Facts.

Ground Address:
(to 1906) Oakey's Oval, Stanley, County Durham.
(From 1906) Murray Park, High Street, Stanley.

Nickname:
(Early Days) 'Stanla'.
(Latter Days) 'Wests'.

Colours:
All White - as Oakey's Lilywhites.
Red Shirts, White Shorts - as West Stanley.
(Pre-war - Red and White hoops, White Shorts)

West Stanley.

First Games:
As Oakey's Lilywhites - Unknown. (Friendly)
1889 or 1890)
As Stanley versus Jarrow (Away). 0-1.(North.Alliance)
Sept.12 1896 (Attendance 3,000).
At Murray Park versus Stanley United
(Durham Challenge Cup). 1-1 (1-0)
Sept.27 1906.

Last Games:

As Oakey's Lilywhites versus Birtley. (Home) 3-1
(2-1). (Friendly) 29th August 1896.
At Oakey's Oval versus Hull City. (Friendly) 5-3
(1-3). 30th April 1906.
At Murray Park versus Alnwick Town.
(League) 1-1. 25th April 1959.

Record Attendance:
12,585. versus Leadgate Park. 27th October 1921.
(1920/21 Final-North West Durham Chall. Cup. 2nd rep.)

Main Achievements:

Founder Members - North Eastern League: 1906/07.
North-Eastern League Runners-up: 1949/50.
North-East Lge. 'Non Reserve' Medal Winners:
1929/30. 1949/50.
Durham Benevolent Cup Winners: 1927/28.

F.A. Cup.
2nd Round Proper:
1919/20. (Beat Rotherham and Gillingham.)
1st Round Proper:
1925/26. 1931/32.

Notable Players:
T. Barber (Bolton Wanderers and Aston Villa))
B. Brown (Middlesbrough)
D. Herron (Stoke City)
H. Holdsworth, N. Thompson (Notts C. and Forest)
T. Fish (Sheffield Wednesday)
C. Stephenson (Aston Villa, and England)
L. Stoker (Birmingham C. and England))

The Football achievements from the North East of England are Legend both in it's Sons and it's Clubs. The story of the game however goes far back in time, back even to 1363 when 'Football' of a sort was recorded as being played in Durham. More recently, but still before the advent of the modern game, another variety between the 'Upstreeters' and the 'Downstreeters' was regularly contested every Shrove Tuesday, in the Town of Chester-Le Street, a few miles from Stanley. The games were so strongly contested that a ban on the playing of the 'sport' was made in 1933 - for the safety of all those concerned - and the Police were stationed all over the Town on the first Tuesday in February 1934 to ensure that the ban was complied with!

The first organisation to control Football proper in the North East area was the Tyne Association in 1876, aided by the Northumberland & Durham Association in 1879, and finally separate Associations for these two Counties in 1883.

The rise of Football in the late 19th Century in this part of the Country was no doubt influenced by the numerous Coal-mining Communities who turned to this competitive sport to alleviate the extreme hardship, with scant reward, that the workforce had to endure. There were numerous teams representing not only every Town and Village but every Colliery as well as many Pubs in the localities. Taking 'our' Stanley area as just one example, pre-1890 records show Clubs such as South Moor Albion, Stanley True Blues, Stanley Temperance, Headley Harriers, South Moor Headley Harriers, to name but five were located in the town and it's immediate surrounds. However, to add to the confusion and difficulty in tracing the origins of West Stanley F.C., the Town of Stanley Crook, (now barely a Village) also in Durham but some miles distant from West Stanley, also has to be accounted for. In this locality there were the likes of Headley Hill Terrace Rangers, Stanley United, Stanley Albion, etc. To further compound the confusion, the Headley Hill Terrace Club played in the Crook, Stanley & District League, whilst the 'other' Headley Club (The Harriers), were evolved from the Coalmine at Headley Pits, Stanley. Stanley United were a notable Club in the Northern League until 1974 before the Club - on the point of extinction -joined the Durham City League.

Records concerning individual Junior Clubs in the
Durham area around 1890 are few and far between, and
there appears to be no way of verifying the match details
for Oakey's Lilywhites first match. Occasional references
to the Club playing Friendly games can be traced, notably
the local derby away to Shield Row Juniors. In this early
match, the play produced by the home team was so rough
that the Oakey Supporters were provoked into invading the
pitch and were reported to have used "bad language"!

Other local sides met in friendly matches included
Headley Hill - who played at South Moor and were probably
the strongest of local opponents - Stanley Lilywhites,
West Stanley True Blues and South Moor Headley Harriers.
Despite the similarities in the names, each Club appears
to have been a separate organisation.

Oakey's Lilywhites played home games at Oakey's Oval,
which was situated within the Town of Stanley, and
although abandoned as the home venue in 1906, the site of
the original pitch was later to become a football field
again. The first Club Secretary was one Tom Wood, and
George Lee was the Chairman. The 1890/91 season produced
a few reported friendly matches. One notable game was the
6-0 home victory over Stanley Cripples, that was recorded
as being - perhaps not surprising in view of the
opponents name - as a " One sided match"!

By the early 1890's, Leadgate Exiles, Consett Swifts,
Dipton Wanderers, Hobson Wanderers and South Moor Albions
were prominent opponents, although the most keenly
contested games with large enthusiastic crowds were
usually reserved for those versus Lizzie Celtic. The
Lizzie team became the modern-day Annfield Plain. Notable
'Stanla' (the nickname of the team in the early days)
players of this era were the three Cunningham brothers -
Matt, Jack, and Dick - and Jack Swan, who was destined to
become the Barnard Castle M.P.

The 1891/92 season included matches versus Tanfield
Lea Reserves (an indication that Oakey's were still very
much a Junior Club) which produced an eight goal home win
and a four goal victory at Witton Gilbert. A match with
Stanley Headley Harriers (of the North-West Durham
Alliance League) was also featured; the Harriers could
attract four figure home attendances. The opening
'Stanla' home match in the Autumn of 1892 enticed, "a
large muster of people", to the Ground, and they
witnessed a 4-2 victory over Usworth Swifts.

West Stanley.

The 1893/94 season was the first in serious competition when the Durham Junior Cup was entered, and the first game produced a surprise 4-0 win over Hobson Wanderers. The celebrations were short-lived however for a challenge from the Wanderers that Oakey's had included unregistered Players in their team was upheld, and this together with evidence of having played matches during the 'close' season resulted in the Club being expelled from the Competition! The rest of the season consisted once again of Friendly games, including opponents Ouston Institute and Dipton Wanderers Reserves (the latter's first team attracted crowds of 700 to 1,000 for their Northern Alliance matches). Two other (short-lived) teams in the Town, were West Stanley United and West Stanley Athletic, who despite the similarities in names had no connection with each other.

For the next season, a Reserve team was formed, and following a further period of Friendly matches, which were generally successful for the Club, the plunge was taken and a League was entered in the Summer of 1895. Several of the Club's previous opponents had been playing in the North-West Durham Alliance, and this was the obvious choice for Oakey's Lilywhites. Whilst no honours were won in League competition, it was a successful start, and the enthusiasm for the team was present right upto the last fixture when Allendale Park were beaten at The Oval by 4-1 (despite a 4-0 half-time lead) before a "Good gate of several hundred".

It was in the Durham Junior Cup that the Club first came to local prominence for the 5th round - the final round of the Northern Section - was reached. Playing in the Consett Division, Consett Town were beaten by 4-1 on January the 18th, followed by an 8-2 thrashing of Marley Hill St. Cuthberts. Before a good attendance of 500, Headley Hill Terrace Rangers were then overcome by four goals to two, followed by a 5-2 victory over Craghead Rangers. This was to be the last win in the Competition, for Oakey's then bowed out by the odd goal in three at Leadgate Park.

To provide enough matches several Friendlies were played, one of which was a 2-1 away victory over Tantobie Co-operatives; the home team however were poorly represented, for despite the close result, two spectators from the crowd had to be seconded to the team to make up the numbers! The 1896/67 Season was to be the first in truly Senior football, for the Club's application to join the Northern Alliance was accepted. An unusual condition - perhaps unique in Football - was imposed upon Oakeys Lilywhites, when the League's Management Committee insisted on the Club changing it's name! The reason probably being that the quaint name adopted by the team was not considered suitable to such a respected Competition! And so for around a decade the Club became plain 'Stanley F.C.'

The last game played, as Oakey's Lilywhites, was on August the 29th, 1896, when considerable interest was shown in the Club's rise in status. Despite the fixture only being a Friendly game a large crowd was present to witness the 3-1 (halftime 2-1) home victory over Birtley. The match started late, for in the second half... "the spectators cried for lamps..." with the game finishing in complete darkness!

The formal name change was effected in time for the first League match and on September the 2nd, Stanley F.C. travelled to Jarrow. At The Monkton Enclosure, an attend-ance of 3,000 was present to see the 'new' Club lose by a single goal. The first home match followed on the 12th of September when Willington Athletic were the visitors, and the locals went away well pleased with the 5-1 victory (three goals up at half-time). It was overall a satisfactory start, and by Christmas a mid-table position was attained, with four victories and six defeats being recorded.

Stanley were now playing in a high standard of football, and were in the company of such Clubs as Ashington (later to become founder-members of the Football League 3rd Division North), Newcastle United Reserves, and the Sunderland 'A' team. The Northern Alliance was one of the first Leagues to be formed - in 1890 - following the Football League which had commenced just two years earlier.

Although no evidence remains today, the Oval was developed into a worthy enclosure including a Grandstand which was started in September 1896. The popularity of the game was reflected with normally good attendances; a 'very large crowd', being present for the fixture versus The Exiles (not a League game) and 1,200 spectators at the end of December when Blyth were beaten 4-3.

West Stanley.

A Reserve team continued to operate, with their entry in the Derwent Valley League.

Whilst no honours were won in the next few seasons, the Club held their own against several larger Town and City sides, culminating in their best season of 1905/06, when a final placing of third in the table of sixteen teams was attained. In 30 games, 16 were won and 4 drawn, with Stanley finishing only four points behind the Champions, Willington. By this time entry was regularly made into the F.A.Cup Competition, and the biggest match occured in December 1906, with a no-score home draw, versus Northampton Town in a qualifying round (after three earlier victories in the Competition). Stanley lost the replay by three unopposed goals.

During the season, Hedley, Joey Smith and Browell were transferred to Hull City - newcomers to the Football League Second Division - and on the 30th April 1906 a Friendly match was played with the Yorkshire team (match entry cost 3d.- just over 1p.) An exciting match resulted in a 5-3 victory to the Durham team, despite being 1-3 behind at half-time. Stanley had by now become an ambitious and well supported Club, and this game became the last played at Oakeys Oval. Plans had been made, and construction was well underway for a new Arena, which became the Club's venue until their demise some 50 years later. Much of the Club's impetus came from the Secretary, and later Durham F.A. President John Bennett, who was the main instigator regarding the aquisition and development of the new Ground. He was also the main mover behind the later forming of the Club into a Limited Company.

Stanley caused a minor sensation when an application was made, and accepted, for their entry into the newly formed North-Eastern League. Members of the League consisted mainly of the Football League 'A' teams in the area, who considered that the Northern Alliance and Northern League did not provide competition of a high enough standard. Other Clubs to join included the first teams of Carlisle United, Workington, Hebburn Argyle and Royal Rovers.

There was now a race against time both in raising sufficient funds - only £15 was in the kitty for a new Stand, whilst the Lease was to cost £40 per year - and in completion of the new Stadium for the first home match of the 1906/07 season.

In view of their new commitments, and with the Club
intending to pay out £10 per week for players' wages in a
now professional set-up, there was already talk of
forming the Club into a Limited Company. It was ironic
that although £130 was spent in fencing around the
Ground, it was considered that, "it is not necessary to
have baths, if Players have a good place to wash in, then
that will be sufficient "!

Another major change was that of a new club name -
West Stanley. This would appear to be a transposition
since the Ground was located in the centre of the town
and in fact immediately adjacent to the East Stanley
Cemetery! However, this new title referred back to the
very beginnings of the town. A settlement existed in the
area during the 17th Century, which was variously spelt
as 'Stanleigh', 'Stanlaw' or 'Standley', although by the
early 1830's little more than a small hamlet had
developed. Just to the West a Farmhouse was located, by
the name of West Stanley, and the 1833 opening of the
first Coal mine nearby (this Industry became the
lifeblood for the area) was named 'West Stanley
Colliery'. With the domination of the Coal mines
influencing the life of the town, various organisations
for several decades adopted the 'West' prefix, although
the later enlarged Community became plain 'Stanley' town.
The Football Club, somewhat belatedly, changed their
name, adding this old - 'West' - prefix.

The completion of the Murray Park Ground was
accomplished just one hour before the kick-off for the
first game of the season. It was perhaps fitting that, by
coincidence, the first opponents were the Club's near
namesake, Stanley United F.C., from Crook. The match on
Thursday the 27th September, was in the first round of
the Durham Challenge Cup, and amid great excitement that
followed the Official Opening Ceremony by a local
personality, Mrs. Benson, the game got underway. As so
often happens the match was a great anti-climax, for
after The 'Wests' (as they were now known) led by one
goal at half-time the final result ended at 1-1. Extra
time was started, but play was abandoned due to bad
light. The Club's first ever game in the North-East
League was played earlier in the month on the 1st of
September at Sunderland when the League Club's third team
won by 3-1.

In this game, West Stanley were represented by: Chipperfield, Bamlett, W. Wilson (number '1'), W. Wilson (number '2'), Daly, Tomlinson, Barnfather, Tully, Riddle, Atkinson and Lavery. The second League game, also away, was lost by two goals to nil to Newcastle 'A'. West Stanley were somewhat overawed by their opponents, for it was reported that:

"The West Stanley team is composed of sound triers but they lacked the finesse which was such a notable feature of their opponents play."

The first home League game produced a goalless draw with the third team of Middlesborough, at which a large number of spectators were present.

Although the fourth game was won, by mid-December, partially due to only having played five League matches, the team found themselves at the bottom of the table. There then followed a successful spell which raised the club to fifth (of ten) just one month later. The locals were relishing the quality of the opposition, and the attendances continued to steadily rise. Approximately 3,000 were present for the 2-0 win over Bradford City 'A', 5,000 for an excellent victory over table-toppers Newcastle, and 6,000 when Sunderland won by the odd goal in three.

On March the 31st, a Ground record gate of nearly 10,000 spectators paid £123 to see the final of the Durham Amateur Cup between Dipton and Craighead.

By the season's close the Club finished in a very satisfactory third position in the League, which prompted the following statement in the local newspaper in April:

"They (West Stanley) are anxious to provide their patrons with the very best class of football that it is possible to secure. There is talk in Stanley of a League Division 2 team there, and I should say that the Club is drawing better gates than many of the present 2nd Division teams..... they have such a large and loyal following..."

Enthusiasm had never been higher, and by the end of the season plans were underway to build large changing rooms (presumably with baths!), plus enlargements to the Grandstand, with banking behind both goals and terracing elsewhere. Additionally the pitch was due for enlargement.

West Stanley.

The Club's playing successes took their toll, and Tomlinson, Walker and Barnfather were lured away to Barnsley, Fulham and Croydon respectively. At this time, the Club were finally formed into a Limited Company, with good financial help coming from the Club's supporters.

The first home match of the 1907/08 season was disappointingly lost by 1-2 to Hebburn Argyle before a 3,000 crowd. This was followed shortly after with a drawn match against, one of the first games played on their Ground, of the newly formed Bradford (Park Avenue) F.C. The Yorkshire team had been frustrated by being turned down with their application to join the Football League, and entered their first team in the Southern League, the most Northern team ever to play in this Competition. The return match with the Avenue was a farce! It was rumoured that several of the visiting players were in a near drunken state, and when the Official Referee failed to turn up, the West's Secretary, John Bennett offered to officiate. Bradford had no objections, but the circumstances led to the homesters running amok in the second period, with a final 'cricket score' victory of 13-0; to save further embarrassment to their visitors, the West's centre-forward was requested, by Mr Bennett, to stop scoring after his seventh success!

Only a mediocre start was made in the thirteen team League, but a most successful run was achieved in the F.A.Cup. On October the 5th, the Stanley Club from Crook were defeated by 3-2 at Murray Park, followed by victory over the Crook F.C. team themselves, and before a home gate approaching 4,000 (receipts £48). The third match resulted in an exciting and narrow win over West Auckland, with a half-time and final score of 3-2. (Attendance 3,500). Fellow-Leaguers Hebburn Argyle were then easily overcome by 4-1, after a two goal half-time lead. The final Cup game drew Second Division Glossop to Durham, although the Football League team asked for the venue to be reversed. On this occasion a three nil reverse was experienced by the locals (all scored in the opening seven minutes), before a somewhat small crowd of only 5,000.

However a new Club record attendance at Murray Park drew 10,000 to witness an Exhibition match between Sunderland and Newcastle United. Even the Pits were shut early in order that the Miners could attend, but the game was somewhat of a let-down, as the two Football League teams fielded mostly Reserve team players.

Whilst no honours were won at the season's end - apart from an appearance in the Durham Senior Cup Final - the Club continued in an optimistic frame of mind, and by the middle of the 1908/09 season a 9th placing in the 18 team League was realised. The 3 goal home defeat to Middlesbrough 'A' team produced injuries which at one time left only nine home players on the pitch. G.Henderson injured his leg which swelled up, forcing him to retire. He changed and spent the last minutes of the first half in the Stand. However, the rest appeared to repair the damage for at half-time he changed back into his football kit, and played in the second half!

All thoughts of Football were completely overshadowed in February when one of the worst ever colliery disasters occured at West Stanley. No less than 168 men and boys died, for which a Monument was erected in 1913 in memory of those that perished. This memorial can still be seen in the East Stanley Cemetry, adjacent to Murray Park. Many of the victims were connected with the Club or were supporters, none less than one of the founder-members and Trainer - Steve Wood.

A few days later on February the 20th, whilst the town were still mourning over their dead, the Club were ordered to play a match at Shildon.This led to a not surprising defeat, with the match report stating that:

"Overshadowed as they were by the terrible results of the pit explosion, it is small wonder that the visitors did not absolutely enjoy the game."

The Club completed the season in good style and finished in a final 4th place in the League, with 17 wins, 3 draws and 11 defeats.

The League contained 17 teams for the 1909/10 season, and the Campaign got off to a good start, with a single goal home win over Spennymoor. But the next success in the League was not achieved until early November. Consequently by the year's end the Club were below midway in the table, although less games had been played than their opponents. This lack of success produced the inevitable drop in support, and with the Players refusing a wage cut, the Club were left in financial trouble. West Stanley had in the past, and were in the future, to rely on good F.A.Cup runs to provide extra revenue. However,

in this season no such revenue was forthcoming. Just one
Cup match was won, over Sunderland Royal Rovers, when the
Wests wanted the tie reversed, but the Rovers insisted on
playing in Sunderland; the paltry gate was insufficient
to pay the Referee's fee !

For the next few seasons, upto the First World War, no
honours were won, with the best League place of fourth in
the last pre-war season of 1914/15. But this in itself
was an honour since the League was dominated - as it had
been since it's inception in 1906 - by the Reserves and
Third teams of the local Football League 'Giants'. The
only breakthroughs by non-League teams being achieved
with title wins by Spennymoor United in 1910 (despite
losing their first game that season to West Stanley!),
Darlington in 1912/13 and South Shields in the two
immediate pre-war seasons. The latter two Clubs successes
did not go unrewarded for both were later elected to the
newly formed Third Division North of the Football League.

The reasonable success of the Club during these early
professional seasons can perhaps be better judged by the
talented players that were lost to League Clubs including
Tommy Fish to Sheffield Wednesday, Clem Spephenson -
Aston Villa and England, Dick Herron - Stoke, Tom Barber
to Bolton and later Villa (with whom he scored the
winning Cup Final goal in 1913); plus L.Stoker and W.
Smith who gained England 'Caps'. The financial benefits
gained by transfers, at a difficult time, obviously
outweighed the possibility of League success during this
era.

The Club attempted to carry on playing during the War
years but with little success. Along with the likes of
Leadgate Park, Jarrow and Swalwell, plus other local
teams - many of whom were unable to complete their
fixtures - the team competed in the Northern Combination.
Mere handfulls of spectators attended matches, and it
came as no surprise at the end of the 1915/16 season when
it was reported that:

*"Local Clubs that kept the flag flying during the
past season had such a trying experience that it
may well be that they will not be anxious to go
through the same ordeal again. "*

West Stanley didn't, and football at Murray Park for the
Club was suspended until 1919.

Murray Park did not remain completely unused during the War, for local amateurs 'Craghead United' used the Ground during the 'dark' days for their Derwent Valley League games. Additionally it served as the Finals venue for the North West Durham Charity Cups.

After the cancellation of a proposed Friendly match with Annfield Plain, which had been planned as the first post-war fixture, it was not until the 18th of April 1919, (Good Friday) that West Stanley kicked off for the first time for several years. They were hosts to Durham City, before an attendance of 3,000 - 'quite like old times' stated one report. Six pre-war players put in an appearance, and after a scoreless first half, the final result was a one goal reverse. Further Easter matches produced a 1-4 defeat at Ashington, and a victory over Leadgate Park.

North-Eastern League games re-commenced for the 1919/20 season, and with ex-Oakey's Lilywhites Player Joe Smith at the helm as Player/Manager, a home victory (with 'much support') over Shildon on August the 30th signalled the start of the campaign. After four games the Wests lay in 3rd place with the first defeat coming at home to Newcastle Reserves. A bizarre game at Spennymoor was played, when the Club went a goal down after 3 minutes, conceded three penalties in the first half hour (all of which were missed) and had a Player sent off after 10 minutes! The result was a 1-3 defeat. Despite the promising start not being maintained, good average attendances for this era - around 2,000 - were realised. The final placing was a disappointing low mid-table in the League.

The F.A.Cup exploits however were a different matter with the Club progressing to the 2nd round proper, the last 32 Clubs. Starting in the preliminary rounds, victories over local teams were recorded including a two goal to nil win at Scotswood - the third week in succession that the Clubs had met in competition. Before the best of the season home crowd to date, Leadgate Park were overcome by two unopposed goals in the fifth qualifying round.

The next round, played on the 20th of December, brought Rotherham County of the Football League Second Division to Stanley for the biggest match ever held in the town. Rotherham were keen for the venue to be switched, but the Wests kept faith with their fans, and at 1.00 p.m. on the day all nine entrance gates to the ground were opened. The Non-league team went in at half-time, one goal up, and despite the County pressing hard in the second period, it was the home side who scored again through Austin, roared on by over 8,000 fans (£227 receipts).

After the match several Rotherham players expressed their admiration of the facilities provided at Murray Park, admitting that they were better than their own. A newspaper stated that:

"Very gratifying is the victory over Rotherham in the competition as the South Yorkshire Club is in membership with the Football League second division, and the success of the homesters taken in conjunction with Darlington ought to shake the judgement of those who vainly imagine that all the best teams are comprised in the Football and Southern Leagues."

Gillingham or Swansea (both of the Southern League) were drawn to play in Stanley for the 1st round proper of the Competition. After a second replay (on the same day as when they were due to play each other in a League match) the Kent team won and were destined to make the long journey North. Old aquaintances were renewed with Jack Chalmers in the Gills line-up against his old Club.

The supporters of the Wests were confident of beating the team from down South, in view of their previous victory over a Football League team, and on the day, 'The biggest crowd that ever attended a football match in North-West Durham' (over 10,000) were present for the occasion. After 10 minutes the home team went ahead through Bohill, but the visitors had equalised before half-time. Against a strong wind, West Stanley were under pressure for much of the first half, but in a breakaway, Hall was apparently clearly fouled in the penalty area, but this went unnoticed by the Officials, and so the scores remained level after 45 minutes. With Preston and Walton being treated for earlier injuries, the Wests started the second half with only nine men, but with a full complement of players back on the field, they missed a golden opportunity to go ahead when awarded a penalty which was well saved by the goalkeeper from Kent. Gillingham were now under constant pressure, and it came as no surprise when Walton put the homesters ahead. The crowd erupted!

West Stanley.

A party of Players and Officials at the Houses of Parliament.
(31st January 1920. Prior to the 'Spurs F.A.Cup match)
Cen re of picture: Consett M.P. Aneurin Williams, with his daughter.

WEST STANLEY'S BRILLIANT PERFORMANCE

Gillingham Receive Their Quietus From the Cup: A 3 to 1 Victory.

JOY BELLS RING AT MURRAY PARK : BOHILL KEEPS HIS WORD.

By " CROSS-BAR."

The biggest crowd that ever attended a football match in North-West Durham assembled on Murray Park last Saturday to witness the meeting of West Stanley and Gillingham in the first round proper of the English Cup competition. They witnessed a determined encounter with the local lads, always the stronger side, and finally deserved winners by 3 goals to nil. Gillingham arrived in Stanley by the noon train, and had light refreshments at the Commercial Hotel, whilst the Stanleyites, who had been under Trainer Hunter's eyes for the past three days, lunched at the headquarters of the club, the King's Head Hotel, with the directors and other friends, including quite a host of Press photographers, artists, and knights of the pencil.

Prior to the team leaving headquarters for the field of victory, the chairman of the board of directors (Mr. M. Smith) read the following cheery messages:

From Scotswood Football Club: " Scotswood send you the very best of wishes for your game v. G'llingham, and sincerely trust that you will repeat the Rotherham act against them, and the Hotspurs, too."

From the Rev. A. S. Wardroper, Vicar of Walker (and one of the best sportsmen of the North of England): " Best wishes for success on Saturday and then what a gate at Tottenham, which I know well. Be sure and score in the first quarter of an hour,

and rub it in. It takes two to beat that goal. I congratulate the club and team."

From Darlington Football Club: " Darlington Football Club wire best of good wishes for to-day."

helping them in the opening half, but before the finish 'twas blowing half a gale.

Strung Up to Fighting Pitch.

Thompson kicked off, and from the first stroke it was evident that we were in for a great fight. Both teams were strung up to fighting pitch, and although they had not received the orthodox "rub nation," they were every bit as keen as if going over the top in days now happily ended. The Southerners at once got going and Steel (R.) forced Austin to handle in the first minute. With characteristic calmness, the home goalie hurled the ball 30 yards and Jim Walton passed on to the home left, but Buchanan beat Bohill for possession. Hall was prominent for a tricky run and neatly tricked Buchanan. The first really exciting moment came when Hall planted over to Bohill who headed for goal the ball striking the bar. Bohill was temporarily rendered horsde-combat through his head colliding with something hard, but he was soon on the warpath again. Pressure by Stanley was well maintained and good placings by Browell and Bussey were cleared by Leslie. Then the Gillingham forwards swept away in line and Steel fired in a beauty which Austin magnificently caught and fisted away. The Kentish men returned to the attack and Feenan hard pressed, found safety in touch. Walker helped to raise the siege by a judicious pass forward. Gillingham did a bit of hard attacking at this stage, but were stoutly resisted by the Stanley halves and backs, who, to a man, were sound tryers and something more. Lee, the tall centre-half, was prominent in helping his vanguard to the assault, but Bussey finally relieved with an accurate pass which Smith seized upon only to be robbed by Leslie. Thompson then led his forwards in a hot rush to the entrance goal and Bohill, taking up a neat pass, was going straight for goal when fouled a little outside the penalty area

(Stanley News)

Arguably the 'West's' greatest triumph. (January 1920)

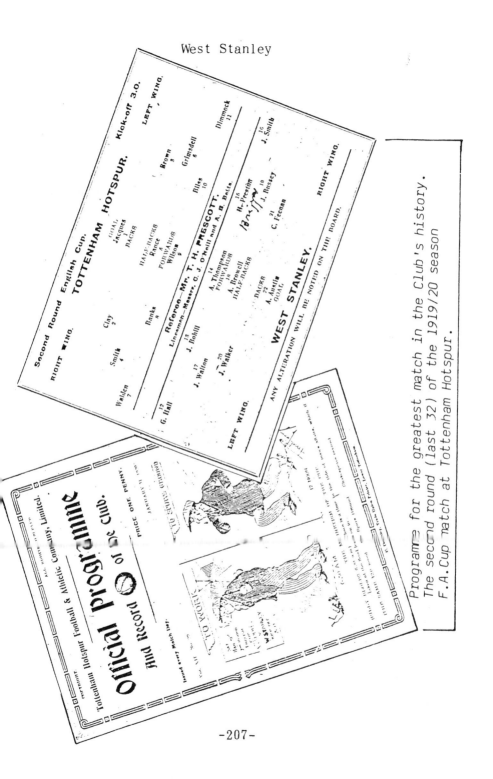

Programme for the greatest match in the Club's history. The second round (last 32) of the 1919/20 season F.A.Cup match at Tottenham Hotspur.

West Stanley.

"Several Ladies in the vicinity of the non-existent press box expressed an ardent desire to embrace him (Walton), and the mere males shouted as if the League of Nations had ended all war for ever."
Thus it was poetically reported by the local press!

With just eight minutes remaining Hall scored his first of the season, and the third for West Stanley to put the tie beyond the reach of Gillingham.
Without doubt West Stanley F.C. had reached their proudest hour, and when the draw for the second round was made, it became obvious that even greater excitement was in store. Tottenham Hotspur F.C. the Club that 19 years earlier had caused a sensation by winning the F.A.Cup whilst still a non-League team, and now topping the Second Division, were to play hosts to the 'little' team from Durham. Whilst admittedly a professional squad with fifteen paid players - eleven of whom also worked in the mines, and all living a maximum of twenty miles from Murray Park - it was a daunting task that caught the imagination not only of Durham, but the whole Country. There was a rumour circulating in the town that several people had booked tickets for ' An aeroplane voyage to Tottenham'! Whether the aeroplane trip was realised or not, many supporters from the North were amongst the 35,000 crowd that paid over £2,500 entrance money.
In drizzling rain, the non-Leaguers hopes were diminished when they went one goal down after only 15 minutes, and virtually dashed completely when Wilson added a second ten minutes later. With this score remaining at half-time, and starting the second period with only ten men due to a first half injury to Feeman, West Stanley started the next half with spirit and determination. However despite the Wests being back to full strength for the last thirty minutes, the Spurs gradually took control again, and added two further goals. 'There is credit in defeat. West Stanley put up a thrilling fight against the Second Division leaders'. Was the fitting report of a thrilling experience. Seven days later, the Wests were well represented at Garden House for the away League fixture with Durham; such was the Club's fame, that a record League attendance was reported!

West Stanley.

A good start was made for the 1920/21 season, and good home attendances of 6,000 (versus Darlington), and 4,000 for Spennymoor's visit were recorded. By mid-October, following a four goal victory over Durham, there was the possibility of the Club entering the proposed Football League Division 3 (North). However, one week later a single goal first home defeat started a slide down the table from which they never recovered, and it was left to the likes of Durham, Ashington and Darlington, with their more consistant playing records, to represent the North-East the following season in the Football League. West Stanley were included in the many applications that were made for election, but the vacancies were few since those from the Central League were accepted en bloc. It was admitted that West Stanley, 'could live and do well in such a Competition', but it was not to be as only four from ten were lucky from 'the rest'. The Wests six votes of confidence were far too few for acceptance, and only Wakefield City (4), Lancaster Town (3), Scunthorpe and Lindsey United (3) plus South Liverpool's solitary one vote, were below them in the poll.

Defeat in the F.A. Cup came at the hands of Bishop Auckland – the first ever meeting of the Clubs – with a 1-3 away deficit, before an attendance of over 5,000.

The start of the 1921/22 season produced three exciting and historic games, versus foes of longstanding – Leadgate Park – in the 1920/21 final of the North-West Durham Charity Cup. Despite it's relatively minor status the final was to attract great support, and in effect more or less signalled the end of the short period of good attendances. On the 29th of September, around 8,500 spectators flocked to Murray Park to witness an exciting match. After going ahead with a sensational free kick scored direct from near the halfway line, the Wests went further ahead after 30 minutes. The visitors fought back in the second half, scoring their second, and the equaliser, 10 minutes from the end. The replay drew 6,500 to Leadgate Park, where West Stanley were forced to start with only ten men due to a car breakdown! This match also finished all square. The second replay held on the 27th of October really captured the imagination of the Public, and an all time record attendance at Murray Park (and for North-West Durham), of 12,585 paid £472 for the privilege. In an exciting match full of thrills, the Wests failed by a single goal.

West Stanley.

Support was by now on a 'high', and community singing at home matches became a feature - until a rendering of 'Pack up your troubles', caused distress to the mourners at a burial at the adjacent Cemetery - and signalled an end to this pre-match entertainment! But the twenties signalled the start of the depression which was particularly deep in the North-East of the Country. In common with many Clubs, West Stanley started to feel the 'pinch' although they maintained a moderate League record. It was reported at the A.G.M. in May 1922, that the member-Club gates were well down. Nonetheless some entertaining matches were seen, particularly the home draw with Blyth (3,000 attendance), and the end of season 2-0 victory over Middlesbrough Reserves which attracted 4,000 to Murray Park. The Wests were still fairly well supported when compared with their contemporaries in the North-Eastern League, for instance there were only 3,000 spectators present at Chester-le-Street despite the game being a local derby with the Wests.

In view of the end of season displays, there were optimistic thoughts for the next campaign, and it was hoped that the finances would be helped by the Supporters Club that had been formed in January. Huddersfield won the F.A. Cup Final that season, and the only goal was scored by W.H. ('Tantobie') Smith - an ex-West Stanley player. The Club's hopes appeared to be fulfilled when a good start was made. The Hare Law Aged Miner's Cup was won in August when 2,000 spectators saw a home victory over Hedley Park - this Final had been held over from the previous season. But this was the only success in Cup games, apart from the F.A.Cup, as all other matches were lost at the first attempt. The 4th qualifying round of the F.A.Cup was reached, following victories over Seaham Harbour, Ferryhill Athletic of the Palatine League (after a scoreless draw) and a 5-0 home thrashing of Spennymoor before a 3,000 crowd. The end came at Durham City - by now in the 3rd Division - with a 1-2 defeat. A good start to the season was followed by defeats, and by mid-November the Club had slipped to 14th in the League. In the final event yet again no honours were won. The 4,000 crowds for the 'top' home games against the Reserves of Sunderland and Newcastle were by now exceptional figures. The next season produced little, save for reaching the semi-final of the Durham Challenge Cup - a defeat to Cockfield.

West Stanley.

Finishing 9th of the twenty Clubs in the League at the 1924/25 season's end was due to a late season flourish, but not without some surprising defeats. Nil-six at Workington in January, and an unopposed seven goal crash at Darlington Reserves; an embarrassing defeat was also suffered in the Durham Senior Cup at the Bill Quay enclosure, the home ground of Wood Skinners F.C.

On September the 1st, 1925, the first ever League match meeting at nearby Annfield Plain was staged, when a 'very large crowd' saw the Wests win by 3-1 - which was followed with a 0-7 away defeat to South Shields Reserves. But it was another good F.A.Cup run that helped to keep the Club's financial head above water in a gradually worsening situation. Rochdale of the Football League were visited on the 28th of November, West Stanley having fought their way to the 1st round proper again. Following appeals by both sets of supporters, the Referee, somewhat reluctantly, let the match go ahead on a quagmire of a pitch, before an attendance of only 4,318, somewhat lower than had originally been hoped for. Unexpectedly the first half 'belonged' to the Wests, so much so that extra police were called in to quell the disquiet of the home crowd. But the visitors could not contain the League team in the second period and were easily beaten by four clear goals.

The following season produced no F.A.Cup glory, with the Club losing by one goal in an early round to Chilton Colliery. It was a topsy turvy season all round. The League record was near disastrous with the Club narrowly avoiding relegation to the Second Division - for its inaugural season! Whereas in the Durham Challenge Cup the position was somewhat better. The final was reached following a semi-final home victory - before a very rare, 'large crowd' - over South Shields Reserves. The Final at Annfield Plain was expected to produce a record gate of around 15,000, but only 6,486 paying £320 turned up in the end. The Referee blew up for half-time after only 42 minutes, and an unprecedented event followed.

On resuming for the second half the match official, realising his timing fault, continued play as for the first half for three minutes before stopping the game, ordering the teams to change ends and playing a full second period of 45 minutes! West Stanley equalised the amateurs of Crook's first half goal, nine minutes from time, but the replay at Bishop Auckland was lost by 2-4.

West Stanley.

However, this end of season treat hardly compensated the Club for one of their worst ever in the North-Eastern League, when a final 3rd from bottom was realised. Included in some best forgotten results was a record 1-10 reverse (at Middlesbrough Reserves) and a last League game defeat of 1-8 at Annfield Plain.

With many new players the 1927/28 season started well, including a moderate Cup run with victories over Spen Black & White and Burnhope - the latter away match producing a record attendance which was mostly composed of West supporters! The end came at Spennymoor. High scoring games were a feature of the season including the most goals ever scored at Murray Park in the League - an 8-4 victory over Preston Colliery in November. The final outcome to the season was a big improvement over the previous one, but yet again no honours.

For some years the pattern of 'little success but few disasters' continued, although the 1929/30 season represented one of the best. In it's inaugural season the Club won the League's 'Non-reserve' Medal, (won by the highest finishing non-League team in the League) by attaining 5th place - the award was brought about by the near total domination in matches by the stronger Reserve sides of Football League Clubs. The medal was won despite a last game defeat by eight goals to nil to Champions (for the fourth consecutive time) Sunderland Reserves. The following season, a mid-table League placing was achieved after 8 matches - despite defeats including 1-3 at home to the Reserves of Middlesbrough (before a, by now, good attendance of over 3,000) and 1-7 at Newcastle. The final outcome some months later however was 16th (of 22) in the League table. In the F.A.Cup a good scoreless draw at Scarborough was followed by a disappointing defeat at Murray Park before a crowd of only 2,000. Some compensation was received with their winning (for the second time) the Holmside Hospital Cup, with victory over neighbours Annfield Plain.

A four-nil half-time lead over newcomers Chopwell in the initial game of the 1931/32 season finished at the final whistle in an eight goals shared draw. However, in the next game amends were made with a 4-0 final scoreline at neighbours Annfield Plain before around 3,000 spectators. Overall, a good start was made, including a rare win over Newcastle Reserves with a gate of £86 (over 3,000). In October another notable victory was gained

over North Shields when a second, and winning goal, was
scored with the last kick of the match. By now the Club
were in a reasonable 8th position in the League, and
there was also another appearance in the 1st round of the
F.A.Cup. On the 13th of November, Scarborough made
another visit to Murray Park but on this occasion were
defeated by two goals; the match produced a gate of over
£165 - 4,116 spectators - one of the best for years. The
Ground entrance charge was one shilling (5p).

This win earned a trip to Tranmere Rovers and a very
welcome share of the £250 gate money; but there was no
shock result as the Wests lost by 0-3. In an extremely
good and sporting game, the Club were described as
'Gallant losers'. The best win of the season occured on
Boxing day with a 6-1 scoreline over Washington Colliery,
the Club to whom West Stanley lost a day earlier! But the
end of season saw the Club in the all to familiar
position, by now, of having won no honours.

The early 1930's, saw the - emergency - appearance of
the Club trainer in one match, a man well into his
sixties! The next few years were to prove to be little
short of disastrous. Local support was dwindling not only
due to the depression throughout the Country, but also in
view of the team's poor performances which were unable to
produce any major honours. The final placing in the
League in May 1935 saw the Club in bottom but one, which
required a (successful) re-election application. One
season earlier, the Club would have been relegated to the
Second Division, but were saved due to the abandonment of
the lower competition!

By the Christmas of 1935, things were again looking
desperate - all three Holiday games were lost, including
that by nine unopposed goals at Jarrow. Things had been
fairly hard for the previous ten years or so, but never
so bad as at the start of 1936. Last but one in the
League, poor gates, no money, and no professional
players! An appeal was made to the public to support the
Club, following which there was a paltry 200 present for
the Durham Challenge Cup match which was lost to
Hartlepool Gas & Waterworks. The local newspaper reported
that: "The Directors of West Stanley will have to realise
the uselessness of carrying on until the end of the
season.... ". But carry on they did, aided by a general
revival in results and attendances. The last home match
produced a 5-1 victory over Darlington Reserves, although

West Stanley.

earlier a 2-10 defeat was suffered at the hands of Middlesbrough Reserves. From hovering around the bottom of the table, the Club elevated themselves to a final 18th position.

Somehow the Club carried on, but as Amateurs pitted against the higher quality professional players of most of the opposing Clubs. The most humiliating defeat was by two goals to ten versus The City of Durham (the reformed former Football League Club) - a team that had only won a single game in their previous ten! The Wests team were rooted to the bottom of the League by the end of 1936 and even more stringent measures had to be taken.

Greyhound Racing was becoming a popular spectator sport, and West Stanley F.C. were thrown what on paper appeared to be a lifeline, with the chance for such an organisation to become tenants of Murray Park. The extra revenue undoubtedly helped the Club to continue. This future extra cash was critical in view of the second half of the 1936/37 season with the Club apparently immoveable from the bottom of the League - they finished 10 points below the next Club with 2 wins, 3 drawn games and 33 defeats; and a goal difference of 37 - 189. On the 25th of February for the home match versus Eden Colliery (who were in dire straits themselves and disbanded soon afterwards), just 200 spectators were present. The last match was lost at Middlesbrough, 1-9!

Despite the experiences of some, who found the dual use of the Ground to be to the detriment of the Football Club, the Wests had little alternative but to accept the situation - or disband! And so in late August 1937, the first Greyhound meeting took place (and still does to this day), before a crowd of some 5,000. Although the average dropped to between 3 and 4,000, these attendances were far in excess of the support for the football team. Murray Park had the undoubted benefit of improved spectator accommodation - including a new high covered stand - (financed by their 'tenants'), but it was necessary to reduce the length of the football pitch in order to provide the required dog track oval. A feature that was to have a definite bearing on the eventual demise of the Football Club. Perhaps the greatest indignity was the re-naming of the Ground to 'The Stanley Greyhound Racing Stadium'!

The possibility of a new era in the annals of the Wests encouraged a crowd in excess of any that had

attended League games during the previous season, to the
trial game for the 1937/38 campaign. And the first home
League match, a draw versus Darlington, attracted a 2,000
gate. Attendances showed a marked overall increase, and
although the coming months could hardly be considered as
highly successful, the Club managed to lift themselves
well off the bottom of the League ladder at the finish.

1938/39 promised to be a further improvement, with the
Club in eighth position (of twenty teams) as 1939 dawned.
But despite a good run upto early March, a season's end
slump - six successive defeats - produced a final placing
below mid-table. The following season got off well, with
a 5-2 win over Throckley Welfare in a thunderstorm before
a 1,500 crowd; the same opponents were later met when
ex-Partick Thistle player, and Wests Player/Trainer since
1909 - Tommy Hunter - played for the Club at the age of
63 years! Surely the oldest Player ever to appear in a
Senior competitive match. In 1939 he relinquished his
active role, joining the Board of Directors before his
death in 1953.

Storm clouds were by now raging over Europe, and with
the declaration of War, the Ground was commandeered by
the Military, with football ceasing for the duration.
Greyhound Racing was also curtailed of course, and with
fresh meat at a premium, it was sadly necessary to
destroy most of the dogs.

The prospect of an end to the War signalled the
resumption of the North-Eastern League for the 1944/45
season, and although West Stanley F.C. in common with
most Clubs saw a renewed interest in the sport - with
average crowds around the 2,000 mark - the performances
of the team showed a similarity with those in the pre-war
period. However five straight wins during March and April
1946 - marred later by a 1-6 home defeat before newcomers
Murton Colliery before the best gate of the season - at
least gave rise to some optimism for the future.

The first match of the 1946/47 season appeared to
justify the supporters faith, when before a 2,000 home
crowd, Throckley Welfare were crushed by nine goals.
Further victories ensued, including a 6-4 top of the
table win over Sunderland Reserves before 4,000
spectators at Stanley. By the end of the year the team
found themselves in the hitherto unimaginable position of
heading the League table, but a bad patch in the latter

half of the season prevented the team winning any
honours. Any hopes of a sustained revival were short-
lived, and there was little in the way of success, apart
from a mid-table placing by January 1949. This was
improved upon to 6th position following a seven games
without defeat run, including an exciting 7-5 home win
versus Workington Reserves. But as so often had happened
in the past, this uplift was not sustained and the final
place in the League was a drab 14th. Then without
warning, during the next season the Club enjoyed one of
their best ever campaigns.

The North-Eastern League with it's regular composition
of twenty teams, including the Reserves of six Football
League Clubs, saw North Shields as Champions for the
first time in 1950, but only two points behind stood West
Stanley.
The season started with a 2-1 away win at Blackhall
Colliery, and further good results produced a 6th placing
in the table after the same number of games. In the F.A.
Cup - a competition which was soon to be denied the Club
- a no score draw at home was followed by a 1-2 defeat at
Hexham Hearts before a record 2,000 attendance. In this
match the Wests had no less than four goals disallowed!
However, in the League things were far more encouraging,
for despite a November lapse, the team were still placed
in a respectable 8th position. An improved second half to
the season produced a final record of 23 wins, 6 draws
and 9 defeats with surprisingly low goals figures of 65
to 45 - the Club being placed above both Middlesbrough
Reserves (3rd) and the Sunderland second string in 5th
place.
Whilst this achievement was worthy of celebration, a
high placing was shortlived for twelve months later the
Club were in the more familiar bottom half of the League
- in 14th position! This in itself was hardly a disaster,
but once again finance was causing concern. The post-war
attendance 'bubble' had burst and attendances now seldom
reached 1,000. Whereas in the past the Club had relied on
several lucrative F.A. Cup runs, these were now denied
them, for the reduced size of the pitch - smaller than
the minimum required - prevented the Club's further entry
in the Competition.
The 1951/52 campaign, although with an improvement to
8th place in a reduced League of 18 teams, saw a further

drop in home attendances which by now were rarely reaching 700. Six places lower was realised one year later, only 4 points clear of wooden-spoonists and neighbours - Annfield Plain. The warning bells started ringing in January 1953, with the Club sending an urgent S.O.S. for support in order to carry on. The Club's plight was not unique for amongst others, Consett and South Shields were only just hanging on, and for West Stanley's visit to the latter in late April the lowest Tynesider's attendance of just 226 was recorded.

There appeared to be little chance of survival, at least in this senior League, for with little money from low gates, the Club were unable to retain the worthwhile players on their books. Although a good start to the 1953/54 season was made, the run up to Christmas was disastrous and by this time the Club had dropped to bottom place. From January onwards just 4 wins and likewise in drawn matches of the seventeen games played resulted in the same position at the end. Support for the Club continued to dwindle and at the season's end a large financial deficit was shown. The 1954/55 season was even worse for the same final position in the League was the outcome, this time however with only 18 points and a goal difference of 45 - 106.

Hopes of a recovery a few months later were raised with the biggest win for many years, a 6-0 drubbing of Whitley Bay, but this was proved to be the exception, for an unenviable completion of a hat-trick of bottom places in the League was the final grim story. On this occasion a paltry 12 points were obtained (nine below next Club, Horden Colliery) with a worse goal difference of 37 - 107. Further drastic cuts had been made over the previous twelve months, with notably the retention of only four professional players (whose wages had been cut). At least the losses on the season had been reduced, but with a total income of £841 - only £435 in gate receipts - the Club could clearly not carry on much longer. Perhaps more surprising was the Club's continued acceptance into the North-East League after such a dreadful period !

Prior to the commencement of the 1956/57 season, a plea went out to the Town's people from the Working Men's Club, which at this time was the venue of the Club's A.G.M. :

"*If the football enthusiasts of the district will only support the Club better by attendance at games, the Directors of West Stanley A.F.C. are convinced that a more successful season will be enjoyed.*"

There was little response at the gate, but the Club did get off to a fair start, and two excellent wins were achieved over the might of the Sunderland and Middlesbrough Reserve teams - but also a 0-6 defeat at North Shields! The Football League Clubs had by now become disenchanted with their Reserves being pitted against generally weak opposition - which included several purely Amateur teams - and there was soon to be a split that would mean the end of this old established League. At least West Stanley managed to lift themselves above the lowest rung, but there was still little to celebrate.

The 1957/58 season was to be the penultimate active one for West Stanley, and also the last for all of the Football League Reserve teams in the League; the big Clubs resignations lead to the eventual disintegration of the Competition. As Founder-members half a century before, the Wests had no alternative but to change to a League more in keeping with their capabilities.

An entry into the Northern Alliance for the 1958/59 season became the last ever for the West Stanley F.C. The season commenced well enough at this lower level, and the Club found themselves in a high placing at Christmas. The second half however was a different matter and a series of defeats included home reverses against Morpeth Town (2-7) and Ashington Reserves (1-7). The first win of the year and the first home victory since December the 6th, came on the 7th of March with a single goal win over Blyth Spartans Reserves.

The last match ever for the Club came on April the 25th, a 1-1 home draw with Alnwick Town, in what should have been an easy home win. The team that day consisted of: Brooks, Reeve, Steel, Stansfield, Simm, Taylor, Batey, Spivey, Hodgson, Jeffries and Hudson. The last named scored the goal, and despite being a more or less Reserve team player with Wests, he was shortly after signed up as a part-time professional with Partick Thistle of Scotland.

On August the 13th an announcement was made, that came perhaps as no surprise to anybody connected with the

Club, that the football team could not carry on. At this time, the intention was that the Club be put in 'Suspended animation' pending provision of a suitable playing field. Whilst lack of finance was undoubtedly the root of the trouble it was also recognised by the F.A., the Northern Alliance and fans alike that the Ground and pitch were no longer suitable for Senior football. The Club had fought a constant battle with the Greyhound Authorities, not only with the occasional clashing of fixtures but more importantly regarding the undersized playing field - that could not be enlarged in the present circumstances - and which prevented the Club's entry into the lucrative F.A. Cup Competition. Not only was the size a problem, but also the condition of the pitch over the years had unevenly sunk (subsidence) due to colliery works below. The Club's opponents, and the team were unhappy, as were the fans who could no longer enjoy skillful games, and the final result was even lower attendances.

The Directors announced that another suitable Ground would be found, and in this endeavour the Stanley Urban Council's help would be sought. However, it was clearly impossible for anything to be undertaken before the imminent season. But fund-raising was to be continued, until such time that the Club could operate a football team again.

****

For a few years the Club were left in limbo. At one time the intention was for the Club to play at nearby Park Field, South Moor with a hoped for commencement in the 1961/62 season. But Louisa Colliery of the West Durham Combination who were using this playing field were evicted in early 1961 as the pitch required a new playing surface. The time dragged on, and in October 1962 it was confidently predicted that Stanley would once again have their own football team - this time with a hopeful re-entry into the North-Eastern League for the 1963/64 season. However, Mr J.W.Kerr, the Secretary since 1938, emphasised that the Club was still in existance, in name at least. West Stanley F.C. was alive due to the efforts of a few dedicated people and it would be necessary for crowds of at least 1,000 at home matches, to ensure survival. "The fans are there, and will flock to Stanley

if entertaining football is provided..." was the
confident prediction.

By now it was intended, with the help of the Local
Council, to fence in the adjacent Kings Head Playing
Field (just off the High Street) and provide changing and
washing rooms at the Ground, at an estimated cost of
£4,000.

But only £600 was raised in three years, and after the
efforts of those few enthusiasts, this was the final nail
in the coffin..... the dream of those fans died, and the
reality of a Senior football team once again representing
Stanley, County Durham, died with it.

PROGRAMMES:

Whilst it is known that programmes were issued both
before the War, and at least in the early years after,
surviving copies are very rare.

MURRAY PARK.

An impressive memorial to this lesser known Club that
once nearly graced the Football League still remains,
despite their passing away so many years ago - the
Stadium at Murray Park. This is still used for Greyhound
Racing and the Ground stands little changed - save for
new social club amenities, seated stand improvements and
the partial loss of the covered enclosure - from it's
football playing days.

The original title of the Club led to the quaintly
named Ground name, Oakey's Oval. This venue, to the West
of Maurray Park, was used until 1906, by which time it
could boast of a Grandstand (which had been started in
1896), but probably little more. Some years later the
site - by now unfenced - was once again used for
football.

With the Club's raised status, a more substantial
Ground was necessary, and with their acceptance into the
North-East League in 1906, a frantic rush developed in
order to undertake the work, during the summer of that
year. The development was only completed one hour before
the Club's first match at the Ground. Although £130 was
spent on providing fencing to enclose the Ground,
suitable dressing rooms and washing facilities were
considered of secondary importance, and were not added

until a later date! For a number of years, the spectator facilities were limited to a small Grandstand on the North side (with the eventual dressing rooms behind), and a raised bank behind the goal at the Western end. Turnstile entrances and exits were provided on the High Street (Chester-le-Street Road) side, at the East and West ends, and at the North-west corner - at the end of Church Street; the latter being the main one. Although limited in facilities, it was considered a better enclosure than several of those Clubs in the Football League.

There was little done to the Ground until 1937, when the Greyhounds Company became tenants at Murray Park. These tenants provided mixed blessings, for whilst the extra revenue was a necessity for the survival of the Football Club, the 'improvements' to the Ground were both beneficial and detrimental. A large Grandstand was built on the South side (which remains today) - where just open grass banking was present - and the original structure opposite was replaced, probably in the 1930's or 1940's, with a full pitch length covered enclosure (part of this still remains). But another change that was necessary was for the Dogs, was far from beneficial to the Football Club. In order to accommodate the required Greyhound racing (oval) track, it was necessary to shorten the football pitch contained within. This new pitch size was considered too small to host F.A.Cup games, and the Wests had to eventually resign from the competition. In the past their F.A.Cup matches had proved to be the Club's financial salvation, the later absence of these games was to hasten their demise. Today, a football pitch complete with changing rooms and a railed off pitch exists at the Kings head Playing Fields (where it was intended that the new West Stanley F.C. would re-commence playing in the 1960's), and is used principally by a successful Sunday team, by the name of .... 'Murray Park'!

West Stanley A.F.C.

OFFICIAL PROGRAMME

Issued   by the
SUPPORTERS'   COMMITTEE
Secretary :   E. MEEK.

Saturday, February 20th.

Nº   73   Programme. 2d.

A reproduction of Stanley F.C. in 1894, soon after its origin. It was then known as Oakey's Lilywhites, but had to change to a more dignified name upon admittance to the Northern Alliance. During the season in which this photo was taken Lilywhites never lost a match. The names are:—Back row (left to right): M. Cunningham, C. Scott, G. Fallaws, J. Bryden, S. Chisholm, J. Smith (senr.), R. Smith. Middle row: J. Shaw, M. Cunningham, D. Welsh, and R. Cunningham. Front row: Geo. Collings, J. Cunningham, W. Gibson J. Shield, and J. Masterman.

Unfortunately the quality is poor, but the significance worthwhile!

West Stanley A.F.C.

OFFICIAL PROGRAMME

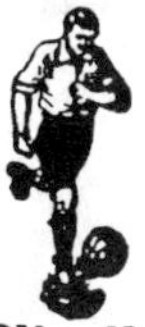

ISSUED BY THE
SUPPORTERS' COMMITTEE

SECRETARY: H. WATTERS.

SATURDAY, OCT. 5th, 1946.

PROGRAMME 3d. **NO. 4**

ALEX. MCKINLAY, Printer and Stationer. Phone 8 Stanley.

Murray Park 1985. Looking South-west.
The covered enclosure (right) was once much longer – the posts remain.
(Photo: Dave Twydell)

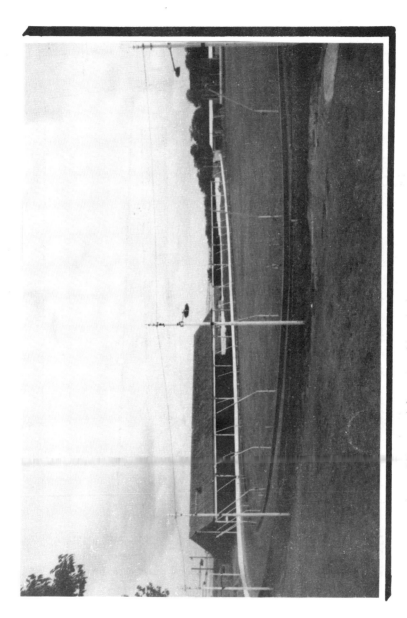

Murray Park 198-. Looking North-east

West Stanley

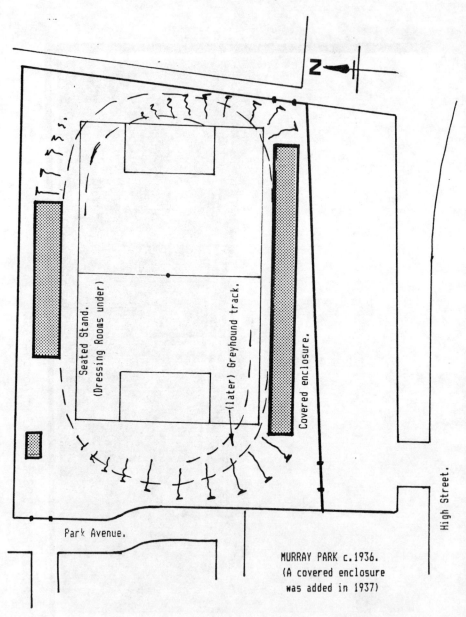

Seated Stand.
(Dressing Rooms under)

(later) Greyhound track.

Covered enclosure.

Park Avenue.

High Street.

MURRAY PARK c.1936.
(A covered enclosure
was added in 1937)

THE END.

Also, From the Author of this Book:

BRENTFORD F.C.- THREE VISITS TO WEMBLEY.
(Joint Author) Published July 1985. 48 Pages.
(Few available: Now £1-00 post free.)
Chronicles Brentford's three matches played at Wembley Stadium, the most recent being the first ever Freight Rover Trophy Final. Also includes the complete statistics of every match played in the first (1984/85 season), Freight Rover Competition..

DEFUNCT F.C.
Published July 1986. 252 Pages.
(Now sold out)
Written in a similar style to 'More....Defunct F.C.' but covering the detailed histories of five Defunct non-League Clubs. Namely - Bedford Town, Chippenham United, Guildford City, Pegasus (includes the full statistics of this Oxford/Cambridge University Club), and Symingtons/Market Harborough Town.

REJECTED F.C. VOLs 1 & 2.
Vol.1: Published June 1988. 368 Pages.
(Now Sold out)
Vol.2: Published July 1989. 488 Pages.
(Few Available - £11-95 plus P/P)
These two books detail the histories of the 22 Clubs that have been 'rejected' (i.e. voted out) from the Football League. The format is similar to that of the 'Defunct F.C.' books.

ALBANIA F.C.
First Published January 1989.
Reprinted November 1989. 44 pages.
(Price £2-00 incl. U.K. Postage)
A lighhearted but factual account of Football in Albania. The Author's experiences of a visit made to the Country in November 1988. Includes an interview with the Albanian National Team Manager.

*** available from: ***
Dave Twydell, 12 The Furrows,
Harefield, Middx. UB9 6AT.

^^^^^^^^^^^^^^^^^^^^^^^^^^^^^^^^^^^^^^^

Future Publication:

'Grounds For A Change' - a detailed look (in words and pictures) at the former Grounds of the Football League Clubs and other famous venues. (Anticipated Independant Publisher, and available late 1990).
(Postal purchasers of the above books will be notified)

OTHER READING:

For many years, there was relatively little to entertain football followers in respect of historical reading. But during the last decade or so, the football public has been bombarded with a veritable plethora of historic and nostalgic offerings. Aside from the professionally produced books, a small army of enthusiasts produce "one-off" (and sometimes more) limited run volumes - from small booklets, to major works or periodicals. In view of the many hours of research necessary, their efforts are to be fully applauded. Many of the subjects and Clubs covered are most unlikely to be reproduced in any other books; they are true 'labours of love'.
This list only represents a small fraction of a variety of publications available, but together I believe they provide a balanced 'read':

"The Footballer":
A bi-monthly, professionally produced magazine, from:
The Footballer, 72 St.Peter's Avenue, Cleethorpes, DN35 8HU.
Historically covering the whole range of football.
"The Association of Football Statisticians":
A quarterly report detailing many fascinating statistical articles.
From: Ray Spiller, 22 Bretons, Basildon, Essex. SS15 5BY.
"Non-League Football":
A professionally produced bi-monthly (from Bookshops or on subscription).
Backed by the Daily Mail, and under the Editorship of Tony Williams who is principally known for his annual Non-League Directories.
"Pyramid Magazine":
Mostly current information (that builds up into a Library of facts) of the non-League scene, from: Pyramid, P.O. Box 553, London, N2 8LJ.
"The Groundhopper Magazine":
A monthly that deals almost exclusively on the Grounds aspects of football, principally related to the non-League 'World'.
From: Flat 1, 64 Hunting Gate Drive, Chessington, Surrey, KT9 2DD.
"Programme Monthly":
From: John Litster, 14 Raith Crescent, Kirkcaldy, Fife. KY2 5NN.
The title is self explanatory!

\~

Most Football League Clubs histories have, or are, being written. Non-league Clubs have their stories less frequently told. Full statistical histories on defunct non-League Clubs are a very rare item! Therefore two from the latter classification that are currently being produced are worthy of mention:

"Guildford City" (1921 - 1978): Available Summer 1990. Details from:
Pete Phillips, 135 Manor Road, Stoughton, Guildford, Surrey.
"Croydon Common" (1897 - 1917): Available May 1990. Details from:
Alan Futter, 89 The Woodfields, Sanderstead, Croydon. CR2 0HJ.